The Terms of
Political Discourse

The Terms of Political Discourse

Third edition

WILLIAM E. CONNOLLY

PRINCETON UNIVERSITY PRESS
PRINCETON, NEW JERSEY

Published by Princeton University Press, 41 William Street,
Princeton, New Jersey 08540

Library of Congress Cataloging-in-Publication Data
Connolly, William E.
The terms of political discourse/William E. Connolly.—3d ed.
p.   cm.
Includes bibliographical references (p.   ) and index.
ISBN 0-691-02223-2 (pbk.: acid-free paper)
1. Political science—Philosophy.   I. Title.
<u>JA74.C66   1993</u>
320'.01'4—dc20   92-45234
76489
First published in 1974 by
D. C. Heath and Company, Massachusetts;
second edition published 1983 by Princeton University Press
First printing of the third edition, 1993

Princeton University Press books are printed on acid-free
paper and meet the guidelines for permanence and durability
of the Committee on Production Guidelines for Book
Longevity of the Council on Library Resources

1   3   5   7   9   10   8   6   4   2

Printed in the United States of America

Contents

Preface to the
Third Edition (1993)

When this book was written, at the beginning of the 1970s, the prevailing conception of rationality in Anglo-American social sciences was becoming an object of critical examination. Rationality had been understood within these circles to require a sharp distinction between analytic and synthetic statements, a clear delineation between descriptive and normative statements, and a neutral method of discrimination (such as falsification or some principle of confirmation) through which scientific (testable) theories could be distinguished from un- or extrascientific doctrines. A series of divisions between rational and irrational, science and ideology, open and closed, testable and untestable, empirical theory and normative theory, realism and utopianism, and so on, was bound up with this conception of rational practice. These standards were widely invoked in debates over the adequacy of key concepts, the promise of alternative theories, and the clarity of thought of young scholars up for tenure or advancement.

It seemed advisable to me, in 1974, to challenge this conception of rationality as a prelude to advancing a set of themes about the theory-embedded character of political concepts, the contestability of key political concepts, the normative implications of conceptual decisions in empirical inquiry, and the primacy of interpretation over law-like explanation. Otherwise, it seemed, my arguments on these fronts would be rejected out of hand by many because they were thought not to correspond to minimal, universal standards of rationality.

But these same standards of rational practice are today no longer shared so widely or self-confidently. Many remain committed to the sufficiency of rationality, but few are foolhardy enough to insist that these particular standards must form its core. Some are committed to some of them; many are opposed to many of them; but almost nobody thinks it is simply irrational to reject any of them. The academic terms of debate over the practice of rationality have changed significantly. It is doubtful that anyone advancing the theme of this book today would feel pressed to begin it as I did in 1974.

Still, some tendencies have persisted. Most practitioners believe the practice of rationality is bound up with the law of noncontradiction; many either assume or contend that rationality is a sufficient condition of responsible inquiry; many believe that any convincing argument that shows the insufficiency of a particular practice of rationality must be followed by an inquiry that will render rationality itself sufficient. It is still only a minority of dissident practitioners who contend, first, that rationality is both indispensable and problematical in every practice of political inquiry, and, second, that folding acceptance of this condition into the terms of academic debate and the practices of democratic politics is a precondition of a viable democratic ethos. "Rationality" has not become widely activated as an essentially contested concept, at least within the operational codes of most practicing social scientists, even though almost everybody would concur upon reflection that the prevailing practices of rationality in academic discourse today vary from those of the early 1960s.

Practices of rationality in political thought are essentially contestable, but these practices have still not become active objects of contestation. The recurrent acknowledgment of the insufficient and problematic qualities of local practices of rationality needs to be converted into debates over possible limits attached to any project that aspires to a sufficient concept of rationality. Deconstruction and genealogy are the best candidates through which this aspiration to the sufficiency of rationality can be engaged critically today, since they strive to enable practitioners to glimpse contingencies, remainders, resistances, and excesses in their own practices. These critical practices might encourage more theorists to engage a paradox arguably installed in rationality itself: namely that practices of rationality are both indispensable to political reflection and highly problematical in their claims to self-sufficiency. The scholarly division of labor in political and social theory today, however, does not encourage such reflection. For while a host of theorists now practice the arts of deconstruction and genealogy, very few rationalists have yet to consider the possible relation of these practices to their own enterprise and aspirations.

Rather than responding to each new exposure of the insufficiency of a particular practice of rationality with a renewed effort to restore closure, more practitioners might strive to come to terms with the ethically productive effects of treating this effect as a persistent, regular feature of the human condition. Rather than treating retrospective recognition of the insufficiency of each particular practice of rationality as simply a lack, loss, or defect to be lamented and repaired—thereby generating pressures to conceal, repress, redress, or, at the very least, whine about this effect—it might be timely to address the productive role "essentially contestable concepts" can play in ethical and political life. For it is possible that extending contestation more actively into established practices of rationality might create more social space for difference.

A positive response to the essential contestability of each concept of rationality might become an avenue through which the political minimalism of liberalism/individualism and the consensual idealism of communitarianism/civic republicanism are challenged. Such a response would prize the element of conflict in politics and cultivate agonistic respect among rivals as a means to foster freedom, generosity, and creativity within the incorrigible disputes of political life. For the most serious threats to the promise of such a mutual appreciation of limits between rivals flows not from irrationalists who refuse to recognize rational limits but from interlocking patterns of aggressive conventionality, closed rationality, and dogmatic faith entrenched in prevailing practices. The problem of evil in politics resides more in closed practices of rationality than it does in the refusal by irrationalists to conform to established practices of rationality.

We might, then, seek to loosen the grip the imperative to "reason" has on our souls in the interests of cultivating generosity in political contestation. We can come thus to appreciate how multiple practices of rationality are simultaneously indispensable and problematical. No argument could force anyone to reach such a conclusion, nor could it compel one to go in the other direction. Political discourse, on the model presented here, possesses a highly limited capacity to reach necessary conclusions through rational compulsion or entailment. Its conclusions acquire the appearance of necessity mostly by covert strategies that draw upon institutional power to secure the universality or sufficiency of particular practices of rationality. Critical engagements with prevailing practices of rationality can make a difference in the presumptions, predispositions, and moods through which practitioners engage political issues. These engagements can enhance reciprocal generosity and forbearance in political debates and struggles.

Chapter six, which was added to the second edition of this book, pursues some of these issues, defending "essential contestability" against a familiar set of objections, pointing to the role genealogy can play in appreciating the persistence and productivity of conflicts in these domains, and reconsidering presumptions about the rational, responsible agent that provided the backdrop to the definitions and contestations offered in the first edition. In the remainder of this preface I will pursue the implications of this perspective for an orientation to ethics and a conception of democracy. I will try to move "contestability" more actively into the domains of ethics and democracy.

Suppose one thinks, as I do, that a persistent problem of evil resides in the paradoxical relation of identity to difference.[1] An identity consolidates and stabilizes itself by distinguishing itself from different modes of being. I am pagan; you are Christian or nontheistic. I am feminine; you are masculine or androgynous. I am gay; you are straight. I am conventional and raucous; you are adventurous and reserved. I am rational; you are irrational or mystical. But the bearers of the differences through which an identity consolidates itself contain their own drives to identity, and these may well take a form that will destabilize, disturb, and disrupt the security of the identity I seek. These alter-drives, then, are required for the stabilization of an identity, but they can also emerge as threats to that same identity.

When these pressures intensify, one or both of the parties involved may move to consolidate its identity by defining a range of differences as evil, irrational, perverse, abnormal, or heretical. Identity requires difference, but difference also threatens to destabilize identity. Evil, as undeserved suffering of the other, grows out of the multiple pressures to conceal or repress the paradoxical character of this relationship by converting a range of differences into a single, totemic otherness that deserves to be conquered, converted, reformed, or reconstituted.

There are two points that connect these comments to those about rationality: first, the recurrent experience of the insufficiency of rationality is one of the signs of the paradoxical element in the logic of identity claims; and, second, the modern problem of evil resides more in the rationalization of prevailing conventions through the regular constitution of difference as otherness than it does in willful, gratuitous acts of evil by evil agents.

If a problem of evil resides in the paradoxical relation of identity to difference, we might strive to relieve its effects by emphasizing the constructed, contestable, contingent, and relational character of established identities, encouraging negotiations of identity and difference to proceed with a more refined sensibility of the limits of claims to self-sufficiency. Some moralists, however, will insist (predictably) that such a strategy is self-defeating. They will adopt the same perspective on this project that critics of essential contestability have done in more restricted zones. They will say: "It fosters nihilism" or, "it is parasitical upon the foundations of morality it opposes" or, "it issues in a relativism that disables it from opposing on moral grounds any response to the very paradox it purports to recognize."

Such replies are familiar. Their familiarity signals either a persistent blindness by those replying or a stubborn unwillingness to face up to the contradictory character of this enterprise on the part of those who press the contingency of identity and the contestability of established practices for ethical reasons.

From my perspective those who offer objections of the above sort implicitly demand ratification of the universal superiority of their own identity. This is detectable in the strong language used to characterize opponents. What can be done, anyway, with a parasite, a nihilist, or an irrationalist if you take these terms seriously and if you have enough power to act upon their implications? To use Nietzsche's language, the carriers of this message are saying "I am morality itself and nothing besides is morality." They insist that they are what morality requires, and they bolster that claim less by affirmative demonstrations and more by trying to show how any perspective that breaks with such an equation falls to pieces. They deploy morality to consolidate the self-certainty and intrinsic superiority of their own identity.

In the first edition of this book I endorsed a loosened version of such a position myself, treating the responsible agent as the ground of morality who would lapse into a pragmatic self-contradiction if it denied this status to itself. It now seems not only that this conclusion was exaggerated (as the addition of chapter six to the second edition indicates), but also that it may be possible to articulate an alternative orientation to ethical life that provides a more positive alternative to prevailing moral imperatives.

One line of response might be to challenge theories of intrinsic *moral order* with a competing *ethical sensibility,* and to open a little space between "morality" and "ethics"—with appropriate apologies to Hegel—so that the latter can become a more active competitor of the former. Conceptions of moral order can take several forms. One type accentuates the verb "to order," treating morality as obedience to an ultimate order or command issued by a god, nature, the dictates of reason, or a categorical imperative. Another type accentuates the noun "order," treating moral order as an inherent, harmonious design of being with which humans can enter into closer communion by practicing the right arts in the proper spirit of piety. Moral order, then, becomes an inherent command, a harmonious purpose, or, very often in the Western tradition, both of those modalities in some unstable combination.

The sensibility I am reaching for challenges both conceptions of moral order, whether they are explicitly defended or, as they often emerge today, implicitly installed in narratives that do not defend them explicitly. The implicit versions, for instance, are often signified through the application of pejoratives of parasitism or heresy to their opponents through terms that presuppose access to an intrinsic moral order founded on truth, attunement to a higher direction, a transcendental imperative, or universal reason.

Perhaps it is useful to open this distance between morality and ethics by considering some points of contact between one of the two moral conceptions summarized above and the orientation to ethics supported here. There may be discrete points of convergence between a teleological morality (the second type noted above) and the "post-Nietzschean" ethical sensibility I am developing, despite the more fundamental divergence between them. Both, first, challenge authoritarian tendencies in command moralities. Both, second, construe the self to be a microsocial structure of voices, replete with foreign relations, implicated in complex relations with the macrosocial structure in which it participates; both thereby deny "the self" as a sufficient ground of ethics or politics. And both, third, are ethics of cultivation rather than command. That is, both draw sustenance—to appropriate the recent words of Charles Taylor—from sources that exceed any settled identity and are irreducible to unfettered translation. [2]

A teleological morality might strive to commune with intrinsic purposes lodged in the embodied self, the language of a community, or the love of a purposeful god. In the Nietzschean tradition, such fugitive, nonpurposive sources might be "life," "will to power," "bodies," "earth," "fundamental difference," "*différance*," or "untruth." A teleologist might anchor his morality ambiguously in the realization of a deep identity and in communion with a higher design exceeding that identity's powers of articulation. A post-Nietzschean might draw her sensibility ambiguously from a contingent identity that incorporates agonistic respect for some of the differences that help to define it and from an "abundance of life" exceeding any particular set of identity\difference relations.

In Nietzsche's work, as I read it, "life" (as with other nonconcepts of its type) is an indispensable, nonfixable marker, challenging every attempt to treat a concept, settlement, or principle as complete, without excess, remainders, or resistances. This projection functions only through contrast and contestation with those concepts that project a commanding god, a designing god, an intrinsic purpose, or the sufficiency of reason into moral and ethical discourse.

A post-Nietzschean ethical sensibility, then, might strive first to expose artifice in hegemonic identities and in the definitions of otherness that help to sustain their self-certainty; second, to destabilize codes of moral order within which prevailing identities are set, when doing so crystallizes the element of resentment in their definitions of difference; third, to pursue generosity—that is, a pathos of distance—in the indispensable rivalries between moral/ethical perspectives by emphasizing the problematical character of each contending position (including one's own) and the unavoidability of such contestations; and, fourth, to counter political visions that suppress the paradox of difference with alternatives that go some distance in specifying the positive vision that inspires them. Since I have so far separated this ethical sensibility from the name "Nietzsche" only by a prefix and that all-important hyphen, let me offer a pertinent quotation from the divine source (or madman) himself:

> Thus I deny morality as I deny alchemy, that is, I deny their premises: but I do *not* deny that there have been alchemists who believed in these premises and acted in accordance with them.—I also deny immorality; *not* that countless people *feel* themselves to be immoral, but that there is any *true* reason so to feel. It goes without saying that I do not deny—unless I am a fool—that many actions called immoral ought to be avoided and resisted, or that many called moral ought to be done and encouraged—but I think the one should be encouraged and the other avoided *for other reasons than hitherto*. We have to *learn to think differently*—in order at last, perhaps very late on, to attain more: *to feel differently*.[3]

The "we" in this quotation is a solicitation rather than a command, and Nietzsche's use of artful techniques to alter corporeal "feelings" functions as a replacement for teleological virtues. For a Nietzschean ethic to function, a revised set of sensibilities must become inscribed in the feelings through tactics applied by the self to itself. This sensibility subdues existential resentment against a world in which the quest for a moral command or a higher purpose constantly meets with rebuffs. To the extent it succeeds in this latter task, the Nietzschean ethic both affirms the relational and contingent character of its own identity and cultivates agonistic respect for those differences that threaten its self-reassurance.

A post-Nietzschean ethic is an ethic of cultivation rather than a morality of command; it cultivates an experience of excesses, resistances, and remainders that calls into question the closures and sufficiencies of established practices of rationality rather than a communion with a higher purpose inscribed in being; it promotes a greater generosity in those valuable relationships of interdependence and rivalry rather than a unified consensus to which everyone subscribes; it strives to come to terms politically with dilemmas posed by the social need to act in concert and the persistent absence of a sufficient rational basis on which to establish consensuality. The above slogans merely provide preliminary bearings for a sensibility that expresses itself through the interpretations of prevailing practices it offers rather than through a set of abstract principles it brings to the judgment of fixed conventions. The post-Nietzschean sensibility shares this last disposition, too, with the teleological tradition that it contests at the ontological level.

Such a post-Nietzschean sensibility might consolidate itself through the elaboration of a *timely* conception of democracy congruent with its basic ethical impulses. This task, obviously, must be an extremely post-Nietzschean enterprise, one that is as opposed to some dimensions of Nietzsche's thought as it is indebted to others, standing in antagonistic indebtedness to the name "Nietzsche."[4] The installation of agonistic respect into the strife and interdependence of identity and difference must occur in a democratic culture today if it is to occur anywhere at all. I will here merely list two dimensions in such a conception of democracy, illustrating how "democracy," as an essentially contestable concept, might become the object of a new and timely contestation.

First, within the territorial state: A viable democratic culture would embody a productive ambiguity at its very center. Its role as an instrument of governance and mobilizer of collective action would be balanced and countered by its logic as a medium for the periodic disruption and denaturalization of settled identities and conventions. Both dimensions are crucial to democratic life and both are bound up with institutions of electoral accountability. But if the second function were to disappear under the weight of the first, state mechanisms of electoral accountability would become conduits for the production of interior, internal, and external others against which moral wars would be waged in order to bolster an artificial consensus.

Second, the limits posed by the territorial state to a democratic ethos: We live during a time when an asymmetry between the globalization of life and the confinement of democracy to the territorial state itself often functions to intensify democratic state chauvinism.

The nostalgia in political theory (and the culture at large) for a "politics of place" in which territoriality, sovereignty, electoral accountability, and belonging all correspond to each other in one "political place" has the double effect today of depoliticizing global issues and weakening the ability to challenge state chauvinism. The collective desire to limit the scope of political discourse to topics and responses that correspond to the effective limits of state action can suppress crucial issues: the suppression within democratic states of discourse over the greenhouse effect merely symbolizes a more extensive tendency. And these issues are likely to return in ways that are statist and exclusivist in character. The return of the repressed is often ugly.

Under the circumstances of late-modern life, productive possibilities might be opened up by a creative disaggregation of the democratic imagination, paying attention, for instance, to how a democratic ethos might exceed the boundaries of particular states, even while institutions of electoral accountability remain confined within states. During a time when corporate organizations, financial institutions, intelligence networks, communication media, and criminal rings are increasingly global in character, and when, as a result, a whole host of dangerous contingencies has become global in character, democratic energies, while remaining active below and through the state, might also extend beyond these parameters to cross-national, nonstatist social movements. A new pluralization of identifications and spaces of action flowing over the boundaries of the state seems needed to compromise the state's ability to monopolize collective identity at key historical moments.

Such boundary-crossing democratic movements with respect to, say, green pressure, gay/lesbian rights, state responses to the international transmission of disease, exposure of international patterns of state secrecy and surveillance, and contestation of statist monopolies over the potent symbols of security and danger can be productive. They can address the interests in question, the democratic drive to have a hand in shaping events that affect people, and the ventilation of politics within states. As cross-national, nonstatist movements already in motion accelerate, they might extend the democratic ethos beyond state boundaries through a new pluralization of political spaces for identification and action. They might compromise the state as the highest or consummate site of collective identity by extending the spaces of democratic action.[5]

These thoughts carry the theme of contestability into regions not thought through in the previous editions by opening up the terms of contestation more actively in the intersecting domains of rationality, ethics, and democracy. Introducing this perspective into such domains might change or alter established terms of debate. The cultivation of such an ethical sensibility would challenge persistent elements in the moral tradition, and do so in a way that consolidates its own implications for democratic theory. Pursuing these questions would bring out the ethical significance of rendering fixed debates and practices more fluid and problematic.

The agenda is to develop an orientation that treats encounters with excess, resistance, and remainders in culture as prized souces of creativity and change, rather than simply lacks, deficiencies, and failures to be resolved. Doing so would cultivate a sensibility that prizes simultaneously the importance of political disturbance to ethical life and the importance of limits to political disturbance.

The path from "essentially contested concepts" to a "post-Nietzschean sensibility" is not that difficult to discern, once some of the underbrush has been cleared by a protean thinker like Foucault. The conception of politics elaborated in the first edition of this book, for instance, is remarkably close to the one I have pursued later. It was, nonetheless, difficult to anticipate this trajectory in the initial context of this study's formulation.

NOTES

1. This thesis is developed in *Identity\Difference: Democratic Negotiations of Political Paradox* (Ithaca, N.Y.: Cornell University Press, 1991), esp. chap. 3. The relation between that study and *The Terms of Political Discourse* can be stated fairly succinctly. While the first study emphasizes the instability and contestability of key concepts, the second emphasizes these same characteristics with respect to the identities

through which we are constituted. The orientation to politics is similar in both studies, though the position is pushed onto new territory in the latter one.

2. Taylor's "sources" reside in intimate relation to the culture in which they find expression and to more fugitive experiences that are susceptible to partial articulation but not to forthright representation as independent objects. "Moral sources empower. To come closer to them, to have a clearer view of them, to come to grasp what they involve, is for those who recognize them to be moved to love or respect them, and through this love/respect to be better enabled to live up to them." *Sources of the Self: The Making of the Modern Identity* (Cambridge, Mass.: Harvard University Press, 1989), p. 96. Taylor does not quite see, as I read him, how nonpurposive, nondirectional sources can inform ethical life.

3. Nietzsche, *Daybreak: Thoughts on the Prejudices of Morality,* trans. R. J. Hollingdale (Cambridge: Cambridge University Press, 1982), p. 103 n.103. Alan White considers this quotation in a parallel way in relation to ethics in *Within Nietzsche's Labyrinthe* (New York: Routledge, 1990), chap. 7. I agree with his reading, adding only that the discussion of "feelings" at the end of the quote is perhaps the most crucial part of it. I consider more extensively how the above quotation from Nietzsche illuminates the sensibilities of both Nietzsche and Foucault in "Beyond Good and Evil: The Ethical Sensibility of Michel Foucault," *Political Theory* 21 (1993).

4. I outline such a relation of "antagonistic indebtedness" in *Political Theory and Modernity* (Oxford: Basil Blackwell, 1988), chap. 5.

5. This theme is developed more extensively in "Democracy and Territoriality," *Millennium* 20 (1991): 463–84.

Preface to the Second Edition

The urge to depoliticize emerges in theories about politics as well as in the political life about which we theorize. It finds implicit expression, for instance, in the wish to construct a neutral matrix for political discourse. While the sources of this urge are readily understandable, recurrent efforts to demonstrate that one particular scheme actually provides the neutral medium sought are constantly open to decomposition. Each attempt to provide a frame both rationally demonstrable and specific enough to guide practical judgment, opens itself to reasonable contestation. This thesis was explored in the first edition of this text by developing the idea of essentially contestable concepts and by pursuing its implications for understanding the terms of political discourse. The notion helps us to understand not only the discourse of politics but also the politics of discourse. It helps us to see how politics becomes submerged in political theories governed by a strong program of rationalism and how struggles over the grammar of crucial concepts plays a prominent role in political discourse.

Though there are changes I would now make in these arguments, I continue to endorse the major thesis itself, and I have thus not revised the original text. Rather I have written a new last chapter which responds to criticisms of my initial account of power and essential contestability, re-examines the role and limits of counter-examples in conceptual inquiry, and considers affinities and differences between the thesis of contestability and the more relentless theory of deconstruction.

William E. Connolly
April, 1983

Preface to the First Edition

The terms of political discourse set the frame within which political thought and action proceed. To examine that discourse is to translate tacit judgments embedded in the language of politics into explicit considerations more fully subject to critical assessment.

My purposes in this study are to explore a set of concepts whose meanings are subject to persistent contests and debates at strategic points, to illuminate the role that such conceptual contests play in political inquiry and political life, and to stake out positions on the contests themselves that, if generally adopted, would help to weave viable norms of responsibility more tightly into the fabric of political life.

In 1970 Felix Oppenheim and I decided to collaborate on a short study of political concepts. The stimulating debates that ensued, though seldom issuing in agreement, convinced me to undertake this study and helped me to identify the pertinent issues more clearly. Steven Lukes has read a preliminary draft of each chapter of this book. His insightful criticisms and suggestions have been immensely helpful in my preparation of the final product. Jean Elshtain, Glen Gordon, George Kateb, David Kettler, and Sanford Thatcher have each read selected chapters; I deeply appreciate their numerous suggestions, many of which have found their way into the final draft. It is clear enough to me that each of these colleagues shares a measure of responsibility for the strengths and the defects of this study.

I wish to thank the National Endowment for the Humanities for a grant during 1973 that enabled me to pursue this study. I should also like to express my gratitude to the editor of *Politics and Society* for permission to reprint a revised version of "On 'Interests' in Politics"; to Mrs. Vera Smith for her very competent typing (and retyping) of the manuscript; and to the graduate students in political theory at the University of Massachusetts who heard and criticized earlier versions of these arguments.

William E. Connolly

Introduction

It is sometimes assumed that language is simply a medium to convey ideas. If too much time is spent examining the medium, the ideas it is supposed to convey tend to get lost in the shuffle. Moreover, it is alleged, once one starts to examine a few concepts the initial task threatens to proliferate into an endless assignment: To define a concept is necessarily to connect it with several others that need clarification if the first is to be clear, and those others in turn are connected to a still wider network of concepts deserving equally close attention. Thus, one soon finds oneself in the position of the cabinetmaker who, after sharpening and cleaning his tools for weeks, is dismayed to discover that no cabinets have yet been built. Time spent examining the concepts of politics, it is feared, is time taken away from politics itself.

There is indeed a point buried in such a line of reasoning, but it is distorted by the fallacious assumption with which it begins. The language of politics is not a neutral medium that conveys ideas independently formed; it is an institutionalized structure of meanings that channels political thought and action in certain directions. Those who simply use established concepts to get to the facts of political life, those who act unreflectively within the confines of established concepts, actually have the perceptions and modes of conduct available to them limited in subtle and undetected ways. Such conceptual blinders impede the work of any student of politics, but they are particularly corrosive of efforts to explore radical perspectives on politics. For to adopt without revision the concepts prevailing in a polity is to accept terms of discourse loaded in favor of established practices.

The connection between the structure of political life and the terms of political discourse is comparable in some respects to the relationship of a jury to a legal system. The jury examines the evidence and reaches a verdict, but prior to its deliberations, the judge, acting as official interpreter of the law, charges the jury with a set of responsibilities, establishes what can be considered as evidence, and specifies what constitutes a punishable offense. If, for instance, the jury is to decide whether the defendant negligently caused or contributed to injuries received by the plaintiff, the judge instructs the jury as to what sorts of conduct legally constitute 'negligence' and 'contributory negligence'; he also informs the jury where the burden of proof rests and screens claims from it, such as 'hearsay' testimony, that are not legally admissible as evidence. In charging the jury and in regulating the presentation of evidence to it, the judge, we might say, specifies the terms within which the jury considers evidence and reaches a verdict.

By the *terms* of political discourse, then, I refer first to the vocabulary commonly employed in political thought and action; second, to the ways in which the meanings conventionally embodied in that vocabulary set the frame for political reflection by establishing criteria to be met before an event or act can be said to fall within the ambit of a given concept; and third, to the judgments or commitments that are conventionally sanctioned when these criteria are met. To return to our legal example, when a jury finds that a defendant was negligent, it is holding that his conduct met certain specified criteria and that the conformity to those criteria justifies or warrants holding him legally liable for the resulting injury. The jury describes his conduct within a legal concept that also conveys a judgment of guilt and liability. Similarly, in political life we describe people as committing treason, instituting tyranny, and engaging in corruption, and in each case the concept invoked to describe the action or practice conveys a judgment about these acts and practices as well. To apply those concepts is to sanction the judgments they incorporate. More generally, to share a language is to share a range of judgments and commitments embodied in it.

Since the discourse of politics helps to set the terms within which that politics proceeds, one who seeks to understand and to assess the structure of political life must deliberately probe the conventions governing those concepts. To examine and accept, or to examine and revise, the prevailing terms of political discourse is not a prelude to politics but a dimension of politics itself.

To probe these connections and to explore the issues they pose it is necessary to subject several methodological postulates of mainstream social science to critical reappraisal. Distinctions between operational and nonoperational vocabularies, descriptive and normative concepts, analytic and synthetic statements, empirical and conceptual arguments, technical terms and the terms of ordinary discourse, the role of the social scientist and that of the citizen, all require adjustment and revision if the role of conceptual contests in politics is to be comprehended. The goal of such a revisionary effort is not to repudiate ideals of clarity, precision, and objectivity but to recast them along lines more applicable to the phenomena of politics.

In the first chapter of this study I launch such an effort. Drawing on some recent work in linguistic philosophy I revise several of these presuppositions and research norms. Reinterpreting these directives allows us to understand more clearly why the central concepts of politics are so often and so intensely the subject of controversy and conflict. While I certainly do not articulate considerations sufficient to resolve each of these controversies rationally—indeed, it appears that definitive resolution is usually impossible—I hope the considerations advanced do enable us to understand these conflicts more thoroughly and to render judgments with respect to them more conscious and reflective.

In the next three chapters, themes developed in the first are exemplified through scrutiny of three concepts implicated both in the discourse of political life and that of political inquiry. A number of concepts are susceptible to the analysis I would propose, such as the ideas of consent (and its cousin in social science, consensus), legitimacy, violence, tolerance, public and private, but I have chosen the concepts of interest, power, and freedom for attention. Not only are these concepts important to both the domains in question, but each has been construed by many social scientists as a neutral, descriptive concept, definable in operational terms and properly acceptable after such tightening to any investigator regardless of his ideology or normative orientation. These concepts provide admirable vehicles for testing competing claims about the terms of political discourse. With respect to each concept I first probe the nature and import of contests over its proper definition and then stake out a position with respect to these contests. The claims I make will remain, to some degree and in certain respects, inherently controversial. Part of my objective is to show why this is so and to explore routes to reasoned judgment in contexts where it is so.

The final chapter explores some additional dimensions of these themes. It is offered, not as a stack of fully developed arguments, but as a set of suggestions in need of further elaboration and development. By focusing on the connection between conceptual revision and political change one can grasp more fully the latent structure of conceptual disputes within political science and within political life; one might also enhance understanding of the sorts of considerations to invoke in deciding to endorse or to repudiate proposals to revise key concepts in particular ways. After exploring connections between conceptual contests and politics I offer some ideas about how one might hope to subject such conceptual contests to a measure of rational control.

The conceptual dimension of political inquiry and political life does not, certainly, operate in a void; to explore it is to make contact with a whole range of issues involved in the larger enterprise of political theory. An examination of political concepts that does not confront each of these related issues is to that extent incomplete. Such a verdict is surely true of this study. To minimize problems that might accompany such incompleteness I will, in what follows, identify some of these related problems and issues, specify points at which they touch the thesis of this study, and indicate generally my assumptions and inclinations concerning each.

1. If one were to concur in the formulations of 'interest', 'power', 'freedom', and 'politics' elaborated here, it would seem clear enough that one would be forced to revise significantly the pluralist interpretation of American politics. The plausibility of pluralist theory, in its various forms, rests to a great extent on the plausibility of key concepts in the theory. In the process of examining these concepts I often indicate how this is so and what implications might follow from accepting alternative readings of them, but there is no sustained effort to develop an interpretation of American politics that incorporates these concepts in the revised form recommended. Close attention to these conceptual issues will enhance and deepen, I believe, the so-called pluralist-elitist debate, but the full development of these implications is yet to be pursued.

2. If the approach to conceptual clarification adopted here is on the right track, and if the concepts of political life help to constitute that life in the ways argued, then it is unlikely that models of explanation derived from natural science can apply to social and political life in unrevised form. More specifically, since the "laws" of social science are designed to explain the behavior of agents who are capable of understanding them and of reacting to that understanding, and since the concepts with which we understand the actions of persons and groups in politics must make contact with the concepts the participants accept, it seems quite unlikely that social scientists can hope to devise explanatory *laws* with close *predictive* power that apply cross-culturally. I do not explore these issues closely here, but the approach taken to the understanding of political concepts moves one some distance away from the covering law model of explanation generally adopted by behavioral social scientists. I think it unlikely that the extreme alternative posed by Peter Winch will prove fully viable either,

but his formulations have served as an invaluable corrective to models of explanation currently accepted by many social scientists.

3. On many occasions I speak of concepts that describe from a moral point of view or, less restrictively, from a normative point of view. Such concepts describe while conveying the commitments of those who share them. The issues raised by these claims are connected to larger questions about the performative dimension of language and especially about how one properly construes the contours of the (or a) 'moral point of view'. I do not discuss these latter issues extensively; I do not, for instance, attempt to specify in detail what I take the moral point of view to be. This does not prove disastrous; though my claims are incompatible with extreme forms of noncognitivism such as emotivism, they are compatible with several other interpretations of the moral point of view. In fact it is quite congenial to my argument to hold that the idea of morality is itself inherently contestable along some dimensions. Here, as elsewhere, I have tried to footnote a literature that seems to me to reinforce and develop a particular aspect of my thesis. Thus I would endorse recent work by Stuart Hampshire, P. F. Strawson, and Charles Taylor, cited in the text, which illuminates central dimensions of moral discourse in ways that are generally congruent with the position articulated in this study.

4. Finally, I believe that efforts to reduce politics to other forces such as psychological factors or economic forces are doomed to produce a serious misreading of the phenomena under investigation. Central to politics, as I understand it, is the ambiguous and relatively open-ended interaction of persons and groups who share a range of concepts, but share them imperfectly and incompletely. Politics involves a form of interaction in which agents adjust, extend, resolve, accommodate, and transcend initial differences within a context of partly shared assumptions, concepts, and commitments. On this reading, conceptual contests are central to politics; they provide the space for political interaction. The use of force

certainly does occur in politics, and the appeal to a range of evidence that might narrow disputes between those who share similar concepts and assumptions is common also, but neither the resort to force nor to evidence constitutes what is distinctive to this dimension of social life. I try to identify some of the distinctive ingredients of politics in this study, but they are not finely analyzed. I would not contend that contemporary pluralist processes of issue formation and accommodation are the quintessence of politics; the mere proliferation of political issues and debates does not ensure sufficient airing of the grievances, troubles, hopes, and ideals of every segment of the society. Indeed, the fact that corporate control over pricing, investment, hiring, and the structure of work life is generally treated as if it were outside the political processes of pluralist society can serve as the beginning of an argument that the internally acknowledged sphere of politics is more restrictive than it should be. 'Politics' itself, on this reading, is construed too narrowly by most participants in our society. As this example suggests, close attention to the biases of a political system requires, among other things, critical scrutiny of the contours of those conceptual contests that help to constitute the life of the polity.

1

Essentially Contested
Concepts in Politics

ESSENTIALLY CONTESTED CONCEPTS

In an important essay written in 1956 W. B. Gallie argues that people committed to partly discrepant assumptions and ideas are likely to construe shared concepts in rather different ways as well.[1] They will share these concepts in the sense that in a number of situations they would agree in calling a particular set of practices a 'democracy', a 'Christian doctrine', or a 'work of art', but in other situations one party might deny that, say, the concept of democracy applies while the other affirms its proper application, or the contesting parties might disagree about the extent to which the concept applies to the situation at hand.

When the disagreement does not simply reflect different readings of evidence within a fully shared system of concepts, we can say that a conceptual dispute has arisen. When the concept involved is *appraisive* in that the state of affairs it describes is a valued achievement, when the practice described is *internally complex* in that its characterization involves reference to several dimensions, and when the agreed and contested rules of application are relatively *open,* enabling parties to interpret even those shared rules differently as new and unforeseen situations arise, then the concept in question is an "essentially contested concept." Such concepts "essentially involve endless disputes about their proper uses on the part of their users."[2]

According to Gallie, 'democracy' is such a concept, at least as it is used in western industrial societies. It is an achievement valued by most. Commonly accepted criteria of its application are weighted differently by opposing parties, and certain criteria viewed as central by one party are rejected as inappropriate or marginal by others. Finally, arguments about its proper use turn on fundamental issues about which reasoned argument is possible but full and definitive resolution often unlikely. Thus, for some the central criterion of a democracy is the power of citizens to choose their government through competitive elections; for others this factor is less important than the equality of opportunity for all citizens in attaining positions of political leadership; for still others both of these criteria pale in significance if the continuous participation of citizens at various levels of political life is not attained. These disagreements proliferate further when we see that concepts used to express them, such as 'power', 'political', 'equality', and 'participation', require elucidation also, a process likely to expose further disagreements among those contesting the concept of democracy.

Gallie argues that mutual awareness among adversaries that some of their shared concepts are subject to essential disputes contributes to the intellectual development of all protagonists. The pressure of opposing interpretations, when each sees other interpretations as capable of some degree of rational defense, is seen by each to contribute to his "own use or interpretation of the concept in question." [3]

We shall have occasion later to assess Gallie's qualified celebration of the diverse use of partly shared concepts. But a crucial part of my purpose here is to expose and refute widely held presuppositions that have discouraged American social scientists from coming to grips with Gallie's thesis and from exploring its implications for their own work. There are several aspects of Gallie's arguments that make them difficult for contemporary social scientists to assimilate and easy for them to ignore. To those accepting prevailing views about the nature and role of concepts in political inquiry it appears that Gallie does not distinguish sharply enough between neutral, "descriptive" concepts, about which intersubjective agreement can be attained, and those "normative" concepts that are open-ended and controversial in the way Gallie asserts; he doesn't seem to see that descriptive concepts, which are after all the ones pertinent to scientific work, can be defined operationally, enabling investigators with divergent ideologies to accept common definitions and to adopt the same impersonal tests in applying these shared concepts to determinate states of affairs; he even takes his examples from the life and discourse of ordinary people, inadvertently bypassing the technically defined terms of political science designed to meet the conditions of objective inquiry specified here. To the extent

Gallie's argument is correct, these social scientists would contend, it does not apply to the enterprise of political science; and to the extent the argument applies, it is wrong-headed. These are the counterarguments I will summarize and refute here. If the refutation is successful, I will have vindicated an approach to the understanding of political concepts and their role in political life quite different from that honored (if not consistently pursued) in contemporary social science.

AN EXAMPLE: 'POLITICS'

'Politics', surely, is a concept central to political life and political inquiry; its very centrality helps to ensure that participants in and students of politics will, within a broad framework of shared rules, debate its proper range of application. We can begin to grasp the nature and import of such disputes by drawing up a list of possible ingredients in (or criteria of) the complex idea of politics. Thus to call something 'political' or part of 'politics' might include reference to the following:

1. Policies backed by the *legally binding authority* of government.

2. Actions that involve a *decision* or *choice* among *viable options,* for instance, an entrepreneur in a perfectly competitive market system who lowers prices in response to a decline in demand is not making a political decision.

3. The sort of *considerations* or *motives* participants invoke in selecting one available option over others, for example, a public official playing down his opposition to abortion in a campaign speech given to a group of feminists is said to be acting politically.

4. The extent to which decision outcomes affect the *interests, wishes,* or *values* of particular segments of the population, for example, a university's admission policy is political if it systematically discriminates against a minority group.

5. The extent to which the outcomes of decision are *intended* or at least *known* by the decision makers, for instance, other things being equal, a policy of discrimination against

minority ethnic groups is more political if the result is intended than if it is not.

6. The *number* of people affected by the decision outcome and the *length of time* for which they are affected, say, if two or three people are affected briefly by a bureaucrat's decision to withhold a visa, we view the act as less political than if a larger class were so affected by such a policy for a number of years (other things being equal here as well).

7. The extent to which the *traditions* and *consensual expectations* of a people acknowledge the matter at hand to be one in which a public voice is legitimately involved, for instance, a strike by organized labor is more political in this sense than a corporate price increase, even when the corporate decision affects many and is not fully constrained by market forces.

8. The extent to which a policy or act becomes an *issue* as groups with different views about it range themselves on opposing sides to influence outcomes, for example, the production of napalm by Dow Chemical Company became more political after it was subject to wide debate and opposing pressures than it had been before.

Certainly a more thorough canvass would uncover further dimensions of 'politics', and the dimensions briefly enumerated here could well be elaborated more fully. But the foregoing sketch is sufficient for present purposes; attention to it reveals several implications pertinent to the understanding of conceptual disputes.

1. *The Internal Complexity and Contestability of 'Politics'.* Perhaps none of these dimensions alone is *sufficient* to establish an act or practice as political, although some of them are surely more important than others. Thus item 1 is normally thought to be crucially related to 'politics', but we would not say that the police practice of enforcing traffic laws is part of politics unless some of the other conditions listed were also met (say, the police are ordered by the incumbent mayor to ticket cars parked illegally at his opponents' rally—items 3 and 4). If none of them alone qualifies an act as part of politics, *any* three or four of them in conjunction are sufficient at least

to make the act or practice a viable candidate for that rubric. Taken together, these two points mean that we cannot specify an invariant set of necessary and sufficient conditions for the proper application of the concept of politics but that we must treat politics as a cluster concept to which a broad range of criteria apply; any large set of these criteria grouped together in a particular act or practice is capable of qualifying the act as political.

Not only is politics an internally complex concept with a broad and variable set of criteria but each criterion itself is relatively complex and open. Each of the dimensions listed in items 1 through 8 makes reference to new concepts, implicated in our understanding of 'politics', such as institution, decision, viable option, motive, outcome, interest, wishes, values, intention, issue, tradition, and consensus. To make the concept of politics intelligible we must display its complex connections with a host of other concepts to which it is related; clarification of the concept of politics thereby involves the elaboration of the broader conceptual system within which it is implicated.

We shall call a concept with these characteristics a cluster concept. We often find that various people jointly employing such a cluster concept weight the importance of shared criteria differently; they might also interpret the meaning of particular criteria jointly accepted in subtly different ways; and some persons might find it advantageous to add new criteria to, or drop old criteria from, the established list, while other groups object to such moves. When one or more of these conditions prevail we have the makings of a conceptual dispute. Such disputes have undeniably arisen in contemporary life over the concept of politics. Radicals, for instance, are prone to call certain corporate decisions political because these practices are thought to conform to items 2, 3, 4, and 6, while their opponents resist these efforts on the grounds that (what are in their view) the more *important* criteria (1, 5, 7, and 8) are either excluded from or very imperfectly manifested in corporate practices. Contests persist over the proper interpretation of the partly shared idea of politics, and we might say that its very characteristics as a cluster concept provide the space within which such contests emerge.

2. *The Limits of Operationalism.* The doctrine of operationalism is often advanced both as a vehicle for specifying more closely the criteria of concepts such as politics and as a standard against which competing interpretations of such concepts can be appraised. The version of the doctrine we are interested in holds that each concept in political inquiry must be associated with a precise and definite testing operation that specifies the conditions of its application, and it seeks to adjudicate between competing definitions by ascertaining which proposal most adequately meets the operational requirement. Karl Deutsch endorses and purports to live up to such a doctrine in the preface to his recent text on comparative politics; he informs us that "each concept," in his study, "is defined in terms of some operation that can be repeated and tested by different people regardless of their preferences."[4]

But Deutsch does not and cannot deliver on either of his promises. A perusal of definitions actually offered by him reveals immediately that none is translatable either into a single operation or a small set of invariantly associated, simple operations. Consider: *Politics,* "the making of decisions by public means," (p. 31); *interest,* "anyone's interest in a situation consists in the rewards he can extract from it" (p. 10); *liberty,* "the ability to act in accordance with one's own personality, without having to make a great effort at self-denial" (p. 13); *power,* "the ability to make things happen that would not have happened otherwise" (p. 24).[5]

This preliminary judgment is reinforced when we explore the extent to which the criteria of a concept such as politics can be rendered operational. For, as we have seen, each of the criteria in items 1 to 8 makes reference to new concepts implicated in our understanding of politics: To make the cluster concept of politics operational is to make each of the cluster concepts that help to define it operational as well. And, it should be noted, the concepts that help to define politics are not simple observation terms either; each of them has complex connections to a host of other concepts that must be understood before it can be used properly.

More important, even if it were established that one proposed definition of politics were more operational than another, this demonstration in itself would not be sufficient to establish it as the preferred definition. For the more operational definition might drop out elements central to our idea of politics; we might transform the point of talk about politics itself in the name of making that talk more precise. *Until we consider the point or purpose in grouping a set of elements under the rubric of 'politics', we lack a basis for deciding that one proposed definition is superior to another.*

If the doctrine of operationalism fails in its stringent form, a more relaxed version can be defended. In this version the *range* of allowable criteria for a concept is broadened and loosened and the standard of what *counts as an observation* for each criterion is relaxed. Instead of limiting "observables" to movements or objects unmediated by interpretation, highly complex perceptions are allowed, such as observing a person "react defensively," "cast a vote," or "reject a bribe." These latter perceptions are understood to require a rich conceptual background both for their occurrence and for the observer's grasp of them. For to differentiate "casting a vote" from different activities superficially similar it is not sufficient to observe marks on papers taken from sealed boxes; one must have reason to believe that the voter has marked the ballot intentionally, voluntarily, with the purpose in mind of contributing his voice to a social decision of importance in a setting where this act makes some difference on the outcome of events, and so on.

The extent to which the original doctrine of operationalism has been relaxed under the pressure of philosophical analysis is suggested by George Schlesinger in his summary of a version that does remain defensible:

> That which is conceptualized need not be completely defined in terms of operations, although it must make contact with the world of public experience.[6]

But while such a formulation saves operationalism, it saves a version that cannot draw a clear line between concepts acceptable in social inquiry and those to be excluded; two concepts, for example, which were prime candidates for rejection according to earlier operational enthusiasts—Marx's concept of false-consciousness and Freud's concept of reaction formation can surely pass the muster of this revised requirement. Neither does the relaxed version provide a rationale for adjudicating between competing uses of partly shared concepts. Any version of operationalism restrictive enough to carry the heavy burden social scientists have imposed on it is false, while any version that is defensible contributes only marginally to the resolution of outstanding problems in the clarification of political concepts.

3. *The Analytic-Synthetic Dichotomy.* According to those positivist models of conceptual clarification that continue to have a grip on contemporary social science, every meaningful statement is either analytic or synthetic. Those statements that help to bring out the meaning of a concept are analytically related to it in the sense that it is logically inconsistent to assert that the concept in question applies if any of its defining criteria is missing. All other statements into which the concept enters bear a synthetic relationship to it in that it is a question for empirical inquiry to ascertain whether the conditions where the concept applies are also associated with the occurrence of these other items. Thus, "all bachelors are unmarried" is an analytic statement because its denial is inconsistent with our understanding of the meaning of 'bachelor', while "all bachelors are frustrated" is a synthetic claim about bachelors to be defeated or established through empirical inquiry. But this dichotomy between analytic and synthetic statements does not square with our discussion of the criteria of politics.

While any three or four of the criteria of politics occurring together are sufficient to establish an act or practice as a candidate for the label 'politics', none of these criteria alone seems sufficient; and *any single one of them might be lacking* in a particular instance where the concept politics properly applies. Items 2, 3, and 4 do not, for instance, have as tight a connection to 'politics' as unmarried does to 'bachelor'; yet if we dropped from the defining criteria of 'politics' all those items that lack such a tight connection, the concept itself would evaporate. The criteria of 'politics', then, do not have a purely analytic relationship to the concept nor do they have a purely synthetic relationship to it. The analytic-synthetic dichotomy itself breaks down when we confront cluster concepts such as politics, when we confront, that is, those concepts most characteristic of political life and political inquiry.[7]

If, in elucidating cluster concepts, the analytic-synthetic dichotomy breaks down, modes of analysis for settling conceptual disputes that presuppose that dichotomy also lose much of their purchase. Here we have an instance of Thomas Kuhn's thesis that methods of analysis are often sanctioned by the basic framework of theoretical presuppositions within which they are developed: The erosion of the framework undermines methods of inquiry associated with it, even though practitioners often preserve a residual commitment to familiar modes of inquiry long after they have explicitly rejected the assumptions warranting those methods.[8] These points will be clarified and their wider implications suggested by reviewing William Alston's discussion of the concept of a want, a notion that might be thought by some to be markedly more simple and somewhat less misleading than 'politics' as an example upon which to peg a thesis about concept clarification.

What a want is, Alston argues, can be brought out only by elucidating an indefinite set of criteria, no single one of which is sufficient to justify the concept's application and any large mix of which is sufficient to do so. Not only can we not specify a set of necessary and sufficient conditions for 'want' but each of the several criteria that help to bring out what it means itself includes concepts "as far away from . . . observable features of actions and situations as the concept (of want) itself."[9] The criteria of 'want' identified by Alston (for example, P is not indifferent whether x occurs; if x occurs P will be pleased; if x-related objects are in the environment P is likely to notice them; if x comes to mind P will be pleased) do not fit neatly within the analytic-synthetic dichotomy. Any single criterion might be absent in certain situations where someone wants something; yet none of them has a simple synthetic relationship to 'want'. To comprehend adequately the complex relationship between a want and its criteria, Alston contends, "we need to replace the analytic-synthetic dichotomy with a notion of the degree to which a statement has the truth status it has because of the meanings of the terms involved." [10] And, he concludes, "To make this view more precise, *we would need a more subtle and complex logic than any in existence*—one which replaces the analytic-synthetic dichotomy with the notion of the degree to which a statement makes explicit some aspect of the meaning of one or more of the terms involved." [11]

This conclusion, applicable to most if not all concepts in politics, deflates, I suggest, methods sanctioned by many social scientists to clarify concepts and to resolve conceptual differences. At the most general level, the breakdown of the analytic-synthetic dichotomy diminishes the utility of formal methods of logical analysis in clarifying cluster concepts. For those *methods* force criteria into an analytic relationship with the concepts they enter into, distorting the actual relationship. It is no coincidence that the later Wittgenstein moved to the use of ordinary language to clarify key concepts after he rejected his earlier more positivist view of the structure of concepts.[12] More specifically, the breakdown of this dichotomy deflates the so-called open question argument classically employed by positivists to defeat various forms of ethical naturalism and to debunk arguments to the effect that the rules governing a particular concept are highly complex or subtle. Thus when ethical naturalists have sought to identify a conceptual connection between, say, the assertion that something fulfills one's desires and the assertion that it is good, their critics have converted this claimed *conceptual connection* into a *purely analytical one* and then demonstrated that such an "analytic relationship" does not hold. They do so by showing that whereas it is not legitimate first to assert "x is a bachelor" and then to ask "but is he married?" it is legitimate first to assert that "x makes y content" and then to ask "but is x good for y?" Since the latter question is always open, 'good', it is said, cannot *mean* 'fulfills desires' or 'meets needs' or any other such descriptive statement; and thus ethical naturalism must be mistaken. This form of argument is often applied to "descriptive" concepts as well, especially to refute claims that such descriptive concepts bear a conceptual connection to the moral point of view. But when we see that cluster concepts such as 'politics', 'good', and 'want' have multiple criteria, many of which do not bear a purely analytic (nor a purely synthetic) relationship to the concept each helps to define, we can see that the open question argument itself has been systematically misused as a tool of conceptual clarification. To apply such an argument to these concepts is to force them into molds imposed by the requirements of a false dichotomy. Put another way, the breakdown of that dichotomy paves the way for a more close and subtle inspection of concepts central to political inquiry and opens avenues to the deeper understanding of the sources and import of conceptual disputes. We shall have occasion shortly to identify instances where apparently forceful arguments become precarious when their dependence upon the analytic-synthetic dichotomy is exposed.

Politics, then, is a concept particularly susceptible to contests about its proper range of application. The internal complexity of the concept, combined with the relative openness of each of its unit criteria, provides the space within which these disputes take place, and because of these very features, operational tests and formal modes of analysis do not provide sufficient leverage to settle such disputes. That is the thesis so far. But why doesn't each investigator simply stipulate definitions suitable to his particular purposes and leave matters at that? Why do *differences* in interpretation of a key concept so often become *disputes* over its proper meaning? Why, when these disputes occur, are they *essential* in the twofold sense that the prevailing use is continually vulnerable to challenge and reassessment and that the disputants find themselves treating the issue as important rather than merely irksome? It is widely known that even social scientists who formally state that the definitions they advance are merely "arbitrary" stipulations preceding the important questions of inquiry become quite disturbed when their own favored definitions of key concepts are challenged; but the model of inquiry accepted by these social scientists makes it difficult to locate the source of that irritation.

We have already implied a partial answer to these questions: The decision to make some elements "part of" cluster concepts while excluding others invokes a complex set of judgments about the validity of claims central to the theory within which the concept moves. If, for instance, it were some day empirically established that all bachelors are in fact frustrated and this fact also were to play a major role in our explanatory theory of social structure, we might eventually find it convenient to embody that judgment in the very meaning of 'bachelor'. The concept of bachelorhood would shift from a simple idea unencumbered by theoretical ties to a cluster concept, and we would use this idea of single, frustrated males in our quest for other generalizations about social life. If it later turned out that a few odd unmarried males were not frustrated, we might well decide to coin another term for them (singles) so as not to upset the cluster concept of bachelors which had by now come to play a central role in our social theory.[13]

In political inquiry, too, the multiple criteria of cluster concepts reflect the theory in which they are embedded, and a change in the criteria of any of these concepts is likely to involve a change in the theory itself. Conceptual disputes, then, are neither a mere prelude to inquiry nor peripheral to it, but when they involve the central concepts of a field of inquiry, they are surface manifestations of basic theoretical differences that reach to the core. The intensity of commitment to favored definitions reflects intensity of commitment to a general theoretical perspective; and revisions that follow conceptual debates involve a shift in the theory that has housed the concepts.

It is in this light that we can begin to understand current debates about the propriety of revising 'politics' to make the idea more suitable for comprehending the conduct of large-scale corporations. According to the proponents of such revision, corporate units can no longer be understood adequately through the categories of neoclassical economics. A suitably revised idea of politics would comprehend many aspects of corporate behavior, and we would be able to place the motivations, institutional constraints, and social effects of corporate practices within the frame of a revised political theory.[14] Corporate activities, in this view, are not identical to those governmental activities we have called political, but they are close enough and their effects important enough to warrant a conceptual shift that would enable us to view their practices and activities from an angle of vision previously obscured.

The connection between the criteria of a cluster concept and the ingredients of a theory goes some distance, I think, in explaining both the intensity and import of conceptual disputes in political life and political inquiry. But there is still more to be said. Before it can be said coherently we must challenge another dichotomy sanctioned by contemporary social science—between those concepts that enter into descriptions and explanations of political life and those that enter into our evaluations of that life.

"DESCRIPTIVE" AND "NORMATIVE" CONCEPTS

Essentially contested concepts, we have said, are typically *appraisive* in that to call something a 'work of art' or a 'democracy' is both to describe it and to ascribe a value to it or express a commitment with respect to it. The connection within the concept itself of descriptive and normative dimensions helps to explain why such concepts are subject to intense and endless debate. We must now ascertain whether allegations about such a presumed connection and its import for our understanding of conceptual disputes are somehow muddled from the start. Have we ignored a line that cannot be crossed without confusion and ambiguity?

To describe a situation is not to name something, but to characterize it.[15] Thus we are not describing when we say "Empire State Building" or "Jim"; we are when we say that the building is very tall and made of grey concrete or that Jim is a quiet, intense person who is quite industrious. It is the tendency to think of describing as if it were the same thing as naming that accounts for so many commentators ignoring a fundamental feature of description: A description does not refer to data or elements that are bound together merely on the basis of similarities adhering in them, *but to describe is to characterize a situation from the vantage point of certain interests, purposes, or standards.*

To describe is to characterize from one or more possible points of view, and the concepts with which we so characterize have the contours they do in part because of the point of view from which they are formed.   Consider some examples. When concepts such as lever, table, or medicine enter into my descriptions, I am describing from the point of view of certain uses or purposes to which these items might be put by people. In the language of Julius Kovesi, whose recent work on these matters deserves the closest attention of social theorists, the 'material elements' of, say, a table can vary widely and still remain a table.[16] A table might be round or any of several other shapes; it might have four legs or none, be made of wood, metal, or other materials, be solid or soft.   But various combinations of these elements unite to form a table if in combination they make a convenient place for us to eat from or to work on and are characteristically used in these ways.   Similarly, a stick of wood, a metal rod, or other elongated object becomes a lever when it is put to the use of prying, and a large and indefinite range of plants, chemicals, and pills become medicine when they are taken with the reasonable expectation that an unhealthy condition will thereby be remedied.   Other concepts are formed from what we might call, roughly, a prudential point of view.   To describe persons or situations as awesome, fearful, dangerous, menacing, or risky is typically to call attention to features in these settings potentially harmful to participants; the features are grouped together under these headings in order to allow these concepts to serve their purpose of issuing warnings about harmful possibilities.   Clearly, we could exemplify concepts formed from other points of view as well.

Now this seems innocent enough until it is claimed that many concepts with which we describe or characterize are formed from a moral or, more broadly, normative point of view. Yet, to say that someone has lied, promised, threatened, or murdered, or has acted violently, courageously, cowardly, rudely, or is innocent, negligent, corrupt is to describe a variety of acts, practices, and dispositions from a moral point of view. These notions enter into description in that certain specified conditions must be met before each applies to a situation, but they also appraise or evaluate the conduct and practices described in the light of those conditions.

These concepts describe from a moral point of view, not in the sense that to say one has broken a promise is *always* to conclude that the described act must be wrong, *but in the sense that the concepts themselves would not be formed, would not combine within one rubric a set of features, unless there were some point in doing so—unless we shared a moral point of view that these concepts concretize and reflect.* Is the concept of a mistake or of acting inadvertently either "descriptive" or "normative" in the way that those who draw a dichotomy between the two would understand that question? Hardly. There are an indefinite number of ways of making a mistake (for example, dropping a book, losing a key, misspelling a word, misconstruing a point). But in each case where we say a mistake has been made we characterize an act from a broadly normative point of view; we assert, by the use of the term, that the act has certain criteria or characteristics in the light of which we have some reason to *excuse* the agent, or to mitigate his responsibility for the outcome of the act. The characteristics and the point are dialectically related; for it is from the point of view of the kind of conduct we deem excusable that the concept 'mistake' is formed, and it is because an act meets these specifications that we say we have a reason to excuse the agent when he makes a mistake. If someone doubts this we must ask: What role, then, does 'mistake' play for us? Why does the concept have these particular contours in our language and not others?

As Kovesi puts it, we always describe from *some* point

of view, never from a perspective we could call the "descriptive point of view." Those concepts that describe from the moral point of view he calls moral notions; for each of them groups "together in one term the morally relevant facts of certain situations." [17]

Just as a family of concepts such as table, furniture, and household items or person, animal, and living thing form hierarchies in which the more limited and specific notions at the lower end are subsumed under more general notions at the upper end, so a similar hierarchy can be discerned for moral notions. 'Misspelling' is more specific than 'mistake', and 'mistake' is more specific than 'excuse'. The most general and open moral notions are concepts such as right and wrong, good and bad, blameworthy and meritorious. These general and rather atypical notions, though, have received by far the greatest attention of those philosophers who would sustain a dichotomy between "descriptive" and "normative" concepts. Many false starts could have been avoided, as Kovesi has shown in some detail, if analytical philosophers had spent less time comparing 'good' (an open concept of the highest generality) to 'yellow' (a most specific color word). The very selection of these atypical notions as paradigms encouraged philosophers to draw an unbridgeable dichotomy between "normative" concepts understood to combine relatively specific *functions* such as commending with a descriptive content that varies indefinitely (for instance, 'good'), and "descriptive" concepts understood to combine quite variable functions or no determinate function at all with a single criterion or a small set of invariant, observable criteria (for instance, 'yellow'). It is not that no concepts conform to this model, but many do not fit into one of its two cells without some strain and many others do not until central aspects of their grammar are either overlooked or massively distorted.

When we compare concepts formed from *different* points of view operating at *similar* levels of generality the limited applicability of this simple model becomes apparent. Thus, in comparing 'kettle' and 'mistake' we see that the properties of each can vary rather widely (but not infinitely) and that each is formed from a particular point of view that provides the basis for lumping its set of elements together under the rubrics 'kettle' and 'mistake'. The first is formed from the point of view of human utility in boiling water, and so on; an object can have various shapes, materials, colors, and sizes and still be a kettle as long as those elements in combination allow it to serve as a convenient receptacle for cooking. Similarly, if one acting hastily, inattentively, or nervously, and so on, creates adverse or unexpected results for himself or others, he has made a mistake, and we now have a reason to excuse him or reduce his responsibility. Neither 'kettle' nor 'mistake' can be adequately understood until we capture the connection between its point and the conditions of its application; neither is comprehended by attending only to its function or only to its "descriptive" criteria. Those who would exorcise from every concept employed in description the point of view from which it is formed would find that they lacked rationale both for using the concept and for adjusting its criteria to meet those new and unforeseen circumstances that persistently arise in a changing society.

Kovesi distinguishes between moral notions that are complete and those that are incomplete. While I am not confident that any moral notion is fully closed or complete, a range of comparative completeness and incompleteness does seem discernible among moral notions. Thus 'murder' is a (relatively) complete moral notion because, unlike killing or natural death, intentionally taking the life of another for personal advantage always constitutes a set of reasons for judging the act to be reprehensible.[18] Other concepts are formed from a moral point of view, but incompletely so. Their incompleteness means that some actions meeting the conditions specified might have additional features enabling them to escape the moral judgment embodied in the concept. 'Lie' is an example. To lie is to say what is not the case with the intention to deceive, and the point of gathering those elements together in one notion is to reflect our judgment that actions that fit these conditions are wrong. We did not, after all, just happen to isolate those particular elements within one notion for no reason at all. But the notion of lying is incomplete when viewed from the point of view from which it is formed. Sometimes statements meeting its conditions are made with the intention of protecting the deceived agent from dangers he otherwise would be exposed to unavoidably, and we accept such a condition as sufficient to override the prima facie judgment embodied in the concept of lying. 'Lying' could be reformed to include this specification; in that event it would more completely reflect the point of view that warrants, for the language community using it, gathering together that particular group of elements within one notion. Most moral notions are incomplete in this way; many are less complete than 'lying'. Their points can be understood only by grasping the way in which they summarize and crystallize shared moral judgments, but their rules of application are not specified finely enough to ensure that every conceivable act falling within the rules specified embodies (for the community that shares these ideas) the moral judgment that most such acts do.[19]

There are other refinements that might clarify this thesis further. But I think we have reviewed it sufficiently to consider its application to concepts in politics.

Not all concepts in politics are formed from a moral or, more broadly, normative point of view, but many are. Some formed from this point of view are more complete than others. Thus in political life when we characterize the action of a protest group as "expressing its *grievances*," the description itself commits us to take those claims seriously; for before we can describe an act in these terms there must be some basis for saying that the claims are justified. If we described the "same act" as an expression of group demands, wishes, preferences, or goals that implication would not be so necessarily or so fully present.

To commit fraud, follow a policy of genocide, participate in corruption, or overthrow a legitimate government is to be involved in political action described from a moral point of view. Only genocide among these notions might be construed as complete moral notion, but the others stand relatively close to that status. *If we subtracted the moral point from any of these concepts, we would subtract as well the rationale for grouping the ingredients of each together within the rubric of one concept.*

Were we to ignore the moral point of view from which each is formed, we would also lose our ability to judge how these concepts apply to new and unforeseen situations. Consider 'genocide'. We surely cannot combine its criteria on the basis of "empirical similarities" that stand out independently of our interests and commitments. That won't work for 'table' or 'medicine', let alone for 'genocide'. Genocide, as characterized by Dr. Lemki in 1944, means, briefly, extermination of a national or racial group as a planned move. The purpose of grouping these ingredients together is to embody in one notion the shared judgment that acts meeting these criteria are deserving of the worst condemnation and most vigorous opposition. But what if we run into a new situation where the extermination is not complete and where the result itself is not intended or planned, but flows *knowingly* from a war policy shaped by quite other objectives? In these circumstances, close attention to the point of the notion might lead us to revise its criteria to include these new conditions, for the latter involve the wanton taking of human life and are as worthy of condemnation as those acts that first occasioned the term. Attention to the point of the concept is in this way required if we are to apply it to new situations that deviate in some way from the case or cases that first occasioned its formulation.[20]

Or perhaps more likely, these new situations might lead some parties to revise the criteria of the concept in this way while others would continue to insist that such revisions are unwarranted. Then 'genocide' would emerge as a contested concept, and the character and import of the dispute itself would be understood by the adversaries insofar as they saw that they disagreed not simply about the proper criteria of a descriptive concept but more fundamentally about the moral judgment appropriate to certain acts. 'Genocide' would now embody less completely a shared moral judgment; one party would speak of a "policy of genocide" while the other would construe the behavior as an action or policy of a rather different sort. In an important sense the disputing parties would not be describing the same *acts* at all.

Many concepts of politics, I want to suggest, have a somewhat looser connection to normative considerations than those just described, yet they cannot be adequately understood without attention to that connection. Concepts such as 'democracy', 'politics', and 'freedom' are bounded by normative considerations; to use these concepts in our society is to characterize arrangements and actions from a normative angle of vision. And if we were to exorcise the evaluative point from any of these concepts, we would be at a loss as to how to clarify or refine its boundaries when new and unforeseen situations arose. We would find eventually that a concept so cleansed would lay idle (unless we illicitly brought such considerations back in). With no point or purpose to serve, the concept itself would fall into disuse.

If we say that a society is undemocratic or that a practice does not meet democratic standards, we are typically characterizing that practice or society critically; we are describing it from the vantage point of accepted standards of political participation, debate, and accountability. Similarly, to say that corporate pricing policies are correctly characterized as part of politics is to call attention to certain dimensions of those practices in order to suggest that the policies and policy makers are properly subject to public scrutiny, debate, and pressure. The dialectical relation between the criteria of a concept and its point or purpose in our language is exactly what makes the notions 'democracy' and 'politics' the subject of intense dispute. So much turns on the decision to apply them that numerous parties acquire different interests or pursue different purposes in shaping those decisions. Generally, the resulting contests take the form of each party emphasizing some criteria at the expense of others; sometimes one of the parties tries to modify the point of the concept in some way. 'Democracy' and 'politics' have been subjected to both strategies.

To say that an appraisive concept is understood by exploring the connection between its criteria and its point is not, remember, to conclude that neither of these dimensions is ever subject to dispute. For it is exactly the persisting disputes surrounding appraisive concepts that our analysis accounts for and that those who accept the descriptive-normative dichotomy find so mysterious. Our approach accounts for another feature of these disputes as well: It shows how these contests are not just *about* the concepts of politics but are *part of* politics itself. For to get others to accept my account of an appraisive concept is to implicate them in *judgments* to which I am committed and to encourage political activity congruent with those commitments.

To clarify the character of these appraisive concepts further, we shall consider briefly two counterarguments typically advanced against the sort of argument presented here.

Proponents of the descriptive-normative dichotomy often introduce a variant of the open question argument when the dichotomy itself is challenged. We cannot ask, they say, "Is that bachelor unmarried?" because 'unmarried' follows from 'bachelor' by virtue of the latter term's meaning. But we can sensibly ask, "Is this democratic polity desirable?" Since, it is argued, the latter question can be posed meaningfully, the normative dimension of 'democracy' *must* be attached to it as a "connotation" and not as part of the concept itself.

But the argument only shows that 'democracy' does not have as tight a connection to its normative point as 'bachelor' does to 'unmarried'. We can also sensibly ask, "Did he notice the new car because he *wanted* it?" but that does not mean that noticing something cannot be *part of* what we mean by 'want'. The open question argument as a general tool of conceptual analysis depends, as we have seen, on the validity of the analytic-synthetic dichotomy, and that *dichotomy* does not apply to the more complex of these concepts that enter into our theories about social and political life.[21]

The open question argument, while giving the critic much less leverage than he seeks, does force us to clarify more carefully the connection between, say, the criteria of democracy and its normative point. Just as we can sometimes argue that a lie is excusable or a mistake inexcusable because these are incomplete moral notions, so 'democracy' is bounded even more broadly by normative considerations that influence strongly its criteria of application. *Even given the conventional judgments embodied in the concept,* there can be cases where democratic arrangements are accepted as undesirable. But the conventions governing the concept shift the burden to the critic. Certain overriding considerations might defeat the prima facie case in its favor (for instance, the country is engaged in war or an authoritarian work structure makes it unlikely at present that citizens could develop the needed skills and virtues of political participation) but for those sharing the concept, it embodies a standard to be applied unless so defeated.[22]

Moreover, a change in our theoretical understanding or historical situation could sever the prevailing connection between the criteria and normative import of 'democracy'. Suppose some of us became convinced that active participation in group decision processes in a society of increasing scarcity of natural resources unavoidably leads to the division of political parties into uncompromising warring bands, and suppose also that we concluded that the structure of blue-collar work life necessary to the survival of dense, mass societies in this situation of resource scarcity necessarily develops a large lower class incapable of participating intelligently in political life. In such an event, where the theory within which the concept of democracy moves is radically altered, we would be faced with three broad options with respect to the concept itself:

1. To revise the criteria of the concept in order to preserve its point, say, revising the criterion of participation to include as citizens only those who pass certain tests of competence and civility.

2. To revise the point of the concept to preserve its criteria, that is, 'democracy' now becomes a condition to be avoided and future adjustments in its criteria take this altered judgment into account.

3. To leave the criteria, the point, and the theory within

which the concept is embedded intact, but then to treat the whole complex as an anachronistic system irrelevant to the modern age.

We cannot predict exactly which course would be followed, and very probably each of these three alternatives would find its advocates. But we can predict that a massive theoretical change of the sort suggested would not leave the concept of democracy untouched. The conceptual contests to which the concept would then be subject would be further complicated if, as likely, some parties were to refuse to accept the theoretical revisions that occasioned the conceptual shift; they would then retain and fight to preserve in the public mind the old concept of democracy as well as the theory that provided it with its old criteria and point.

The clarified thesis, then, is this: 'Democracy'—and other concepts like it—displays in our discourse over a normal range of cases a close connection between its criteria and its normative point. The relation is close enough to allow us to say that if that connection were somehow abrogated by a large number of people for a large number of cases over a long period of time, the concept itself would either fall into disuse or undergo fundamental change. That thesis is not only true, but untrivial. Those who fail to see its significance have not, I contend, followed closely the earlier argument about how awareness of the point of a concept is essential for judging how and whether it applies when new and unforeseen situations arise.

A second and related counterargument builds on the fact that the rules governing the use of these concepts have a conventional basis. Perhaps, the argument goes, there is a conventional connection between the criteria and the point of these appraisive concepts that influences the historical development of these concepts, but there is no *logical* objection to someone accepting the descriptive dimensions of such a concept and rejecting all commitments to *any* pro or con normative implications with respect to it. My approch to this argument, after reminding the critic of serious difficulties that will arise in applying the concept to new situations and wondering why he would bother to use such a pointless concept, is to insist that *both* the points and the criteria of our concepts are sanctioned by convention. Logically these conventions could be altered in an infinite number of ways, but showing that something is logically permissible does not establish that it is also justifiable or reasonable.

What if a friend said, "I take pride in the fact that the sky is blue"? We would first ask whether perhaps he has played a major role in instituting antipollution measures. But if he answered that he had not, and had not indeed contributed in any way to the sky's blueness, nor had his friends, relatives, countrymen, and so on, contributed in any way to it, we would be puzzled. For making a contribution to something that is acknowledged to be a worthy achievement is a central part of what we mean by 'pride'. If the friend persisted in this odd use of the notion, we would suspect him either of trading on the point of the concept while illicitly shifting its criteria (perhaps he is running for public office) or of failing to understand the rules governing the use of that concept in our community. We would say: "Either you are cheating or ignorant; if the latter, what you really mean is that you are *glad* the sky is blue; if the former, we reject and expose your duplicity." If, though, he acknowledged neither of these interpretations and continued knowingly to use the concept in his odd way, we would ask him to provide some rationale or justification for this revised use. For he would have broken established linguistic convention, and if we often broke these conventions *without reasons of any sort,* the shared system of concepts itself would be jeopardized. We would lack a basis for communication and for action. His move, then, is logically possible, but it breaks linguistic convention, and while these conventions can be and often are altered, we reasonably expect significant alterations to be justified in some way.

To agree that the criteria and functions of our concepts are conventional is not to agree that anyone can change those rules for no reason at all. That conclusion applies to both dimensions of our concepts. In proposing a conceptual revision (even if the process is less formal than a proposal), the burden of argument must be on the reviser. Starting from conventional rules of discourse, he might well offer defensible reasons for a revised weighting of a concept's established criteria, for the addition of new criteria, or for a shift in its point. But if he proceeds in this way, he will find himself implicated in the sort of discourse that surrounds essentially contested concepts.

Suppose, though, our neutral observer offers a reason. He refuses to attach any normative point to 'democracy' even though, he acknowledges, such a point is conventionally established, because he wishes to protect the dichotomy in political inquiry between descriptive and normative concepts. This dichotomy, he correctly surmises, is essential to his goal of remaining a "value-free" social scientist. And to indicate clearly his rejection of all normative implications he will surround 'democracy' with quotation marks whenever he uses it in inquiry, just as we do when we talk about the grammar of the idea. How do we respond now? We first reiterate, I suppose, how consistent adoption of such a view will increase the investigator's difficulty in adjusting the concept to new situations, for he will now have no basis for making such adjustments. But then we must press an additional point. An indefinitely large number of concepts in political life reflect a connection between their criteria and the normative points that inform them; if his reason for abrogating that point with respect to 'democracy' is to preserve the descriptive-normative dichotomy, then he must follow this approach with all such concepts. While investigators can, and often justifiably do, mark off any single concept with quotes to indicate that a conventionaly accepted criterion or point is to be questioned or reappraised, matters change significantly when one is compelled to mark off consistently *all* such concepts employed in one's inquiry. Consider: "In the 'politics' of the United States, the intensification and spread of 'corruption' led to a decline in 'democracy' and the 'threat' of 'oligarchical' controls." What is being *described* here? Why use these concepts to describe what has happened, since there is no longer a point in doing so? Has the vantage point of the detached, neutral observer been established, or if we take the quotation marks seriously, has no coherent vantage point at all been established? To preserve the descriptive-normative dichotomy by adopting a vocabulary conventionally laden with commitments and then systematically dropping out the commitments is like eating a chicken-salad sandwich without the chicken. Investigators who adopt such an approach either delude themselves and others, illicitly trading on the conventional dimensions they explicitly reject, or they destroy the ground of communication with users of the very language they have adopted.

Efforts to restrict the terms of political inquiry to those that describe from a "descriptive point of view," while doomed to failure, nevertheless generate adverse consequences of importance for our discourse. For to render this view at all plausible, investigators are forced to populate their inquiries with concepts that are quite open and quite general. Since the program runs into more immediately obvious difficulties for 'genocide' and 'grievance' than for, say, 'politics' and perhaps 'interests', the latter become the concepts of "neutral" political inquiry. In the interest of meeting an unattainable standard of precision (because it is drawn along the wrong lines) mainstream social scientists have rejected exactly the range of concepts that contribute most to our understanding of the subtlety and import of political action. That is one important reason, I think, that studies seeking to adhere scrupulously to the descriptive-normative dichotomy emerge so often as arid and unclear.

THE ROLE OF ORDINARY LANGUAGE

The arguments so far presented presuppose that concepts employed in the political life of a community should play a central role in theories explaining that life. Those concepts selected to illustrate various aspects of our thesis, such as politics, want, democracy, grievance, and murder, are all part of everyday discourse. Many social scientists would argue, though, that while the concepts of political *life* might have some of the features attributed to them here, a technical language of political *inquiry* can be devised that will minimize the troublesome features and amplify the extent to which conceptual agreement can be attained among professional political scientists. Such a view is, I think, seriously defective. I will try to expose its most important flaws in what follows and then indicate how our knowledge of why it is a defective view illuminates our understanding of the nature and import of essentially contested concepts.

May Brodbeck suggests the view of these matters I want to oppose when she says:

> Our concepts may be open textured, but the world is not. If language is to be descriptive, it must indicate what there is in the world, no matter how variably we talk about it.[23]

There is a sense in which this statement is perfectly correct, but it is exactly its tendency to assume that the concepts of social life refer to a process standing out there independently of them that must be modified if the view that the concepts of ordinary discourse properly play a central role in our technical inquiries is to be sustained.

To explain the politics of a society we must be able to make the *actions, projects,* and *practices* of its members intelligible. But a single act or pattern of action embodied in institutions is not made intelligible merely by observing overt behavior. Actions and practices are *constituted* in part by the concepts and beliefs the participants themselves have.[24] The concepts of politics are, that is, part of the political process itself; they give coherence and structure to political activities in something like the way the rules of chess provide the context that makes 'moving the bishop' and 'checkmating' possible as acts in the game of chess.

If a person did not understand the concept of honesty, he might, if he wanted money, simply take it from a purse left open. We could not correctly say that he acted dishonestly, just as we could not properly say that an infant follows advice or behaves politely. For the concepts of honesty, advice, and politeness must be available to the agents themselves before they can be said to act in these ways. If our simple person came later to understand the concept of honesty, he would now confront *decisions* not available to him before. He might, on seeing the purse again, decide to act honestly or to steal the purse, concluding that honesty is a virtue poor people cannot afford. Thus he can now make decisions about being honest or not, and he can form *beliefs* not open to him before about the virtue of honesty. He now has new *acts* available (for example, acting honestly); he can have *feelings* of pride or guilt about these newly available acts; and we, as observers, can characterize his conduct differently than before (for instance, "He acted dishonestly"). The acquisition of this new concept enriches the world of action by making new decisions, beliefs, acts, and critical appraisals possible.

Or consider the distinctions among leaving, departing from, forsaking, abandoning, fleeing, and retreating from another. All of these actions can involve moving away from another; but the differences among them are differences in the intentions, beliefs, and responsibilities one agent can be said to have with regard to the other. We make these *judgments* about relationships between two people when we decide which action-description the behavior of moving away falls under. We cannot always formulate explicitly, of course, the rich and subtle set of rules we tacitly follow in making these delicate distinctions. But make them we do. Thus when it is asserted that the investigator's understanding of the rules of ordinary discourse must enter into his explanations of political practice, it is not the definitions the participants explicitly give that must be privileged in this way, but the rules they actually follow in their actions and appraisals of action. People do, after all, draw subtle distinctions in practice between concepts of guilt and shame, conflict and competition, manipulation and persuasion, inadvertent and negligent acts, without being able to formulate upon request the complex rules governing these distinctions.

These strictures apply to the emotional states available to a population as well. We cannot differentiate among resentment, anger, fear, indignation, annoyance, outrage, and envy merely by reference to differences in affect, raw feeling, or physiological states. In our discourse, the emotion of resentment involves the *judgment* that someone has injured me intentionally and wrongly. The other emotion-concepts are made up of different mixes of belief and judgment; without those differences built into the fabric of our emotion-concepts, our emotional life itself would be simple and brutish.

When we see the extent to which shared concepts and beliefs enter into our emotional states and actions, it is immediately clear that other societies could populate the world of action and emotion rather differently than we do. Thus efforts to construct a cross-cultural language capable of capturing within its net the practices of all societies are likely to achieve limited success. And that is why I intend the discussions of specific concepts in earlier sections to apply particularly to American society—although some aspects surely apply elsewhere as well.

These points apply just as thoroughly to political life. Even a simple relationship of command and obedience, as Peter Winch has shown, requires that the parties in the relationship have the notions of command and obedience. Lightning preceded thunder before we had the concepts of thunder and lightning, but

> it doesn't make sense to suppose that human beings might have been issuing commands and obeying them before they came to form concepts of command and obedience. . . . An act of obedience itself contains as an essential element, a recognition of what went before it as an order.[25]

Suppose we observed a line of people walking in a slow circle around a government building. If those walking lacked the concept of protesting government policy, we could certainly not characterize their activity correctly as an act of protest. We would have to become clear about the ingredients and point of the act as they conceived it before we could begin to explain it or go very far in assessing its broader implications. Perhaps they were parading or mourning.

In our politics people engage in acts of protest and civil

disobedience; they also lobby, dissent, negotiate, blackmail, vote, engage in violence, and strike. Participants in each of these activities must to some extent share these concepts or they will lack the ability to enter into the activities; and any outsider who lacks our understanding of the distinctions among these actions could not possibly participate in or explain our political practices. To understand the political life of a community one must understand the conceptual system within which that life moves; and therefore *those concepts that help to shape the fabric of our political practices necessarily enter into any rational account of them.* It may be justifiable for the investigator to introduce some technical concepts into the established conceptual world; but these will be useful only to the extent that they build upon and are understood in relation to the prevailing system.[26]

Among those concepts that help to constitute the political practices of a society are many that describe from a moral point of view. Since these, too, must be incorporated in studies of the political practices of a people, the normative dimension of political life enters political inquiry, not after the describing and explaining is done, but, as it were, at the ground floor.

Moreover, among these concepts that are constituents of our practices, some are essentially contested by the participants. These, too, must be incorporated by the investigator, for they contribute to the political dimension of social life in a singularly profound way. And here the distinction between describing and participating in our politics becomes even more hazy. To the extent that the investigator stakes out a position on these conceptual contests, and we know about it, he can be said to participate in our politics itself. *For these contests over the correct use of partly shared appraisal concepts are themselves an intrinsic part of politics.* In convincing me to adopt your version of 'democracy', 'politics', or 'legitimacy' you convince me to classify and appraise actions and practices in new ways; you encourage me to guide my own conduct by new considerations. And if I decide to repudiate your use, I am likely to range myself with others opposing the interpretations, strategies, and policies that express the judgments you would have us accept.

When groups range themselves around essentially contested concepts, politics is the mode in which the contest is normally expressed. Politics involves the clash that emerges when appraisive concepts are shared widely but imperfectly, when mutual understanding and interpretation is possible but in a partial and limited way, when reasoned argument and coercive pressure commingle precariously in the endless process of defining and resolving issues. The conceptual debates among political scientists, then, are so often intense because we tacitly understand the relation of these debates to our deepest commitments and we sense as well the import that the outcome of such contests has for the politics of our society.

I have tried to show that there are and why there are essentially contested concepts in politics. Along the way we have had to modify widely accepted distinctions between operational and nonoperational concepts, descriptive and normative vocabularies, analytical and synthetic statements, technical terms and the terms of ordinary discourse, the role of the investigator and that of the participant. I have not, though, tried to specify closely how one can cope rationally with these conceptual contests, partly because I think the role reason can play in these disputes is best exhibited by a close scrutiny of particular concepts. To the extent that this preliminary effort is successful it will clear away the underbrush, making that task more feasible and more clearly imperative.

Perhaps, though, one further implication is suggested by this discussion: Since we often cannot expect knockdown arguments to settle these matters, we must come to terms somehow with the political dimension of such contests. It is possible, and I believe likely, that the politics of these contests would become more enlightened if the contestants realized that in many contexts no single use can be advanced that must be accepted by all reasonable persons. The realization that opposing uses might not be exclusively self-serving but have defensible reasons in their support could introduce into these contests a measure of tolerance and a receptivity to reconsideration of received views. Politics would not be expunged, but its character would be enhanced. These conclusions are themselves disputable. They flow from the assumption that rationality, fragile as it is, is helped, not hindered, by heightened awareness of the nature and import of our differences.

NOTES

1. W. B. Gallie, "Essentially Contested Concepts," in *Proceedings of the Aristotelian Society,* vol. 56 (London, 1955–56). Reprinted in Max Black (ed.), *The Importance of Language* (Englewood Cliffs, N.J.: Prentice-Hall, 1962), pp. 121–46.
2. Ibid., p. 123. Gallie specifies other conditions as well, but those noted here are sufficient for our present purposes.
3. Ibid., p. 142.
4. Karl Deutsch, *Politics and Government: How People Decide Their Fate* (Boston: Houghton Mifflin, 1970), p. ix.
5. It is a bit difficult to find a recent study in political science in which the author explicitly claims to conform to a stringent version of operationalism. The doctrine is most often invoked by political scientists when they criticize the work of others, especially those others who advance ideological orientations with which the political scientist disagrees. In this way the doctrine of operationalism is supported less by displaying its merits in concrete studies than by the repeated charge that others do not live up to it.
6. George Schlesinger, "Operationalism" in *Encyclopedia of Philosophy* (1967), 5:545.
7. Arguing that the *dichotomy* breaks down is not the same as saying that there are *no* analytic statements, *no* synthetic statements. For the very denial that such a *distinction* is valid, see W. V. Quine, *From a Logical Point of View* (Cambridge, Mass.: Harvard University Press, 1953), pp. 20–46.
8. "In learning a paradigm the scientist acquires theory, methods, and standards together, usually in an inextricable mixture.

Therefore, when paradigms change there are usually significant shifts in the criteria determining the legitimacy both of the problems and of the proposed solutions." Thomas Kuhn, *The Structure of Scientific Revolutions* (Chicago: University of Chicago Press, 1962), p. 108.

9. William Alston, "Motives and Motivation," in *Encyclopedia of Philosophy* (1967), 5:404.

10. Ibid, p. 406.

11. Ibid., p. 406, my emphasis.

12. For an elaboration of this connection, see David Pears, *Ludwig Wittgenstein* (New York: Viking Press, 1971). For a similar thesis applied to the policy sciences, see Laurence Tribe, "The Policy Sciences: Science of Ideology?" *Philosophy and Public Affairs* (Fall 1972): 66–110.

13. This example is suggested by Hilary Putnam in an article that has aided my thinking in general about defects in the analytic-synthetic dichotomy: "The Analytic and the Synthetic," in *Minnesota Studies in the Philosophy of Science,* eds. Herbert Feigl and Grover Maxwell (Minneapolis: University of Minnesota Press, 1962), 3:358–97.

14. For a discussion of the import of such a conceptual shift for the theory of pluralism, see William E. Connolly, "The Challenge to Pluralist Theory," in *The Bias of Pluralism,* ed. William E. Connolly (New York: Atherton Press, 1969), pp. 3–34.

15. See Stephen Toulmin and Kurt Baier, "On Describing," in *Philosophy and Ordinary Language,* ed. Charles Caton (Urbana, Ill.: University of Illinois Press, 1953), pp. 20–46.

16. Julius Kovesi, *Moral Notions* (London: Routledge and Kegan Paul, 1967).

17. Ibid., p. 89.

18. In fact, since there are multiple criteria of 'murder', the notion might be morally complete, but it is still open to dispute in particular cases. For its criteria include (1) intentionally taking the life of another, (2) who is innocent and (3) for personal gain or advantage. An act might meet criteria 1 and 3 perfectly, but not 2, and people might then disagree as to whether it is really murder. It might meet 2 and 3 and not be intentional, but done knowingly or unintentionally in a context (some of us think) in which reasonable people would have known about the conse-

quences. 'Murder' is a complete moral notion in that all acts falling under its rubric are deemed reprehensible, but it is still a rather *open* notion in the sense that its multiple criteria of application can be weighted differently by different people. In focusing on the idea of completeness Kovesi seems to discount the possibility of persons variably weighting the criteria of a concept when they share the point of view from which it is formed.

19. It should be clear by now that I am not seeking in this essay to adjudicate the debate between "cognitivist" and "noncognitivist" theories of ethics. The discussion of moral notions developed here is pertinent to that debate, but more must be said before one can stake out a position on the several issues it raises.

20. The same argument applies to concepts formed from the predictive point of view. Think of 'reinforcement', a concept explicitly designed to identify 'stimuli' that predict desired 'behavior'. When behaviorist therapists concluded that painful inputs could eradicate symptoms as well or better than rewards, 'reinforcement' was expanded to include 'negative' forms. Now, 'negative reinforcement' is a contradiction given the use of 'reinforcement' in ordinary discourse, but *not* if reinforcement becomes a technical term formed from a *predictive point of view* and stripped of its conventional point. Why social scientists could not populate their conceptual universe entirely with concepts formed from a predictive point of view will be considered more fully in the next section. One reason is immediately obvious, though. What is to be predicted, that is, what counts as a 'symptom' to be eradicated, is shaped by notions formed from the points of view of our wishes, interests, and moral sensibilities.

21. Consider how the initial plausibility of the open question argument fades when it is applied to more complete moral concepts: "He murdered him alright, but was it justifiable?" "They are practicing genocide, but should we condemn them?" This helps to explain why those advocating adherence to the descriptive-normative dichotomy always select the most open notions for analysis.

22. On first glance it might appear as though I were saying that those moral judgments embodied in our conventional moral notions are *therefore* morally correct. But I am not. There are reasoned arguments, I would hold, that can be given to chal-

lenge and reform conventional moral judgments. *But the arguments will not be given after the critic has accepted a description and explanation of the situation couched in concepts that are neutral on these matters.* The moral argument will itself involve a revision of conventional notions *because* (some of) these notions are formed from a moral perspective. This feature of our discourse makes moral discourse less avoidable and more difficult than some have supposed. But that is not my fault.

23. May Brodbeck, "Explanation, Prediction, and 'Imperfect' Knowledge," in *Readings in the Philosophy of the Social Sciences,* ed. May Brodbeck (New York: Macmillan, 1968), p. 396.

24. My thinking about these matters has been influenced by the following works: A. R. Louch, *Explanation and Human Action* (Berkeley: University of California Press, 1969); Alasdair MacIntyre, *Against the Self Images of the Age* (New York: Schocken Books, 1971), chs. 18–23; Charles Taylor, "Interpretation and the Sciences of Man," *Review of Metaphysics* (Fall 1971): 4–51; Peter Winch, *The Idea of a Social Science* (New York: Humanities Press, 1958).

25. Winch, *The Idea of a Social Science,* p. 125. I don't mean by this quotation to endorse completely Winch's idea of a social science. I accept it only as amended by MacIntyre in "The Idea of a Social Science" and "Rationality and the Explanation of Action," in *Against the Self-Images of the Age,* pp. 211–29 and 244–59.

26. The fact that the practices of a polity are composed in part of the concepts and beliefs of the participants suggests that those recent efforts to construct one general and neutral language of political science fully applicable to the politics of all societies are doomed to failure from the start. For a thoughtful illustration of this point, see Charles Taylor, "Interpretation and the Sciences of Man."

2

Interests in Politics

THE IMPORT OF CONTESTS
OVER 'INTERESTS'

To say that a policy or practice is in the interests of an individual or a group is to assert both that the recipient would somehow benefit from it and that there is therefore a *reason* in support of enacting that policy. Of course, the reason may be overridden by other considerations. But it is important to see that, as it is used in our society, 'interest' is one of those concepts that connnects descriptive and explanatory statements to normative judgment.

One way of seeing the connection between talk about interests and normative appraisal is suggested by Charles Taylor.[1] That is, although to say "x is in y's 'interest' " is not *equivalent* to saying it is good, it is one of the licenses for making the prima facie judgment that x is good or desirable. Another route to understanding this connection is to note the role that wanting, choosing, and preferring play in the concept of interests. For although the latter concept has been variously defined, all definitions seriously advanced make an important reference to the wants, preferences, and choices of agents somewhere in the definition. We generally accept the principle that people ought to be able to do what they choose or want to do unless overriding considerations intervene. And talk about interests carries that presumption into political discourse; indeed it strengthens the presumption, since the sort of wants that enter into the meaning of interests are exactly those deemed to be somehow important, persistent, basic or fundamental in politics. Disagreements about where and how these conative states are included in the concept of interests reflect, I suggest, disagreements about which conative states under what conditions deserve the normative sanction 'interests' provides.

It is notorious that social theorists have disagreed extensively about the proper meaning to assign to 'interests' in political and social life, but the participants in these disputes have typically tried to limit themselves to lines of argument permitted by a positivist disjuncture between descriptive statements and normative appraisals. The debates thereby take the form of arguments over which proposed definition is more 'operational' or, vaguely, of greater 'theoretical importance'. But when we state explicitly, what even positivist social scientists have tacitly known, that talk about interests has a *normative function* in our discourse, we can understand more profoundly just why disagreements about the descriptive conditions or *criteria* of its application are so intense and persistent. For one set of criteria will draw our attention to a particular set of conative states formed under certain conditions, while other proposals will divert our attention from these conditions and toward others. The effect of such definitional proposals is to privilege certain actual or potential conative states for purposes of normative appraisal in politics and often to blind us to possible considerations operating outside of those boundaries.

Now, if the very *notion* of interests shapes our normative priorities in the way suggested, an explanatory theory employing that notion will generate more definite and detailed normative conclusions. For such a theory purports to tell us what interests citizens in various settings have, how the political system nourishes some interests, protects others, and dampens or suppresses yet others; it tells us why and how particular segments of the society fail to recognize some of their interests, whether and to what extent some of these unrecognized interests could be revealed and promoted through political pressure; it tells us what costs are likely to be incurred by efforts to reveal and promote these suppressed interests; and finally, it purports to tell us to what extent some of the existing demands and pressures on the political system reflect not the identifiable interests of citizens but their projection of unattainable fantasies and wishes onto public arenas. The explanatory theory, in short, "sets the crucial dimensions through which the phenomena (of interests) can vary" and through its assessment of the possibilities, costs, and risks of satisfying the interests it identifies, it informs us "how we are to judge of good and bad." [2]

I certainly do not want to suggest that the concept of interests is the only one in political inquiry that serves as a bridge between explanatory theory and normative judgment, but it is one of those concepts performing this crucial function.[3] Our inquiry into the various efforts to prescribe criteria for the application of this concept will be more conscious and illuminating if we keep its normative function in mind. In this way, we will grasp the extent to which debates about the *criteria* of 'interests' are a part of larger debates about the structure and style of the good society. When we judge proposed definitions in this way, we will be able to confront directly factors and considerations that typically remain in the shadow of contemporary debates.

I will explore four alternative efforts to elucidate the criteria of 'interests', arguing that the notions improve successively as we move from the first to the last.[4]

INTERESTS AS POLICY PREFERENCE

Most American political scientists, working largely within the confines of a pluralist theory of politics, do not explicitly define 'interests', but tend to equate the notion in practice with the political pressure an individual or a group brings to bear on government; often, too, 'interests' so understood are located by the investigator by identifying the policy preferences of the agents involved. Since the criticisms advanced here apply to either of these formulations, I will treat them as interchangeable, speaking in general of interests defined as the policy preferences of individuals and groups.[5]

Typically the tendency to define interests as policy preference is sharpened when the scholar is presenting a methodological critique of explanatory theories that purport to find "false consciousness" among some segments of society. Thus Nelson Polsby rejects on methodological grounds C. Wright Mills's assertion that "false consciousness" is "the lack of awareness of and identification with one's objective interests." Polsby's alternative view holds,

> at least presumptively, that decisions affect people's interests differentially, and that people participate in those areas *they*

care about the most. Their values, eloquently expressed by their participation, cannot, it seems to me, be more effectively 'objectified.'[6]

The notion of interest as policy preference is open to several telling criticisms.[7]

1. The debate between pluralist theorists and their critics hinges in strong measure on the extent to which specific groups in the society fail to identify and press policy proposals that could substantially improve their well-being. But by defining interests merely as policy preference, pluralists help to push the issue dividing them and their critics outside the reach of empirical inquiry. For given that definition of interest, there simply cannot be "unarticulated interests"; those without particular policy preferences in certain areas must be viewed as not having an interest in a given policy result. If it is possible to formulate a concept of interest, meeting reasonable methodological standards, which does enable us to ask questions such as "Does group Q have unarticulated interest y?" that explication will be preferable on the grounds that it avoids settling by definitional fiat an important question that might be studied empirically.

2. Equating 'interest' with policy preference collapses an important distinction sanctioned in ordinary discourse between one's support for a policy because of a perceived moral obligation and one's support for it solely on the grounds of self-interest. Failure to sustain this distinction clearly in political inquiry lends illicit (because unargued) support to the view that political man must act only, or at least primarily, in self-interest. The pernicious effects of such an unexamined assumption, both for political inquiry and for the considerations governing the political commitments of citizens, can hardly be overstated.[8]

3. If, as already suggested, to say "policy x is in A's interest" is to provide a prima facie justification for that policy, then to define interests in terms of policy preferences and then view actual political participation as the best indicator of policy preference is to sanction perverse normative judgments. Since

a high level of participation is correlated with high socio-economic status, this view of interests supports the claims of various segments of society in inverse proportion to their needs. By thus restricting the application of the concept while tacitly retaining its conventional function in normative assessment, a significant bias is insinuated into materials from which normative conclusions are forged.[9]

Yet such criticisms, impeccable though they may be, fail to speak to the central counterargument wheeled out by those adopting this notion of interests. The argument, suggested by Polsby's statement quoted previously, is that alternative notions of interest generally advanced incorporate the possibility of attributing false consciousness to citizens, thereby encouraging researchers to impute arbitrarily to groups interests that the groups themselves do not acknowledge. The more modest notion of interest as policy preference forces the investigator to confront the hard facts about the preferences and behavior of people in political life. It is a more operational definition.

It is not my intention here to argue generally against the myth of operationalism, which has unjustifiably confined the scope of contemporary political inquiry.[10] Two points, though, are particularly pertinent to the question at hand.

1. Even if the notion of interest as policy preference is more operational than alternative explications to be considered, this advantage might well be outweighed by its other manifest deficiencies.

2. That notion of interest, when elaborated more fully, is not as neatly operational as its proponents suggest.

Since a reasonable assessment of the first claim must await arguments yet to come, I will limit my attention here to the second.

There is, initially, the obvious problem of discovering the policy preferences people actually have. The preferences people express are not always the same as their unexpressed and latent preferences. A survey of blacks just prior to the Detroit riots surely would not have detected 'preferences' clearly discernible during the riot and in studies shortly thereafter. Also, policy preferences expressed to middle-class researchers by members of maverick groups bearing on legalization of dope, protection of homosexuality, legalized prostitution, and so on, may well distort the actual orientations of these groups. Distortions of these types are likely to lead the investigator to overplay the extent and depth of consensus in contemporary politics.

More important, the term 'preference', in this usage, ranges over choices of at least two kinds, and these differences must be unsorted in any appraisal of interests. We have noted the distinction between supporting a policy because one prefers it for oneself and supporting it because it seems morally appropriate to do so even though one would choose otherwise if moral considerations had not intervened. Hence, a farmer might prefer to continue using DDT on his crops when considering only his own benefit, but he might decide, on balance, to vote in favor of making its use illegal. Surely an advocate of interest as policy preference will accept this distinction once drawn, for otherwise he would allow an important question deserving empirical study (that is, when people's policy preferences are self or other regarding) to be obscured by conceptual sloppiness or, more likely, settled by definitional fiat. But then he is forced to distinguish between 'self regarding' and 'other regarding' preferences, and the problem of applying that distinction in research practice will be severe indeed. It will force the dissolution of those crude indicators of interest commonly employed, such as collecting statements from interviewees about their policy preferences or observing the participation of group leaders in support of particular policies. To apply this distinction in research practice will require the subtle assessment of multiple cues in concrete settings.

Finally, since one always *prefers* something to other specified alternatives, the range of alternatives taken into account is crucial to the preference adopted. I might prefer democracy to communism, communism to death, and death to prolonged torture by the secret agents of a democratic society. But attention to this conceptual point complicates the effort to "operationalize" policy preference as interest. Is the range of alternative preferences considered to be limited to those issues that reach governmental arenas for serious attention? If so, the terms of comparison within which policy preferences are stated will be biased in favor of whatever groups benefit the most from existing processes of issue formation. If the range of preferences considered is broadened beyond these limits, the question of how far must be faced. For surely a policy preference must be distinguished from a mere wish. If a trade union leader lobbied in favor of a policy that would ensure the immortality of blue-collar workers, Professor Polsby, for example, would surely concur in labeling that a "pipe dream" rather than an interest of the workers. Such distinctions must be made, but no set of *operations* has been specified that enables investigators to determine even roughly the point in contemporary politics where policy preference shades off into political fantasy.

In practice, these multiple discriminations are presupposed by research assumptions rather than tested by impersonal operations. Such presuppositions generally go unnoted when shared by a community of scholars. But when the theory of pluralism embodying this notion of interests is challenged, when the props are exposed, the impressionistic status of the discriminations themselves becomes apparent. Among the central disagreements between, say, a C. Wright Mills and a Nelson Polsby are diverging interpretations of the unexpressed and latent preferences of the underclass in American society, of the occasions when political actors are guided by moral imperatives rather than self-interest in their political conduct, and especially, of those aspirations within contemporary society that can properly be construed as political preferences rather than mere wishes or pipe dreams.[11] The notion of interest as policy preference does appear moderately operational when appraisals of interest are made within the framework of the theory in which this concept functions. When that context itself is in dispute, the tenuous connection between the concept and any particular set of operations becomes apparent.

UTILITARIAN INTERESTS

Utilitarianism, narrowly defined, takes the wants, desires, and inclinations of persons as given and asks how to maximize their attainment. In this sense, Brian Barry can be said to advance a utilitarian notion of interests. He considers a

> policy, law, or institution (to be) in someone's interest if it increases his opportunities to get what he wants . . . whatever that may be.[12]

Now, this definition, once the term 'want' is appropriately clarified, is a clear improvement over the first notion of interest considered. First, in line with usage in ordinary discourse, the definition makes it possible for an agent to be mistaken about his interests. For misinformation, poor calculation, or failure to consider feasible but unarticulated policy alternatives might lead one to prefer a policy that does not, on a comparative basis, maximize one's opportunities to get what one wants. A low-income citizen, for example, might want to maximize his disposable income but then favor a state sales tax over an income tax because of a mistaken view about the relative effects of each type on the amount of his disposable income. His policy preference, in this instance, would be at odds with his interest.

The definition, as clarified by Barry, also sustains the distinction between supporting a policy because of self-interest and for moral reasons. And since one's interest in a policy on this view has no conceptual linkage to one's participation in the political process, the illicit normative bias built into the first definition is avoided.

The limitations of this notion, though, become more apparent when we probe the phrase "opportunities to get what he wants." With one qualification, Barry takes the prevailing wants of persons as given for purposes of appraising their interests.[13] But the wants we have, as Barry knows, are shaped to a large degree by the society in which we mature. Without regard now to questions of truth or falsity, there is surely a prima facie meaningfulness to the claim that a perfectly adjusted slave or a well-socialized consumer has wants at odds with his real interests. Social theorists as diverse as Karl Marx and Emile Durkheim, José Ortega y Gasset and John Kenneth Galbraith, have advanced interpretations that rest upon just such claimed distortions in processes of interest articulation. We should not accept a notion of interest that excludes such statements unless serious efforts to explicate the concept in ways that accommodate them are shown to be vitally flawed.

Barry's use of 'want' limits 'interest' in another respect. For the kind of wants Barry considers relevant to ascriptions of interest seem to be egoistic wants. Put more clearly, although Barry emphasizes that persons can consciously choose to act against their own interests, the paradigm case of 'doing what I want', is that of securing objects and advantages for my *private enjoyment*. When I act as a want-regarding creature, other persons are viewed merely as means or obstacles to my attainment of "life, liberty, health, and indolency of body, and the possession of outward things such as money, houses, furniture, and the like." [14] As Barry states the point elsewhere while distinguishing an interest from an ideal, "Results concerning people other than A are not directly relevant" in the ascriptions of an interest to A.[15] This restriction, I shall argue, is too confining.

To be clear about interests we must specify the kinds of persons we are talking about and what aspects of their activity we have in mind. Some definitional statements draw our attention to the 'interests' one has when one acts egoistically, but it seems to me that we can also speak sensibly about the interests a person has as a social being. When I act egoistically I seek such things as food and leisure for myself; the satisfactions (or dissatisfactions) I attain do not themselves involve a reference to other people. They are private gratifications, not in the sense that I am the one who experiences them (for that is true of all my states) but in that other people are seen only as *means* or *obstacles* to my states and not as themselves implicated with me in mutually gratifying *relationships*.

When my interests as a social being are at stake, more

than private wants are involved. Certain kinds of relationships with others are fostered—relationships involving trust, friendship, shared conventions, and the like. One who cherishes the social dimension of life may often be willing to sacrifice purely private satisfaction for the mutual benefits of social life. For instance, a person might decide to forgo certain material benefits in the interests of maintaining a relationship of trust with another. He might simply cherish for itself the kind of life implied by sustaining such relationships more than he prizes the sacrificed material benefits. He is surely acting in his own interest in this case. There is a *sacrifice* here, of course, but not in the sense that an act of altruism is the sacrifice of one's own interest. The person is simply sacrificing a lower-order interest for the higher-order interest he has as a social being.

Interests I have as a social being are those that make "essential reference to reciprocal states of awareness among two or more persons." [16] Thus workers might, as Marx contends, have an interest in policies supporting a work life in which they interact creatively in the productive process. Citizens might, as Herbert Morris believes, have an interest in a system of legal punishment that treats one, when accused of a crime, as an agent capable of acting responsibly in his relations with others.[17] Human beings in general might, as Durkheim believes, have an interest in policies enabling each to share with others a set of social norms that give regularity, purpose, and direction to their interaction. It isn't that Marx, Morris, and Durkheim are necessarily correct in their assessments of the interests we have as social beings or in the extent to which those interests override purely egoistic interest, for these three theorists disagree among themselves, and one or all of them might indeed be seriously mistaken in his assessment of interests. But if a reasonable notion of interest can be advanced, enabling us to cope with conflicts between egoistic and social interests on the same plane, so to speak, we will be able to sharpen and clarify those fundamental issues lying beneath the surface of contemporary debates about political life. We will be able to make sense of the kind of claim advanced when someone says, "John favors that policy because he wants to increase his income, but his real interest would be promoted further if the social conditions of his work life were reformed."

With these distinctions in mind consider Gerhard Lenski's use of 'interest'—a concept crucial to his description and explanation of inequality in complex societies. His identification of 'interest' with my category of egoistic interest is exemplified in the following statement:

> In time, of course, the normal child learns to take the wishes of others into account. But this does not mean he is any less motivated to maximize his own satisfaction. Rather, it means that the attainment of his goals is inevitably linked with interests of others.[18]

In Lenski's view one needs others primarily as instruments for private satisfactions, and one is generally *motivated* by a desire to maximize these private interests. The pertinent distinction for him is between self-interested action (in the narrowest sense), which is very common, and altruistic action, which is very rare. That concept of interest in conjunction with his theory that human behavior is motivated by self-interest accounts for Lenski's first "law" of distribution: "Men will share the product of their labor to the extent required to insure the survival and continued productivity of those whose actions are necessary or beneficial to themselves."[19] And because most people generally pursue their egoistic interests, a society with a large "surplus" will find that surplus distributed to those with the most power.

But this dichotomy between egoistic and altruistic action is too crude to capture the richness of human relationships and motivation. People might also have interests as social beings, as I have argued, and when this dimension of social life is understood, Lenski's theory of motivation and his explanation of inequality itself become less plausible. For people might have interests in community relationships that, to be attained, require the loss or diminution of possible material benefits for those involved. And in some societies, where particular conditions make the mutual gratifications flowing out of such social ties apparent to many, the citizens themselves might be *motivated* by exactly these considerations. In these circumstances, Lenski's central postulate that "man has an insatiable appetite for goods and services" might not apply as stringently as he supposes.[20]   Since that postulate flows naturally from Lenski's dichotomy between self-interested and altruistic conduct, we can see how the very concept of interest Lenski adopts impedes his ability to explore patterns of motivation that are neither purely egoistic or purely altruistic.   Forced by his *categories* to assimilate observed conduct to selfishness or altruism, Lenski naturally concludes that the former dominates in every society.

These considerations bear on the difficulties Lenski encounters in explaining why benefits in industrial societies are distributed *less* unequally than his general theory would lead one to expect.   He explains this "discrepancy" in large part by reference to a "democratic ideology," which has somehow captured the sentiments of the masses and now operates also as a constraint on privileged elites.   Acknowledging difficulty in explaining the rise of this ideology, he thinks its role in industrial society is nevertheless crucial.

Two points are pertinent here: First, the rise of a democratic ideology is more readily explicable if one refuses to assume that human beings must always and everywhere be governed by egoistic impulses, assuming instead that under appropriate conditions of social life, people can and will be motivated as well by desires to support their interests as social beings (and by a stronger measure of altruistic principle than Lenski allows).   Second, if one then concludes that certain communitarian relationships would be fulfilling to participants were they to experience them, a set of questions ignored by Lenski now becomes pertinent. Do the present distribution of power and prevailing patterns of motivation in our industrial society obstruct citizen awareness of more fulfilling possibilities?   Do certain structural arrangements (for instance, patterns of work life, social mobility in a competitive economy, rise of the nuclear family, the isolation and psychological deprivation of older people) encourage egoistic motives and discourage attention both to interests we have as social beings and ideals we might otherwise support as moral agents? Could reduction in the existing range of inequality be accomplished if such structural sources of insecurity and narrow self-concern were modified? In this way a revision of Lenski's concept of interest opens one to a re-examination of central postulates in his theory and encourages an exploration of alternative ways to explain prevailing inequalities.

These large issues cannot be explored here, but it should be emphasized that the suggested conceptual revision is not *alone* sufficient to establish an affirmative answer to the new questions posed. It could turn out that the *concept* of interest offered here is viable, but that in fact most people in most settings almost always subordinate interests they have as social beings to their egoistic interests. Or maybe certain communal arrangements are in the interests of most people today, but structural requirements of industrial society make these arrangements unattainable. Or maybe the envisaged relationships are in fact compatible with extensive and steep inequalities. Each of these possibilities is debatable and that is exactly the point: For rejection of the dichotomy posed by Lenski between egoistic interest and altruistic action enables one to raise new questions and possibilities bypassed by a theory reflecting Lenski's *notion* of interests and his *postulates* about the self-interested motivation people everywhere must have.

To fix more concretely the way in which the notion and theory of interests adopted by Lenski loads the conclusions of his analysis, consider his argument that inequalities in job opportunity and salary between men and women are explicable in large part by reference to the opportunities women have for status and material comfort through marriage. In a society where marriage is a way of life,

> a woman may obtain half interest in a very substantial income, entrée to exclusive circles, and leisure to do most of the things she wishes. Even a woman whose marriage is less successful by economic standards is usually provided with a measure of economic security.[21]

Because *these* satisfactions are available to women, he concludes (1966), it is unlikely that existing inequalities between the sexes "will be eliminated or greatly reduced beyond the present level." [22] Lenski's failure to perceive that women might have interests beyond those enumerated and that they might also become motivated to press militantly to fulfill them flows in large part, I contend, from the poverty of his notion of interest and the theory of human nature to which that notion is attached.

INTERESTS AS NEED FULFILLMENT

We can speak rather easily of the interests one has relative to an accepted standard of social life. Thus, given the principle of respect for persons, it is in the interests of the slave to be freed even if he has been conditioned to accept slavery. But is it in the slave's real interest to be treated with such respect? How could we warrant or undermine such a claim when advanced by another for the slave?

American social scientists who have approached this problem have most often posited a set of universal human "needs" that are thought to stand above and beyond variations in social structure and patterns of socialization and to provide a standard of achievement against which particular social arrangements can be assessed. [23] The term 'need' is not always defined carefully in this literature, but Christian Bay's definition typifies a wider usage: A need is "any *behavior tendency* whose continual denial or frustration leads to pathological responses." [24] Needs are not reducible to wants here, for wants are specifically oriented to particular goals, while an unmet need *may* find expression as malaise, vague anxiety, or unfocused tension. Bay, for example, takes suicide, alcoholism, psychosis, delinquency, and drug addiction to be among the symptoms of need frustration. And he holds that these pathologies sometimes develop when 'higher-level' needs are frustrated, such as those to develop cognitive capacities, to act as responsible agents, and to enter into intimate relationships with others.

Even if this notion of needs were fully serviceable, 'need' and 'interest' would not be synonymous. For innumerable personalized and localized cases of need frustration might remain beyond the reach of effective public policy. But, on this view, a *policy* would be in someone's interest to the extent that it, by comparison with other alternatives, promoted need fulfillment or increased opportunities to promote need fulfillment.

Such a definition does underline deficiencies in the first two formulations considered. For there are situations where people have, as C. Wright Mills would say, "troubles" not yet translated into firm wants, let alone into a set of political claims that could speak to them. "Instead of troubles defined in terms of values and threats, there is often the misery of vague uneasiness; instead of explicit issues, there is often merely the beat feeling that all is somehow not right." [25] To the extent that the first two concepts of interest slide over situations such as this, they divert conceptual attention from possible tensions simmering just below the surface of pluralist politics. Conceptual blinders of this sort help to explain the failure of liberal social scientists of the last generation to anticipate the political crises of the 1960s and 1970s, to detect those troubles shuffled out of pluralist politics, and to formulate political issues implied by their presence (Mills, of course, is the exception).

And yet this definition, too, has serious deficiencies. For a simple test will show, I think, that the suggested conceptual connection between needs and interests may well impose severe limits on the theory of interests that results. These limits are both contrary to the intentions of those who advance the notion of human needs and, I shall later argue, unwarranted.[26]

Consider a hypothetical situation in which we (as investigators) have full and direct knowledge of the tensions and behavioral inclinations of a subservient population. We find the population to have all its needs met (defined as behavioral tendencies); there are no "pathological" responses, no blockage of felt inclinations, and no vaguely felt tensions. The creatures we are to visualize are well fed and clothed; they exhibit a strong sense of security; they even express a doglike warmth in their personal relationships. What they lack, though, is the ability to choose reflectively among alternative courses of conduct, to act responsibly, to express the complex reactive attitudes of love, resentment, grief, guilt, remorse, and outrage that we associate with the social life of human beings.

I am not concerned to argue that the condition described is likely to occur anywhere. But if it were to occur, we would surely be tempted to say that the population's lack of felt inclinations to develop, say, their deliberative capacities to a high pitch was not conclusive proof that it would not be in their interests to do so. This is not only because they might find such skills necessary to the fulfillment of other vaguely felt inclinations—a consideration need theories could easily accommodate. But human beings might, in some settings, lack inclinations or urgings of any sort to achieve states they would prize for themselves once attained; they might possess strong dispositions to resist the attainment of those very modes of life they would find the most gratifying once having experienced them; and they might even find that certain arrangements prized for themselves necessarily include tensions and anxieties as part of the prized condition.

Need theories typically start with a plausible statement of primary needs tied to observable behavioral tendencies and inclinations. But as one advances up the hierarchy of postulated needs a subtle conceptual shift emerges. From 'needs' as a noun defined in terms of inclinations we shift increasingly toward 'needs' as a verb construed as those conditions instrumental to the attainment of one's full development as a person. And at the upper end of the hierarchy, the connection between what one needs to become a person and any set of behavioral inclinations becomes increasingly tenuous. Indeed, need theorists tend to tolerate those tensions and anxieties that might accompany attainment of the highest postulated states.

To avoid this tendency toward equivocation—a tendency supported by ordinary usage—it is advisable to treat 'need' as a verb in our theoretical work. This form calls attention to the fact that need statements are always triadic: "Person A needs x *in order to* (do, be, or become) y." And y in this triad is always the crucial variable. One might need something in order to survive, to survive comfortably, to develop the capacity to act responsibly, to polish his shoes, or to eliminate all sexual urges. Thus when we translate need statements into this form we can see that to say "A needs x" is not necessarily to say that A is inclined towards x nor that it is a worthy object for him to pursue. Such judgments must await consideration of what x is needed for.

My charge, then, is this: The conceptual connection between needs and interests seems plausible only when the equivocal use of the term need in need theories goes unnoted. But when 'need' is defined consistently in terms of behavioral inclinations we can both imagine inclinations that it might not be in our interests to promote and identify possible interests not manifested by our most inchoate behavioral tendencies. Any view that anchors interest exclusively in felt behavioral tendencies runs the risk of celebrating uncritically those inclinations cultivated by dominant socialization processes while deflecting conceptual attention from possible gratifying modes of existence bypassed by those same processes. If the intellectual enterprise aims to recover worthy aspirations that have been lost, to render intelligible modes of life that are now only dimly glimpsed, then a definition of interest *restricted* to felt behavioral tendencies can hardly suffice.

REAL INTERESTS

It has not been my intention to claim that all of the notions of interest examined so far are completely mistaken. Each is able to handle adequately a range of cases in which all parties would agree that the language of interests properly applies. More specifically, when we confront circumstances in which neither the broader objectives adopted by the participants nor the basic dimensions that shape their way of life is at issue, the utilitarian and need models of interest will often handle questions posed about interests effectively enough. Thus we can speak of the interests any individual or group has *relative to* an accepted objective or set of institutional arrangements in which the individual or group is securely implicated. It is, in this sense, in the interests of the blue-collar worker, relative to the established expectation that he will pay for his family's housing, health care, food, and recreation out of private earnings in a system where such goods are relatively scarce and income is unequally distributed, to press for an increase in wages; it is in the interests of the prisoner, relative to the conditions of his imprisonment, to have visiting hours expanded; it is in the interests of a prostitute, relative to her need to ply an unlawful trade, to see that the police are not payed so highly that they refuse to accept bribes. But on occasions such as these we also sometimes legitimately ask, "Are the background conditions and/or accepted objectives within which those assessments are made in the *real* interests (or *really* in the interests) of those persons who now live as blue-collar workers, prisoners, and prostitutes do?" The qualifiers 'real' and 'really' signify first, that our discourse is moving to a more basic level involving interests that are fundamentally important and often prerequisites to a range of other possible gratifications; second, that judgment at this level is inherently more problematic and contestable than judgments advanced within more restrictive contexts; and third, that the perspective of the agents caught within and to some extent shaped by those circumstances might be enhanced by considerations that transcend those confining circumstances. The happy slave is happy because alternative possibilities in his real interests are effectively screened from him, and that *could* be true, to a lesser extent, of the contented blue-collar worker, the apathetic prisoner, and the happy hooker: at least we should not exclude such possibilities by definitional fiat.

But must the resort to the language of real interests necessarily mean that one party projects the arbitrary values he simply "happens to hold" onto others? Must reasoned discourse and the discipline of evidence inevitably be displaced, when we move to this level, by mere rhetoric and arbitrary commitment? With respect to these questions I wish to support two related answers: (1) There are considerations available that can inform judgment and often reduce (although not eliminate) the area of disagreement at this level among students of politics who will carefully consult them; (2) the issues themselves cannot simply be expunged from our inquiries, for judgments about real interests are woven, in ways explicitly acknowledged or only implicitly assumed, into every explanatory theory of politics. I will support the first contention now and turn to the second in the last section of this chapter.

We need to articulate a standard to be consulted when we seek to appraise or assess the real interests of ourselves or others. Before I formulate such a standard, let me emphasize one further feature of all such definitional efforts, too often ignored by analysts of political concepts. As Friedrich Waismann has shown, no concept is ever completely defined; every concept is incorrigibly "open textured." In our definitional statements we limit a concept in particular directions, but there are "always other directions in which a concept has not been defined." [27] The definitional statement I will make, then, is only a first approximation. The accompanying text will help to make the import of the initial definitional gloss clear but will not "limit the concept" in all important directions. That gloss will be useful if it provides a basis from which further clarifications and adjustments can be made when new circumstances are confronted. To say that is not to preface my definitional effort with an apology but merely to point to a little-noted dimension of all such efforts. As a first approximation, then, consider the following statement.

Policy x is more in A's real interest than policy y if A, were he to experience the *results* of both x and y, would *choose* x as the result he would rather have for himself.[28]

Several clarifying comments are in order.

1. The definition focuses on the results of policy rather

than on attitudes toward the policy itself, bypassing problems posed in the first definition considered. Furthermore, following Barry's lead here too, it treats interest as a comparative concept because for "any given proposal there is nearly always one that compared to it is in someone's interest and at least one that compared to it is contrary to someone's interest." [29] Defining the concept in this way encourages people to state explicitly the terms of comparison implicitly adopted when they tell us something is or is not in our interests.

2. The key criterion is the choice of the agent involved, but the privileged choice is one made after the fact, so to speak, rather than before it. This does require investigators to make difficult judgments, in many situations, about the choices a person would make if he had had the relevant experiences, but such a reference to counterfactual conditions is required by most concepts employed in contemporary political inquiry (for instance, power). And the definition does enable us, I think, to *say* all of the things about interests we find people in ordinary discourse saying, thereby retaining for political inquiry not only the function that 'interests' plays in normative discourse but the full range of activities it covers in performing that function. [30] It allows one to say that something *might* be in another's interests even though the other does not now (or might never if prevailing social conditions persist) want it. It allows, further, for the possibility of having an interest in some result against which I have strong inclinations at present. And, as I shall argue next, it allows persons to have interests as social beings as well as in those results whose enjoyment does not essentially involve reciprocal states of awareness.

3. Clarification of the phrase "the result he would rather have" is required to understand what *kind* of choices made after the fact are relevant to ascriptions of real interest. If the phrase is interpreted too loosely, we risk merging "interest-regarding" choices with those that reflect a sense of obligation, selfless benevolence, and perhaps fear of reprisal. Interpreted too narrowly, it would rule out the kinds of considerations people tacitly have in mind when they counsel us about our "real interests" or our "best interests" as social beings. Thus

Erik Erikson clearly thinks that social arrangements and policies that help to nourish a relationship of "mutuality" (that is, the sort of relationship that "strengthens the doer as it strengthens the other") are in the real interests of the parties involved even if neither party fully recognizes that fact. For, in a relationship of mutuality between parent and child,

> a parent dealing with a child will be strengthened in *his* vitality, in *his* sense of identity, and in *his* readiness for ethical action by the very ministrations by means of which he secures to the child vitality, future identity, and eventual readiness for ethical action.[31]

As I see it, then, the distinction between interest-regarding choices and other kinds of choices social beings might make can be formulated, if roughly, along the following lines: An agent's choice is interest-regarding when or to the extent that (for many choices will reflect several kinds of considerations) it takes into account the quality of the result for the agent himself and includes a reference to others insofar as his relationships to them are of the sort he would choose as gratifying and fulfilling in themselves. Much more could probably be said about the demarcation line I seek to sustain here. For example, I would hope to argue that it is in my interests to develop the *capacity* to act as a morally responsible agent even though the very perfection of that capacity could, on particular occasions, enjoin me to act against my interests. Even with further clarification, though, boundary problems will persist between those actions that are in my interests in one role or another and those that are indifferent or contrary to them. This, however, is not a problem peculiar to the definition I propose; those definitions couched in terms of preferences and private wants face, at different points, their own boundary problems, as in sorting among "privately oriented," "publicly oriented," and "ideal-regarding" wants.[32]

4. What if a person, after experiencing the results of a policy that legalizes heroin, chooses that as the result he would rather have? Does this apparent counterexample, and others

like it, undermine the proposed definition? It does not, in my judgment, undermine the original formulation, but it does require us to clarify the meaning of 'choice' further and to contain the first approximation offered within a necessarily loose set of boundary conditions that inform reflection about the real interests of *persons*.

First I must clarify the meaning of 'choice'. If the person now regrets those previous decisions that have made him an addict, if he wishes he could choose to give up the habit but knows he cannot, or even if we have very good reason to suppose that he would now choose otherwise were he fully capable of choosing freely, then we can properly say that his present capacity to choose freely has been impaired. The appropriate question in this context is not "What does he now want?" but "What would he choose, if, knowing what he now knows, he could freely make that choice again?"[33] Situations like this raise difficult questions of judgment that we must approach with great humility, but it is also certain that occasions do arise when such judgments cannot be avoided, occasions when the question becomes not if, but how and on what grounds. We are focusing here on the grounds; those who for the sake of methodological purity refuse to confront such questions are the ones most likely to allow the issues themselves to be settled on the basis of conventional wisdom or arbitrary impulse.

The privileged status we give to the current and future exercise of deliberative choice in the clarified definition draws our attention to the sort of creature we have in mind when we speak of the real interests of persons. It might be advantageous to both a caterpillar and a person to avoid being squashed by a huge boulder, but only the person can be said to have an interest in an educational system that cultivates his reflective potential. This is so, of course, because a person is pre-eminently a creature who has the capacity or potential to deliberate and to choose reflectively, to remember past experiences and to project future plans, to enter into complex social relationships of mutual recognition and reciprocal responsibility.

The idea of real interests, then, is bounded by a set of core ideas we share, if often imperfectly and to a large extent tacitly, about those characteristics particularly distinctive of persons. Initial disagreement about these core ideas is amenable to some degree of rational adjudication through close scrutiny of the assumptions and commitments built into complex reactive attitudes such as love, trust, resentment, and indignation that persons express toward one another but do not apply to things or (in any full sense) to lower animals. To prize the ability to receive and to express such attitudes, and to participate in those reciprocal relationships they make possible, is tacitly to believe in and to prize the distinctive capacities they presuppose. It is to adopt certain beliefs about the way *persons* are to be understood and treated. Within the loosely defined boundaries established by such considerations, important differences in emphasis and accentuation can be expected. These differences in turn will be connected to differences in assumptions about the extent to which certain drives, tendencies, instincts, or desires are programmed into all persons independently of any *specific* social context, and to differences in judgment about the extent to which such drive-states function either as imperatives that must be expressed or as tendencies that can be subjected to control and constraint. To disagree about these matters is to disagree about which facts must be taken into account in the assessment of the real interests persons have.

To accommodate these considerations we must circumscribe the choice criterion more closely. What we aspire to, but do not expect to attain completely, is a choice between alternative experiences that is *fully informed* about the factors entering into those experiences and helping to make each what it is. Such a choice is more fully informed if it reflects the agent's conscious awareness of those *tacit beliefs and commitments about persons* that have entered into relationships he has prized for themselves and if it includes the agent's explicit recognition of any *drives or inclinations basic to his nature* that must somehow be confronted (that is, expressed, repressed, sublimated, deflected) in any social setting. When such self-awareness is approximated, the choice criterion still remains fully operative. For one who chooses in the light of such self-awareness does not necessarily give each of these previous commitments and persistent inclinations full rein: He simply chooses after confronting these facts about himself and his setting. Since it is inevitable that no choice will ever be *fully* informed in this way, we must say that the most informed choice available to one in a particular context constitutes a judgment in serious pursuit of one's real interests.

It is quite clear that the issues posed by discourse into real interests are profound and are unlikely to be fully resolvable through reasoned argument and the play of evidence. But this fact does not justify a retreat into complete skepticism; it does not justify a withdrawal from arguments and evidence that promise to render judgment with respect to these issues more informed. We will indicate briefly in the next section and more extensively in Chapter 5 some of the ways in which reflection into the idea of a person can be informed and disciplined through analysis of the depth assumptions and commitments embedded in the language and relationships of social life. At this juncture it is sufficient to point to the connection itself between the idea of a person and the idea of real interests; for it is now clear that to illuminate one of these ideas is to shed some light on the other as well.

With this background we can return to our limiting case of the agent who locks himself into debilitating drugs (or the child who accepts mind-destroying work in order to live, the refugee who accepts slavery, and so on). The implication of the connection between real interests and persons is this: Any current choice whose import undermines one's capacity to make future choices or seriously restricts opportunities to act upon a range of possible future choices weighs heavily against the real interests of the person or class of persons involved. For one of the things we include as part of being a person is the ability to make choices based upon reasoned deliberation *and* to reconsider those deliberations and those choices on future occasions. A person who acts, or is acted upon, in ways that seriously undermine such future capacities and opportunities is hardly acting (or acted upon) in his real interests.

APPRAISALS OF REAL INTERESTS

We must confront, if briefly, the question of testability. There are some easy cases where the choice criterion can be applied in ways that would settle the issue for most investigators. Thus the worker who changes his preference scale as between more income and a more creative work life after having experienced benefits produced by the latter can be said to provide solid evidence in support of the view that the policies promoting a more creative work life were more fully in his interest after all. Even here the contextual setting within which the test is made would have to be understood thoroughly by the investigator. Perhaps the worker would choose the second option if he could, but he is now so deeply in debt that he must opt for the first. A test, then, which overlooked this factor, and hundreds like it, would run the risk of misinterpreting a contingent choice reflecting immediate constraints for one representing the more basic and stable interests of the agent. Or perhaps the worker "chooses" the second option after experiencing both, but his choice reflects in part the pressure of the group to which he is attached. Even in this apparently simple situation, then, appraisals of interest require the careful assessment of the social context within which the appraisal is made. But this is true of all the notions of interest considered.

Surely with regard to the broadest and most fundamental questions about the higher-order interests of persons and classes of persons, the conclusions we reach will rest necessarily on an assessment of indirect evidence and will have a more or less precarious status.

The kinds of indirect evidence we can draw upon are varied. Consider, for example, the claim that it is in our interests as citizens to have a legal system that provides punishment for crimes committed by responsible agents, against our interests to treat every criminal as a victim of circumstances who needs therapy. Assume also that the therapy and punishment models of punishment are equally effective as deterrents, so the issue will have to be settled on other grounds. A line of inquiry pursued by J. D. Mabbot, P. F. Strawson, and Herbert Morris into the tacit commitments built into our use of such terms as responsibility, guilt, love, and resentment suggests that the application of these concepts to people treats them, under appropriate conditions, as persons having a capacity to form intentions, deliberate, enter into relations of trust, and so on.[34] If we were to expunge these concepts from our language (provided that were possible) we would indeed strip ourselves of the ability to view each other as members of a moral community; we would impoverish our lives by restricting the variety of shared experiences within our reach. Since the "preparedness to acquiesce in that infliction of suffering on the offender which is an essential part of punishment is all of a piece with this whole range of attitudes," our operating commitment to treat each other as persons tends to support the institution of punishment.[35] And once we peer into these conceptual connections carefully we are more likely to choose a *system* (not necessarily individual acts) of punishment as in our real interests as social beings. I am not trying to argue for this particular conclusion here, though I find arguments in support of it persuasive. The point is that conceptual clarification can inform the choices we make about our most basic interests by helping us to see more profoundly what turns on each alternative.[36]

A second line of inquiry involves one's vicarious and actual immersion in alternative modes of social life, in various life styles. A participant study of kibbutzim, various tribal forms, feudal communities, and alternative styles in industrial society provides the materials from which comparative judgments can be made about possible interests not actively sustained by prevailing social arrangements.

These lines of inquiry surely help to bring suppressed presuppositions to the point of more conscious deliberation and choice, but what is the evidential status for the ascription of interests of such choices once made? The problem is not only that investigators must ask what the result would be if a particular practice or institution were introduced into an alien setting; nor is it merely that the persons who undertake these lines of inquiry are likely to have a deep investment in protecting a certain interpretation.

The paradox is this: The very process of preparing oneself to make the most reflective choice about one's interests affects the evidential status of the choice itself. Consider the judgment of the girl radicalized by her experiences in the antiwar movement of the middle 1960s. She was not only morally obligated to join the movement, she now believes, but her involvement generated results that were, in a profound sense, in her own interests.

> Now that I look back on that job, if I had known what I was accepting, I probably would not have done it, because of the insecurities and what seemed so many threatening things.... (Kenneth Keniston: Was it a rough time then?) No, it was great. I was totally absorbed in the work. (K. K.: You mean that now you would do it again, but at the time, if you had known, you wouldn't have done it?) Yes, that is what I am saying. I think that one of the valuable things was that I was open. I was looking....[37]

In one sense this judgment, made *after* having experienced two styles of life, is impressive evidence in favor of the latter alternative. But, in another, a changed person is making the choice and that affects its status as evidence. For her recent experience is mediated through new orientations, expectations, and investments that themselves are supposed to be part of the conditions to be appraised. Even under ideal conditions of choice, then, certain elements of conjecture and speculation will enter into our assessment of the extent to which alternative modes of social life are more or less in our real interests.[38] This incorrigible feature of efforts to appraise higher-level interests should be reflected in the way we hold and defend views about these matters; we must accept a policy presumption in favor of the judgment of those who, even after consulting our arguments and evidence, understand their own interests differently than we do.

INTEREST-REGARDING
EXPLANATIONS

Every assessment of real interests is mediated through the way of life of those making the assessment and, as a result, such judgments promise to remain controversial to some degree. If this is so, why should we not drop such speculative questions from the agenda of political inquiry and stick to more manageable and operational problems? We should not because the attempt to do so must fail. Every explanatory theory of politics includes somewhere in its structure assumptions about persons and their real interests. Such assumptions might be formulated quite explicitly, as they generally are in the classic tradition, or they might remain quite implicit, as they often are in contemporary inquiry, but they cannot be avoided in an explanatory effort that purports to be complete.

Suppose someone explains the tendency of blue-collar workers in our society to press for higher wages by contending that the workers recognize it to be in their interests to do so and are motivated by that recognition. Suspending for now questions about its truth or falsity, such an explanation remains *incomplete* until we know if it is merely thought to be in the workers' interests relative to a restrictive range of alternatives available to them or if it would remain in their comparative interests even though the available alternatives were significantly expanded.

The explanatory incompleteness is perhaps a bit difficult to see for those who share tacitly a set of background assumptions within which the initial explanation-sketch is posed. But this barrier can be eliminated by postulating a more extreme situation in which investigators representing opposing theoretical perspectives agree that the alternatives available to the workers are indeed restrictive. Thus if the same workers were to press the legislature to reduce the minimum wage their employer could legally pay, no one would accept as *sufficient* the following answer to the question "Why are the workers lobbying for a lower minimum wage?": "Because it is in their interests to do so." Something more is needed. Our understanding is enhanced by the further reply "The workers believe that unless their wages are lowered the employer will be forced out of business and they will be unemployed." Now the explanation is more nearly complete. But if we later discovered that the employer could in fact raise wages and yet stay in business, our explanation of the workers' conduct would not be complete until we explained how they had been duped, how they had come to accept the false set of beliefs within which their comparative assessment of interests was made. For to *explain* the conduct of an individual or group is not merely to describe the congruence between the agent's beliefs and actions but also to assess the rationality of the beliefs that inform the action. When such beliefs are judged to be irrational, or to be formed on the basis of unnecessarily limited information, the action is not fully explained until we know why the pertinent beliefs are irrational or why the relevant information is unavailable to the agents.[39]

Exactly the same principle applies in our first case, where the workers are pressing for higher wages. One way to complete the original explanation is to contend that most persons everywhere are governed by desires to get roughly the sorts of goods and services that high wages can buy in our society. The workers, we are now told, recognize and act upon their real interests in a context where a broad range of available alternatives allows them to do so. Gerhard Lenski, whose theory we earlier discussed briefly, makes just this sort of assumption about real interests and explains the behavior of workers (and others) in approximately this way.[40]

Now suppose another investigator contends that the real interests of those workers would be more fully promoted by reforms in the structure of work life and, to simplify our example, suppose too he contends that it is not possible to reform work life and raise wages at the same time. Again waiving questions of truth and falsity for the time being, the explanation of why workers pursue higher wages is now *incomplete* until it is explained why they do not recognize or pursue policy objectives more fully in their interests. To simplify again, if it is contended that management, holding impressive power resources, will bargain on wage claims but not on the reform of work life, the explanation now becomes more nearly complete. We know why the workers pursue one set of claims and we have some understanding of why they fail to recognize, or merely fail to pursue, another set more fully in their interests.

The *competing explanations* of why workers pursue higher incomes proceed from alternative assessments of their real interests. Neither explanation is complete until such assessments are made and we cannot decide between them until we decide which judgment of real interests, if either, is more nearly correct. (There are other considerations relevant to the assessment of each theory, but those do not now concern us.) Moreover, once both explanations are completed in the ways specified, we can see that they support conflicting normative conclusions, with the differences flowing in part from disagreements in the assessment of real interests. The former explanation justifies the workers' activities and the larger system that makes these practices possible, while the latter may justify the workers' activities as the best within available alternatives, but it will also project a critical appraisal of a system that circumscribes alternatives in this way.

Advocates of a particular explanatory theory might explicitly formulate the interpretation of real interests embodied in the theory, or the interpretation might work in the background as a set of latent assumptions. The former approach is surely more responsible intellectually (and methodologically), since it opens some of the most important and controversial ingredients of a theory to public examination and criticism. But to approximate such standards of intellectual responsibility one must break with methodological purism: A complete explanation explicitly projecting assessments of real interests will include claims that are necessarily speculative to some degree.

Clarity about what 'interests' means does not ensure that disputes over what is in the interests of an individual or class can be neatly resolved. But it does help to sharpen the issues implicated in those disputes; it does point to kinds of evidence most fruitfully pertinent to an informed judgment of the core issues; and it does encourage investigators to be explicit about a range of judgments woven into the theories they accept, which may not be fully amenable to the constraints of reason and evidence. That is the best, I think, we can expect. To promise more, to offer to "translate" these issues into a series of neat hypotheses amenable to precise and impersonal testing is inevitably to corrupt the enterprise undertaken. The outcome would join surface precision to profound obscurity.

NOTES

1. Charles Taylor, "Neutrality in Political Science," in *Philosophy, Politics, and Society*, 3d ser., ed. Peter Laslett and W. G. Runciman (New York: Barnes and Noble, 1967), pp. 25–57.

2. Ibid., pp. 30, 40.

3. For examples of essays that explicitly place "interests" in the center of moral discourse, see Stanley Benn, "Egalitarianism and the Equal Consideration of Interests," in *Justice and Equality*, ed. Hugo A. Bedau (Englewood Cliffs, N.J.: Prentice-Hall, 1971), pp. 152–67; and John Rawls, *A Theory of Justice* (Cambridge: Harvard University Press, 1971).

4. I omit reference here to "explications" of the following sort, which seek to bypass the issues involved: "Well, what is an *interest* then? . . . But for our purposes in this volume at least that is exactly the kind of question we have tried to avoid. The *scientific procedure* is to observe and isolate certain acts (or behaviors) and actions, and connect these into 'bundles' whose interconnections may prove fruitful. 'Interest group' being just a convenient label for one such 'bundle', it need have no connection at all with the meaning of its two constituent terms." (!) Graham Wootton, *Interest Groups: Foundations of Modern Political Science Series* (Englewood Cliffs, N.J.: Prentice-Hall, 1970), p. 18.

5. Probably because the concept has received increased attention lately in philosophical literature, few political scientists today argue as confidently for interest as policy preference. But the

concept is still commonly *employed* that way, largely on the grounds to be considered shortly, of operational rigor. For earlier statements, see David Truman, *The Governmental Process* (New York: Knopf, 1951), pp. 50–51; and Glendon Schubert, *The Public Interest* (New York: Free Press, 1960).

6. Both quotations are from Nelson Polsby, "The Sociology of Community Power," *Social Forces* (March 1959): 235; my emphasis. I should note that in private correspondence Polsby has denied that he defines interest as policy preference and has suggested that "interest" is not a central category in his work on community power. While it is not central to my argument whether he does or does not employ the term that way and while he has not given an explicit definition of the term in the works considered here, the following two points are relevant: (1) "Interests" must be a central category for Polsby, for "proposition" 4 of the "stratification theory" that he is out to refute holds that "the upper class power elite rules in its own interests." Polsby, *Community Power and Political Theory* (New Haven: Yale University Press, 1963), p. 11. (2) Statements such as the following are found at several junctures in his book when he is criticizing "stratification theorists" for imputing interests to groups which the groups themselves don't acknowledge: "However, 'real' conflicts apparently can take place in the view of stratification analysis without overt disagreements. ... For the moment, rejecting this presumption of 'objectivity of interests', we may view instances of intraclass disagreement *as* intraclass conflicts of interest and interclass agreement *as* interclass harmony of interest. To maintain the opposite seems perverse." Ibid., p. 22; my emphasis.

7. I deal with the criticisms briefly here in order to get to more intriguing notions. For other criticisms with which I largely agree, see Isaac Balbus, "The Concept of Interest in Pluralist and Marxian Analysis," *Politics and Society* (Summer 1971): 151–78; Brian Barry, *Political Argument* (New York: Humanities Press, 1965), ch. 10; and Richard B. Flathman, *The Public Interest* (New York: Wiley, 1966).

8. Pernicious for inquiry because, accepting that assumption, students of political "socialization," for example, forget to explore the central question perplexing Rousseau: Under what conditions of social life and education do citizens develop the capacity to support justice and the public interest even when that

support requires a sacrifice of private advantage? Pernicious for political conduct because the assumption that political acts (almost always) will be self-interested helps to justify particular acts of *selfishness* as part of the human condition. For an intriguing effort to raise the Rousseauian question, see Lawrence Kohlberg, "Moral Development," in *International Encyclopedia of the Social Sciences* (1968), 10:483–94.

9. There are many arguments for the presumption to remain close to ordinary discourse in explicating conceptions such as power, interest, and politics. One argument stands out sharply here: Concepts, as vehicles for thought and action, have complex rules governing their use, which are never fully stated. Since a particular concept receives its full meaning only in relation to the entire conceptual system in which it is embedded, a change in one of its dimensions is likely to produce unnoted implications for its ability to perform its several conventional functions. Such a consideration does not militate against conceptual revision, but against such revision lightly undertaken. Concept revision is more analogous to a heart transplant than to a watch repair.

10. In addition to the arguments offered in the first chapter, see William Alston, *Philosophy of Language* (Englewood Cliffs, N.J.: Prentice-Hall, 1964), last chapter; Max Black, "Reasoning with Loose Concepts," in *The Margins of Precision* (Ithaca: Cornell University Press, 1970), pp. 1–13; George Schlesinger, "Operationalism," in *Encyclopedia of Philosophy* (1967), 5:543–47; and especially Friedrich Waismann, "Verifiability," in *Logic and Language,* 1st ser., ed. Anthony Flew (Oxford: Basil Blackwell, 1951), pp. 115–45.

11. Thus, even the equation of interests and policy *preference* makes "false consciousness" of a sort possible. Polsby, *Community Power and Political Theory;* C. Wright Mills, *The Power Elite* (New York: Oxford University Press, 1959). Such comparisons are developed in William E. Connolly, *Political Science and Ideology* (New York: Atherton Press, 1967), ch. 2.

12. Quoted from Brian Barry, "The Public Interest," in *The Bias of Pluralism,* ed. William Connolly (New York: Atherton Press, 1969), p. 163. Barry is not, of course, strictly a utilitarian. For he considers ideals that are not "want-regarding" relevant to the appraisal of public policy. He is utilitarian only in the sense

that he makes interest a want-regarding concept. See Barry, *Political Argument*, ch. 3.

13. The qualification is this: It might be in one's interest to sacrifice the satisfaction of a current want if its attainment would impede one's ability to satisfy future wants one might have (Barry, *Political Argument*, p. 184). Thus legalization of heroin might help me to get what I now want but limit my ability to attain future wants (and even affect my future wants themselves?). But a qualification posed along a *purely* temporal dimension is necessary but insufficient to handle conventional uses of interest. We need to specify, in addition, conditions that enable us to ask, and bring evidence to bear on, whether it is in the slave's interest to escape slavery even if he now prefers that state to all known alternatives and *always will as long as he remains a slave*. A purely temporal qualification will not handle this paradigm case or the numerous other situations that more or less approximate it.

14. Barry's quotation from John Locke to illustrate the "kinds of ways in which a policy, law, or institution must impinge on someone before it can be said to be 'in his interest'." Barry, "The Public Interest," p. 163.

15. Barry, *Political Argument*, p. 182.

16. Robert Paul Wolff, *The Poverty of Liberalism* (Boston: Beacon Press, 1968), p. 181. See also Balbus, "The Concept of Interest in Pluralist and Marxian Analysis."

17. Herbert Morris, "Persons and Punishment," *The Monist* (Fall 1968): 471–501.

18. Gerhard Lenski, *Power and Privilege* (New York: McGraw-Hill, 1966), p. 27.

19. Ibid., p. 43.

20. Ibid., p. 31.

21. Ibid., pp. 405–406.

22. Ibid., p. 406.

23. Thus Amitai Etzioni, in his defense of a theory of basic human needs, describes the function of such a theory: "Theories which assume autonomous human needs provide an independent basis with which to compare societies to each other, as more or less consonant with basic human needs." Etzioni, "Basic Hu-

man Needs, Alienation, and Inauthenticity," *American Sociological Review* (December 1968): 878. See also Christian Bay, "Politics and Pseudo-politics: A Critical Evaluation of some Behavioral Literature," *American Political Science Review* (March 1965): 870–84; and James C. Davies, *Human Nature in Politics* (New York: Wiley, 1963).

24. Christian Bay, "Needs, Wants, and Political Legitimacy," *Canadian Journal of Political Science* (Fall 1968): 242.

25. C. Wright Mills, *The Sociological Imagination* (New York: Oxford University Press, 1959), p. 11.

26. The next two paragraphs are a somewhat revised version of my critique of a paper given by Christian Bay at the Ripon Conference on Rights and Political Action, Ripon College, October 8–10, 1970. The critique, along with the rest of the conference proceedings, is published in *Inquiry* (Winter 1971): 237–43.

27. Friedrich Waismann, "Verifiability," p. 126.

28. Since I am especially indebted to S. I. Benn's views about how one should construe interests in political inquiry ("Interests in Politics," *Proceedings of Aristotelian Society* 60 (1960): 123–40), I should specify the point at which I disagree. I agree that "to say something is in a man's interest is not to say that he will be glad of it immediately; but it does seem to imply that one would expect him to be glad of it at some time" (p. 130). But Benn then suggests that there "may be a sense" in which something is in a person's interest even if he doesn't want it, would not want it if he rightly understood the position, or even that, want it or not, he would be pleased if he got it" (p. 130). It would be in his interests, Benn thinks, *relative to* a valid norm of conduct, even if that norm is one the agent could never prize for itself. But if he himself did not, once he understood and "lived up to" the norm, come to be pleased with it for itself, then I don't see how we can appropriately say that policies that help him to see and achieve it are in his interests, even though it might be *right* for him to support such policies.

29. Brian Barry, "The Use and Abuse of the Public Interest," in *The Public Interest*, ed. Carl Friedrich (New York: Atherton Press, 1966), p. 198.

30. I do not accept ordinary language as the final court of appeal here, especially since an atomistic view of human nature continues to infect talk about interests. But I do not think any

definition should at least cover the paradigm cases of "interest" sanctioned by ordinary discourse (remembering that "ordinary discourse" means not the definitions people give but the rules they actually follow), and then give reasons for any proposed extensions or modifications. To the extent I modify usage, my reason is simply that the atomistic conception of human nature (partially) reflected in contemporary usage is faulty; when those faults are recognized we can also see that relationships we prize as social beings have much in common with other conditions and objectives we cover with the language of interests. My general approach here reflects, I hope, the spirit of John Austin: "Certainly, then, ordinary language is not the last word: in principle it can everywhere be supplemented and improved upon and superseded. Only remember, it *is* the first word." Quoted from "A Plea for Excuses," in *Ordinary Language* ed. V. C. Chappel (Englewood Cliffs, N.J.: Prentice-Hall, 1964), p. 49.

31. *Insight and Responsibility* (New York: W. W. Norton, 1964), p. 233.

32. See Barry, *Political Argument,* pp. 35–41 and 295–99. For formulations that move in the direction I seek to sustain, see William Alston, "Pleasure," in *Encyclopedia of Philosophy* (1967), 6:341–47; and Alasdair MacIntyre, "Egoism and Altruism," in *Encyclopedia of Philosophy* (1967), 1:462–66.

33. I realize, of course, that the charge of elitism will be hurled here. But the charge moves too far too fast. First, all of the definitions adopted finally end up, as I have noted, acknowledging that people might be mistaken about their interests on occasion. And on most usages most people would agree that certain actions that go against the inclinations of individuals are nevertheless in their interests—as in the cases of some policies toward children and idiots. One only needs one example to raise the question I pose here *of the grounds for making such judgments.* Second, for me to say that you are mistaken about your interests is not necessarily to imply that I will jam my view down your throat. Only authoritarians leap to that implication. I might simply try to persuade you or to bribe you. Indeed, persuasion is usually the most justifiable approach to take for one who celebrates cultivating the capacity for choice. Third, there are some occasions in politics when we simply cannot avoid taking positions on issues that affect the interests of others. Here we simply must exercise our best judgment, remembering human

fallibility and privileging to some extent the views of those affected by that judgment.

34. J. D. Mabbot, "Punishment," in *Justice and Social Policy*, ed. F. A. Olafson (Englewood Cliffs, N. J.: Prentice-Hall, 1961), pp. 39–54; Morris, "Persons and Punishment; and P. F. Strawson, "Freedom and Resentment," in *Studies in the Philosophy of Thought and Action*, ed. P. F. Strawson (New York: Oxford University Press, 1968), pp. 71–96.

35. Strawson, "Freedom and Resentment," p. 93.

36. The ways in which conceptual clarification can inform choices of the sort discussed here are explored with some care by Richard Flathman in "From Therapy to Theorizing: Conceptual Analysis and Political Philosophy," a paper delivered to annual meeting of the American Political Science Association, Los Angeles, California, September 8–12, 1970.

37. Quoted in Kenneth Keniston, *Young Radicals: Notes on Committed Youth* (New York: Harcourt, Brace and World, 1968), p. 121.

38. To focus the problem more sharply, consider the case of a rather contented person who is convicted of a crime and several years later comes to prefer the security and routine of prison life to freedom in the larger society. Many of us would want to ask if that choice could be explained away as the result of the prison's constricting influence on the convict's perception and understanding. Steven Lukes explores problems inherent in making such judgments in the context of deciding between a Marxist and Durkheimian view of human development in "Alienation and Anomie," in Laslett and Runciman, *Philosophy, Politics, and Society*, pp. 134–56. The comparison is particularly pertinent, since I suspect that Marx and Durkheim share the *notion* of interest elucidated here but diverge significantly as to what is most in our real interests as social beings.

39. I am omitting reference to action informed by moral commitments because that would complicate the examples without affecting the basic argument. For a more general statement of this thesis, see Alasdair MacIntyre, "Rationality and the Explanation of Action," in *Against the Self Images of the Age* (New York: Schocken Books, 1971), pp. 244–59.

40. Lenski, *Power and Privilege*, especially the first several chapters. Lenski's work is illuminating because he is so explicit about his

assumptions. But I must add that I think they are seriously mistaken. I have explored the connection between such basic assumptions and the structure of explanation further in "Theoretical Self-Consciousness," *Polity* (Fall 1973): 5–36. The explanation sketch posed above could be made airtight by claiming that the real interests of the workers would be damaged by successful pressure for claims outside the range now available because the system that protects important interests now would then be undermined. And, of course, the workers would have to be interpreted as restricting their claims because they understand that fact. The *social theory* they accept plays a large role in their assessment of interests and how to promote them.

3

Power and Responsibility

FORMS OF POWER

In context, we usually know what someone means when he says that a person or group "has power," is "in power," or is "powerful." Thus we might say that a chairman of a research committee is powerful if he is able to get research projects he favors funded while other members of his committee often find it difficult to do so. But when one advances a theory of power applicable to the operations of an entire society, these shorthand phrases require more careful and explicit clarification. Approaching this problem, several social analysts have noted the need to specify the *scope* of an agent's power (the values or issues over which it ranges), its *magnitude* (how "much" difference he can make with respect to those issues), its *domain* (the number of persons affected by its exercise), and so on.[1] But prior to these specifications another question must be answered: What is it we are saying one has, does, or exercises when we attribute to him *power* of magnitude x, with respect to scope y, over domain z? What changes in meaning occur, if any, when the predicate power is replaced in statements of this sort by predicates such as authority, persuasion, or influence? The statement, "Colonel House's *power* derived not from any constitutional *authority* but from his *influence* over President Wilson,"[2] changes its meaning when we scramble the underlined terms to read "Colonel House's *authority* derived not from any constitutional *influence* but from his *power* over President Wilson." Now Colonel House stands in a quite different relationship to people around the President; his relationship to the President himself is significantly changed; and the clause about his constitutional influence hovers on the edge of incoherence.

Even if we become satisfied about what sorts of relationships fall within the ambit of the concept power, there are still distinctions of importance to note. Thus if I say "A has power *to do* or *attain* some x," I do not always or necessarily refer to the same dimensions that are covered by "A has *power over B* with respect to some x." It is not necessary, in the first locution, for A's power to involve him in limiting or otherwise affecting the life of some B (though he might), and that locution strongly implies that when A acts to get x, x is an outcome he intends or desires to attain. When we use the locution 'power to' we could often substitute 'ability' for 'power' without changing the meaning of the statement.

When we use the locution 'power over' a larger part of our attention turns to those on the receiving end of the relationship; Agent B (a person or group) must be limited or otherwise affected by Agent A before this second locution is easily adopted. Moreover, it is not necessary that A attain *his* objectives for us to speak meaningfully of A exercising power over B, nor is it always necessary for A to intend to limit or otherwise affect B before we can conclude that he has power *over* B.

The locution 'power to' is quite congenial to the classic definition of power offered by Hobbes:

> The power of a man (to take it universally) is his present means to obtain some future end.[3]

And it provides the starting point from which contemporary social scientists typically analyze power relationships. Indeed, it is not unlikely that debates between radicals and moderates about "who has power?" are complicated by the fact that one side is especially interested in knowing which groups have power *to* attain their objectives while the other wants especially to know to what extent those at the bottom levels of income and status hierarchies have power exercised *over* them by those in higher positions. Since they are tacitly asking overlapping but somewhat different questions, it may be that neither of these two sides in such debates makes full contact with the other. It is also likely that the debates within certain organizations (such as universities) between administrative officials who purport to feel powerless, and their subordinates, who purport to feel constrained by the power of administrators, are compounded by the fact that each of the parties has somewhat different aspects of power in mind. The administrators are impressed by limitations on their *power to* achieve specific goals, while the subordinates are impressed by the *power* of the administrators *over* them with respect to the latter's goals and interests. It could turn out that each is more correct than the other imagines, because each tacitly has a somewhat different question in mind when he asks about the "distribution of power" in the organization.

In this essay I shall focus on those who are on the receiving end of a power relationship, on those who have power exercised over them. This focus does not force me (or others adopting such a perspective) to conclude a priori that one segment of the society is always on the receiving end; it does not, that is, force the conclusion that power is stratified or concentrated in an elite. For you might exercise power over me in one respect and I over you in another. But it does shift the focus of our attention from the bidder to the complier in any particular relationship, even though, as we shall see, the conduct of the bidder must also meet certain specifications before *he* can be said to exercise *power* over others.[4]

I will explore a set of cases in which A exercises power over B by putting B in a position, or getting him to do something, that increases B's burdens. And I will include (but not exhaustively define) among "increasing B's burdens" outcomes that make activities consonant with B's wishes, interests, or obligations less available to him. In this section I will restrict the cases to those in which A is an individual, delaying until later the more difficult cases in which A is a group, class, or other collective. Consider, then, the following:

1. An employer convinces his employee through presentation of evidence and reasoned argument that a candidate for local office will, if elected, work to institute a progressive income tax. Since the employee favors such a tax, he is *persuaded* by these arguments and decides to support the candidate. The employer surely does not exercise power over the employee in this instance; for the employee is convinced by arguments given in good faith by the employer, and the employee freely chooses to campaign for the candidate. Except where 'persuasion' is used in an extended sense to include manipulation, identification, and so on, I will hold that instances of persuasion are not instances of power.

2. The employer threatens (and the threat is credible) to

lay off the employee unless he actively supports the candidate. The employee had planned to remain inactive, but the threat convinces him to change his mind. The employer *coerces* him to support the candidate. Even had the employee refused to comply with the threat, it would still be appropriate here to speak of the application of coercive pressure. For the introduction of the threat has made a range of conduct the employee might otherwise find attractive or obligatory less eligible to him. The employer may or may not by this threat enhance his power to get the candidate elected, and he exercises *power to* gain the active support of the employee only if the employee complies with his demand. But he exercises *power over the employee* (with respect to specified activities) if, because of the threat, the employee complies effectively, or complies conscientiously but ineffectively, or gives the appearance of complying but covertly signals to others his reluctance, or refuses to comply but quits his job to join the ranks of the unemployed, or enters into a prolonged depression precipitated by the introduction of this new source of tension, or commits suicide. Note that the locutions 'power to' and 'power over' converge without strain on only one of the outcomes listed— when the employee complies with the demand. In each of the others, one locution is clearly superior to the other, and had we limited ourselves to 'power to', several possible outcomes of importance would not easily or naturally be considered in relation to our thinking about power.

3. The employer gives his employee arguments and evidence that convince the employee to support the candidate. But now the employer consciously withholds pertinent information not easily available to his employee from other sources. He *manipulates* the employee, thereby exercising power over him. As before, the behavior of the employee is not closely predictable. He might try to support the candidate but bungle the effort, actually hurting the chances for election; he might earnestly support him but in an unimaginative and marginally effective way; or he might support him effectively. But to the extent the employee's conduct is guided by these new beliefs foisted on him by the employer, we can say that the employer

has exercised power over him. Whether the employer has effectively improved the chances that the candidate will be elected is another, though related, question.

4. The employer knows something about the motives and life situation of his employee. Judging that the employee cannot easily be manipulated or coerced to support the candidate, and knowing that he is now inclined to campaign for the opposing candidate, the employer decides to use advantages attached to his status as employer to *deter* or *impede* the employee in his efforts. Accordingly, he requires special reports from the employee, which are due just prior to the election; he plants rumors about the employee designed to undermine his credibility with the candidate; he issues a memorandum forbidding political activity during working hours; he takes the employee on an obligatory, lengthy business trip as a "reward" for excellent service in the past.[5] He exercises power over the employee to the extent that he increases the costs, risks, or difficulties the employee must face in supporting the candidate. Even if the employee succeeds in surmounting these obstacles, *deterrent power* has been exercised over him—though the *respect* in which that power is exercised will depend on the success and failure of the employee in recognizing and coping with these obstacles. Moreover, while coercion implies that the recipient be aware of a threat, and (successful) manipulation implies that he not be so aware, deterrent power can be exercised both when he is aware of the deterrent and when he is not.

5. The employee, who has had this job for several years, knows that others have been in the past coerced, manipulated, and deterred by the employer around election time. Concerned about the security of his family and himself, he decides to surrender to the employer's wishes prior to facing such pressures and their incumbent risks. He surrenders in *anticipation* of feared sanctions, and as a result, we can say that the employer *has* power over him in this instance.[6] Ironically, when the employee responds in anticipation of possible sanctions he is often obliged to respond even more energetically than would be expected if he were coerced or manipulated. For

otherwise the employer might not notice the employee's activities on the candidate's behalf and might thus apply the very coercive or deterrent pressure the employee had sought to avoid. Power wielded in this way is often, from the bidder's point of view, the most effective of all: It requires little overt effort on his part; it encourages others to take the initiative; it is likely to generate a more energetic favorable response; and it is one of the most difficult forms of power for outside observers (such as social scientists) to detect. Power as *anticipatory reaction* is parasitic on other forms, such as coercion and deterrence, but it is not less effective because of that dependence.

There are difficult borderline cases with respect to each of the forms of power identified. But this is especially true of anticipatory surrender. What if the *employee,* wishing at once to protect his self-esteem and his job, *deceives himself* into believing that he willingly and voluntarily does in this instance what the employer would have him do? When this description fits the situation, we have to say that the employer exerts power over the employee with respect to specified activities; and one of the many problems facing power analysts is in deciding just when such a description does apply. What if the *employer,* to protect at once his candidate and his self-esteem, *deceives himself* into believing that he does not care and would not react negatively were the employee not to comply with his desires? Again, if that description truly fits the case, the employer exerts power over the employee with respect to that issue.

6. The employer, through intermediaries who hide their relationship to him, has the employee held at gunpoint in his home for two days just before the election. He thereby *forces* the employee to desist from supporting the candidate at a strategic juncture. The use of force is a notoriously blunt and limited way to exercise power over another, blunt because the instrument used is so obvious and thus opens its users to possible reprisals in the future, limited because, unlike coercion, manipulation, and anticipatory surrender, it is generally useful only as a means to restrain someone from doing some-

thing. But by comparison to manipulation and coercion, force is a very *predictable* means of control *within those limits*. When I coerce or manipulate you there is usually a range of choices still open to you, even though some of those choices are thereby rendered more risky or costly. But when I apply force, your effective choice itself is narrowly limited; I can thus predict what you will do during that period very reliably. Contrary to some contemporary views, I will say that when A restrains B forcibly he exercises power over him, even though the restraint itself might mean that A has given up in his efforts to get B to promote actively some objective of A's.[7]

7. The employer, by a combination of manipulation and coercion, gets the employee to see a psychiatrist regularly, who is in fact a fraud, and the psychiatrist subjects the employee to a combination of hypnotic control and shock treatment. The employee in this way is *conditioned* to respond affirmatively to conservative personalities and statements and negatively to their liberal counterparts. Conditioning is not always a form of power, but in this context it is. For now the employee responds to behavioral cues in a manner selected by the employer. The result, of course, is not always or uniformly advantageous to the employer; for while the employee responds consistently to the appropriate cues, his responses are crude and often poorly geared to the nuances of the situation in which those cues are presented. Put another way, the employee's *behavior* is very predictable, but its connection to the candidate's chances for election is not. He says and does the "right things," but he is not always intelligent or persuasive about what he says and does. Conditioning as a form of power has a restricted range of uses.

Items 2 through 7, with different qualifying clauses around each, are forms of power. But to say that is not to say that the exercise of power over others is equivalent or reducible to these forms. Just as the specific forms of vice that we identify by means of special concepts (for instance, graft, collusion) do not together exhaust all the practices we might put under the general label 'vice' so the exercise of power over others does not always fit neatly into one or some mix of these categories.

For example, there may be occasions where identification with another as a model of conduct can be described as a situation in which one is in the power of the model. Moreover, when we say that a person *has power over another* (sticking to personal relationships for now) dimensions are insinuated into that statement that are not so fully or clearly present when we simply say that the first has manipulated or coerced the second. Unless explicit disclaimers are offered, use of the former locution implies that the bidder can draw on several of these forms in conjunction (recall how anticipatory surrender is parasitic upon coercion); it implies that the relationship is durable; and it suggests that the matters with respect to which the bidder can or does limit the recipient are rather extensive and important. The fact that we have both a verb and a noun form for each of the forms of power, but only a noun form for power, signals, I think, that our ideas about 'power' are closely connected to, but not exhausted by, our ideas about the forms power can take.

POWER AND RESPONSIBILITY

Consideration of the similarities and differences among persuasion, manipulation, coercion, deterrence, anticipatory surrender, force, and conditioning helps us to understand more clearly *why* some of them are subsumed under 'power over' and others are not, and that understanding in turn brings into the open rules covering the use of 'power over' that are often missed or underplayed by those analysts who define the global concept 'power' without prior attention to forms its exercise typically takes. We can now ask questions about this family of concepts and their connections to 'power'. What is the point of these distinctions? Along what kinds of considerations is this family of concepts graded? Why is persuasion not a form of power?

Consider, first, an important element common to all these ideas. Each notion presupposes that the agents involved have a capacity for choice; and in those cases where the predicate 'power' is applicable, either the recipient's capacity for choice or his ability to act as he chooses has somehow been impaired. To persuade another (when we use that notion in its narrower sense) is to give him reasons that help to inform his choice. Neither his capacity for choice nor his ability to act on his choice has been impaired by persuasion. To coerce another makes it dangerous or costly for him to act on his choice; to deter him is to obstruct his ability to act on choices he has or might make; to force another is to make it impossible for him to act on a range of choices; and to condition him is to impair his capacity for choice itself along a particular dimension. Our thinking about power, then, draws upon prior conceptions about the characteristics of *persons* capable of forming intentions, acting upon beliefs and ideals, being guided by reasons, and worthy of being held responsible for the consequences of their own actions. The distinctions among these forms of power embodied in our language reflect our shared understanding of a set of capacities characteristic of persons and of the various ways in which such capacities can be nourished, impaired, promoted, and frustrated by the actions of others.

Moreover, the distinctions among such notions as persuasion, coercion, manipulation, and conditioning are built around, and reflect, shared moral considerations. Without the moral point embodied in each, there would be little reason to distinguish among them. From the vantage point of amoral Martians lacking our (partially) shared views and commitments about persons it would indeed be odd and useless to distinguish as we do between manipulation and persuasion. But when one of *us* is convinced that he was in fact manipulated when he thought he had been persuaded, the tenor of the shift in his response outstrips any "quantitative" difference between persuasion and manipulation. Put another way, for those tacitly or explicitly committed to the principle that persons are worthy of respect, *the distance between persuasion and manipulation is a moral distance; it reflects the judgment that there is a moral presumption against the latter that does not obtain for the former.*

Because of the ways in which manipulation, coercion, anticipatory surrender, deterrence, force, and conditioning impinge on the choices of recipients, we shift, in some degree, responsibility in these cases away from the recipient and toward the person initiating these pressures. Only in the case of persuasion, which is not a form of power, does such a shift not occur; and this suggests that there is a particularly intimate connection between alleging that A has power over B and concluding that A is properly held responsible to some degree for B's conduct or situation. Our shared judgment that there is a moral presumption against limiting or impairing the choices of others is reflected in the manifold and subtle distinctions we draw among ways of getting persons to do things (note the paucity of such distinctions for our relationships to animals and things). That presumption can be overridden, but until adequate reasons are given, coercion, manipulation, and the others stand as presumptively wrong acts. And even after adequate reasons are given to justify these forms in context, responsibility for the changes in conduct among the recipients is shifted to some degree to the bidders.

To support these claims we shall look at some of the criteria of 'coercion' more closely. Suppose A says to B, who is fond of him, "If you take that job I'll have a heart attack." [8] If it is not possible for A to *choose* whether or not to have a heart attack under the stipulated conditions, his statement is not a threat but a (nonthreatening) warning. And we do not speak in this case of A coercing B by threatening *to do* something but of A informing B of a certain event beyond his control, which *will happen* if B leaves home. This difference between a threat and a nonthreatening warning allows us to hold the agent responsible for the event he threatens, while he escapes responsibility for the event he merely predicts. That difference is reflected in the rules governing our use of 'coercion'; it is itself part of the difference between coercing, predicting, and warning.

Suppose an employer *informs* his workers that he will go out of business if they unionize. And suppose he is actually *predicting* what will happen to him rather than *threatening* what he will do if they unionize. That is, he knows that his business will fail under the conditions of unionism, and he is simply informing the workers of that fact. His statement may act as a deterrent to the workers, and they might even decide not to unionize. But has *he* exercised power over them if they are deterred by this warning? I think not. It could be that both he and they have power exercised over them by other individuals or collectivities that contribute to the situation; but he, in this instance, is calling the worker's attention to a probable event—quite outside his control. The connection between power and responsibility helps us to distinguish, in this case, between a situation in which the predicate 'power' is not applicable and other situations, remarkably close to it in many ways, in which that predicate does apply. And the very subtlety of the difference itself affects the relations between employers and employees in such contexts. For if the employer claims to be predicting an event beyond his control but in fact has some leverage with respect to it, then we would surely describe the situation as one in which he exercises power over the workers—power that takes the form of coercion and manipulation and that is more effective to the extent that the workers mistakenly interpret it as a mere prediction. It is just this kind of possibility that makes workers very wary of the "predictions" made by employers in such contexts.

Finally, in the movie *The Godfather* the audience finds the mafioso's phrase, "I'll make him an offer he can't refuse," so amusing just because it is not an offer he will make but a threat he will deliver. We do not, except in rare circumstances, consider offers to be coercive, but threats always are. And, once again, I typically am held responsible for my decisions to accept or reject offers, but if I do the same thing because someone has threatened me, a portion of the responsibility for my act shifts to him. And to threaten someone successfully is to exercise power over him, while to make him an offer in a context where other options are reasonably open to him is surely not to exercise power over him.

Our exploration of the forms of exercise of power over others supports, then, two related conclusions. First, such an exercise involves the limiting or impairing of the recipient's choice in some respect, and second, before such effects are manifestations of some person's or collectivity's *power* over the recipient(s) there must be some reason to hold the bidder *responsible* for the limitation.[9] These two conditions are not the only ones that must be met before we can speak of the exercise of power over someone, but they are important conditions often ignored in the formal definitions of power offered by contemporary political scientists. Attention to these two conditions will help us in making judgments about the applicability of the idea 'power over' in those relationships where the agent is not an individual but a group, class, or other collectivity.

When we see the conceptual connection between the idea of power and the idea of responsibility we can see more clearly why those who exercise power are not eager to acknowledge that fact, while those who take a critical perspective of existing social relationships are eager to attribute power to those in privileged positions. For to acknowledge power over others is to implicate oneself in responsibility for certain events and to put oneself in a position where *justification* for the limits placed on others is expected. To attribute power to another, then, is not simply to describe his role in some perfectly neutral sense, but is more like *accusing* him of something, which is then to be denied or justified. Attention to these two conditions surrounding 'power' shows power to be a concept bounded by normative considerations. It *is* used in description: Certain observable conditions (in a broad sense) must be met before it is applicable. But once we decide that the description correctly applies, there is a presumption against that relationship that puts those against whom the attribution is made on the defensive.

Those who exercise power over others typically seek to deny it or to hide it. This desire encourages them both to argue for quite narrow definitions of the concept and to exercise forms of power that are not easily detectable. Where feasible, elites of power will favor deterrence, manipulation, and anticipatory surrender over coercion and force. For others can often be *deterred* by placing before them obstacles emanating from hidden sources. Similarly, when subordinates *anticipate* possible sanctions and comply in advance, it often looks to third parties as though the action is voluntary; the very willingness of the subordinates to comply signals a probable unwillingness to admit to third-party investigators (or perhaps to themselves) the nature of the relationship within which they are involved. And when some *manipulate* others effectively, both the recipients and third parties will find it difficult to grasp the role played by the manipulator. Interested in denying power, elites of power favor exactly the forms most difficult for recipients or third parties (for instance, journalists and social scientists) to identify with confidence. Even the methodological standards of contemporary social science are not neutral in this respect. For the acceptance by social scientists of the methodological requirement to meet precise and easily observable conditions before attributing power to an individual or collectivity plays into the hands of any elites who might seek to veil their exercise of power.

Those in nonelite positions, and those who identify with them, also understand tacitly the connection between attribution of power and charges of responsibility. They will often seek to extend the criteria of 'power' accepted by the public at large and to relax methodological stipulations that must be met before power can be attributed to an individual or group.

Power, then, is a contestable concept, partly because of its conceptual connection to our ideas about responsibility, and these contests themselves form a part of our politics. For to accept the criteria of power advanced by critics is to take one large step into the critical perspective they articulate; and the same holds for the acceptance of criteria advanced by apologists. These contests are constrained within limits, limits imposed by broad and general rules governing 'power' accepted by all parties, but the space within which the contests take place is large enough to be of great importance to the contestants.

One of the advantages of this analysis of 'power' is that we can understand more clearly disputes surrounding the concept itself, which have remained a mystery to those who believe they can discriminate neatly between those neutral, descriptive concepts about which all rational people can agree and those emotionally charged normative concepts that are subject to endless dispute.

The contests surrounding 'power' (as a concept) are over its criteria of application, but similar contests emerge over the form its exercise will take. Thus public officials in Brazil in 1972 instituted stringent censorship over the press. The officials, clearly, preferred to establish guidelines and then to have the journalists monitor their own journals to meet these guidelines. Some leading journalists, however, refused to accept self-censorship, preferring the overt censorship of police officers assigned by the regime to delete objectionable passages. The contest between the regime and the journalists reflected their mutual understanding that the censorship would be more secure, less identifiable, and less open to third-party criticism if the journalists conformed to regime expectations in anticipation of expected deletions. As liberal journalist Raimundo Rodrigues Pereira said to a *New York Times* reporter (1972), "The greatest danger for the country now is the institutionalization of self-censorship." [10] If, as one must expect, the journalists were eventually to give in or to disappear quietly, the regime could then begin to claim to third parties that the press had a rather free hand in reporting the news; and eventually members of the press themselves might become half convinced that the professional code recently internalized was in fact informed more by an ethic of journalistic responsibility than by the constraints of the regime. Power would be both more complete and less identifiable in this case because of the regime's victory in the contest over its *form*.

One further implication of the connection between power and responsibility deserves comment. For this connection helps us to see why power analysis has limited utility in a science of politics that aspires to predict human behavior rigorously. In his critique of power as a concept of political science James March asks "under what circumstances the concept of power does, or can, contribute to the effective prediction of social choice." [11] He is dismayed by the results of his analysis: "On the whole, however, power is a disappointing concept. It gives us surprisingly little purchase in reasonable models of complex systems of social choice." [12] But March is disappointed because he set objectives for power analysis that the notion itself is not designed to meet; he should not be disappointed in the concept 'power' but in the predictivist model of political inquiry from which he appraises its utility. If I exercise power over another, I impose obstacles to his ability to act in support of his wishes, interests, or obligations, but I do not thereby ensure that I (or social scientists observing our relationship) can closely *predict* his resulting behavior (or assign a probability to some act x). He could do any number of things depending, first, upon what other elements are introduced into the "open system" of political life; second, upon how he interprets or understands the limits I have imposed; third, upon how he, as a creature capable of revising his goals, aspirations, and self-understanding, *chooses* to react to the situation so understood. Thus, he might *mistake* the message sent and fail to comply; he might *understand* the message fully and, *strengthening his will* amidst adversity, pursue the course originally intended; the new obstacles might *convince* him that his ideological critics were right all along, and thus he might radically *revise* the interpretive framework within which his understanding and conduct have hitherto moved. In each of these cases his conduct could vary from my expectations, but as long as the element introduced did in fact increase the costs or risks in meeting his interests, wishes, or obligations, I would have exercised power over him. Thus he might accede to my wishes; he might accept suffering in the pursuit of higher objectives; he might misread the message and suffer heavily because of his ignorance; he might deflect costs to others, increasing the load of guilt he carries; he might refuse to comply and flee the country; or he might refuse and commit suicide. I exercise power over him in each of these cases, but because he is a creature of self-interpretation with a capacity for choice, courage, cowardice, ideological revision, making mistakes, and so on, I cannot predict with any certainty how he will respond. The same principle applies to relations among collectivities: We can sometimes predict successfully in social inquiry, but the problematic nature of the relationship between the introduction of new factors and the decisions of persons with respect to those factors makes prediction in principle a more hazardous, limited, and vulnerable enterprise in the study of politics than in the natural sciences.[13]

When power takes the form of conditioning or force, behavior patterns can be predicted reliably, but those very forms of power, as we have seen, are of limited value in complex social systems exactly because they so narrowly limit the recipient's ability either to assess reflectively the situation at hand or to act on the basis of his reflections. Power is a disappointing concept to predictivists because predictivism itself provides a defective model of social inquiry. March would be equally disappointed if he were to subject to a similar analysis other concepts that play a role both in social life and in the explanatory theories of social scientists. To put the point concisely: 'Power' is formed less from the point of view of predicting the future behavior of recipients than from a perspective that enables participants and investigators to locate responsibility for the imposition of limiting conditions by linking those conditions to the decisions people make, or could make and don't.[14]

TOWARD A PARADIGM OF 'HAVING POWER OVER'

We need a model or paradigm of 'power over' that will help us to see what rules we tacitly follow in classifying some (aspects of) acts and relationships within the ambit of this notion while excluding others. While such a paradigm will inevitably be controversial at certain points, the paradigm itself should help us to locate those points of controversy and to suggest considerations of assistance to us in our efforts to cope with them. I will here move toward formulating a paradigm of *having* power over'. This locution is basic, for in some contexts to have power over another is to have a potential for limiting him; in others it is to exercise that potential actively; and in still others it is a passive condition in which the recipient responds to the potential bidder in anticipation of pressure. The three contexts, indeed, are not unconnected, for the active exercise of power in one domain often builds up its potential in other domains, and the increase in power potential enhances its passive exercise through anticipatory reaction.

Consider, then, criteria for asserting that A has power over B (with respect to some domain z):

1.   Of agents A and B, at least A must have access to resources or skills x that, if introduced, would limit the range of options (of sorts to be specified) normally available to B. By "normally available," I mean options that B, in the absence of these factors, could select without undue cost or risk.[15]

2.   The presence of x makes it more difficult, costly, or risky for B to advance or recognize his *interests,* attain his *desires,* or meet nontrivial *obligations* than it would be if x were not present.

3.   To meet the condition of responsibility, A must
   (a)   Introduce x as an intentional act, where A could have done otherwise; or
   (b)   Introduce x as an unintended by-product of action governed by other objectives, where A could reasonably have done otherwise and could reasonably have foreseen the possibility of the consequences of x for B; or
   (c)   Stand in a strategic position to introduce x and have a history that reasonably leads B to believe that an x might well be introduced unless B acts to limit his interests, and so on, in anticipation of its introduction; or
   (d)   Stand in a strategic position to modify or eliminate some present x but fail to do so in a context where it is reasonable to assume that he could understand, if he sincerely tried, the adverse implications of x for B.

Briefly stated, A exercises power over B when he is responsible for some x that increases the costs, risks, or difficulties to B in promoting B's desires or in recognizing or promoting B's interests or obligations. A has power over B as *potential,* then, when he could, but does not, limit B in the ways specified; A *exercises* that power when the constraint x is so introduced or maintained.

The paradigm is *not* designed to be exhaustive. First, there are special cases that it does not fully cover. For example, we would surely consider it an exercise of power if you made me unable to recognize some obligation, but what if you imposed obstacles against my ability to live up to an obligation I recognize but have already decided not to meet? I am inclined to say that you exercised power over me in the latter case, since if I were to change my mind, your obstacle would still limit me. But these are exactly the sort of cases that the paradigm leaves open for further elaboration and for consideration of particular contexts.

Second, not every dimension of this paradigm must be fully present in each case before we can speak of A having power over B. The purpose of the paradigm is to allow us to compare particular relationships to a "paradigm case," so that we can decide whether they count as qualified or imperfect instances of power. Thus we can have cases where the responsibility condition is perfectly met but the limit imposed is very modest, or where the limit is quite severe and the responsibility condition minimally met. In each of these cases we would want to decide whether the relationship is indeed best described as a power relationship, and if so, what sort of qualifying phrases would be needed to indicate that it was less than a pure case of power.

Acknowledging these problems does not constitute an argument against the construction of a paradigm of power; rather it illustrates the very complexities surrounding the idea, which make the construction of a paradigm a fruitful way to proceed.[16]

Included within the paradigm itself are several dimensions of exercising power over others that are at odds with criteria of 'power' often advanced by contemporary power analysts. Attention to these discrepancies will further clarify the structure and import of the paradigm presented here.

Many pluralist social scientists view a *conflict* of interest as a necessary condition for the exercise of power; and since many of them also define 'interest' as policy preference, it follows that a relationship of political power cannot be said to exist until groups range themselves on different sides of a public issue.[17] The concept of interest plays a central role in clarifying 'power' in the paradigm offered here as well. But since we have already seen that people might be mistaken about their interests and that policies and institutions can impinge upon their interests without their realizing it, it follows that power can be exercised over people without that exercise manifesting itself in explicit political conflicts. Indeed, if, as we have argued, manipulation and deterrence are among the important forms power can take, we must acknowledge that overt conflict is not a necessary condition for its exercise.

The paradigm proposed here does not require, as many do, that the agent who exercises power over others himself must *benefit* from that exercise. Stanley Benn, for instance, thinks that it would be "odd" to deny that "the crashing financier who brings down thousands with him in his fall" suffers anything other than a "loss of power."[18] But the oddness recedes when we recall the distinction between exercising power *to* attain what one wants and exercising power *over* others. Certainly the financier does not possess the former, but he *might*, depending on further specifications, exercise power over those others who suffer because of his actions. Thus if his actions result in severe hardship for others in a situation where other options were reasonably available to him and where he was in a reasonable position to foresee this result, his contribution to the crash would constitute an exercise of power over those who suffer because of it.

A closely related issue is posed by Bertrand Russell's famous and influential definition: "Power is the production of *intended* effects."[19] To produce an intended effect is not identical to gaining benefits for oneself, for I might intentionally use resources to promote outcomes harmful to me. This proposed criterion of the exercise of power, then, deserves separate attention.

It is illuminating to ask, first, why so many theorists have felt compelled to include a reference to intentions somewhere in their definitions of power. Why haven't more social scientists, especially those influenced by a behaviorism that is suspicious of talk about "mental states," defined power as a simple species of cause, in which A exercises power by changing the probability that B will act differently than he otherwise would —regardless of whether the change is intended by A or not? The most obvious answer is that such a definition would generate intuitively unacceptable results. Thus if a disturbed man is moved to rape a woman who has eyes like his mother, we would have to say that *she* exercised power over *him* in this case by getting him to do something he would not otherwise have done.[20] Definitions fostering such results are unacceptable, then, and even behaviorists draw away from their implications. But, and this is the further question behavioristic social scientists fail to confront, what makes them unacceptable?

The results of the foregoing example are unacceptable because they diverge sharply from rules tacitly governing the use of 'power' in ordinary discourse, and those are the rules that connect our ideas about power to those about responsibility. By requiring that acts of power be intentional, behavioristically inclined theorists retain some contact with ordinary discourse, for there is an important connection between being responsible for some outcome and having contributed to it intentionally. Closer attention to the connection between responsibility and power, though, would have revealed that intentionality is not a necessary condition of responsibility. There are cases of negligence, even perhaps of strict liability, where the agent is deemed responsible for an outcome even though it is not the outcome he intended. I conclude, then, that the emphasis on intentionality by behaviorist social scientists reflects a residual and blunted recognition of the very connection we seek to represent more sharply and explicitly here.[21]

Surely A can exercise power over B without intending to create the consequences for B that he in fact does. To take a close counter-example first, suppose A *intends* to help C and in the process *knowingly* takes action that harms B severely. Certainly, if the other specified conditions were present, we would conclude that A had exercised power over B even though the outcome he promoted was not, in any strict sense, intended by him. Suppose, to take a case further away, as a white employer in control of important and scarce job opportunities, I fail through inattention and habit to consider candidates for employment other than lower-class white males. I could do otherwise if I were to attend carefully to the consequences of my actions, but I don't, contributing thereby to the high unemployment of minorities. My inaction poses obstacles for the excluded group, and because I hold a strategic position with regard to their employment chances, I can reasonably be said to exercise power over them.

I contend, then, that A can exercise power over B in some situations where there is no overt *conflict* between A and B, where B is not *aware* that A is limiting his interests, where A does not (necessarily) *intend* the results he creates for B, and where A does not *benefit* from the exercise itself. To include, under the conditions specified, these possibilities within the ambit of 'power' better enables us to capture conceptually some of the most subtle and oppressive ways in which the actions of some can contribute to the limits and troubles faced by others.

But perhaps it will be suggested that this paradigm is too permissive. In the interests of capturing veiled and subtle forms within the ambit of 'power', it converts everything into a power relationship. Such a charge is false. The paradigm advanced here excludes relationships of persuasion and, as we shall see, authority from power; it allows a somewhat different set of conditions to apply when we speak of someone having *power to* gain an objective; it requires that we consider the consequences of A's actions for the interests and wants of others before A can be said to exercise power over them; and it insists that A meet certain conditions of responsibility before the pertinent consequences for B are attributable to his *power over* B. The definition is certainly more restrictive than one that defines power simply as A getting B to do what B otherwise would not do. And within these restrictions it still succeeds in calling attention to those very forms, ignored or discounted by many other definitions, that power holders themselves often prize the most: forms that allow them to limit others covertly with maximum effectiveness.

Definitions that require conflict, intentions, benefits, and awareness in the ways here criticized are built, I suggest, from a model which focuses primarily on the *bidding* side in a relationship of power. Though such a focus is often congenial to elites, close attention to those on the *receiving* side of such relationships suggests a different paradigm of power.

AUTHORITY AND LEGITIMATE POWER

While we cannot give the complex idea of authority the full attention it deserves in its own right, our understanding of the relationship that obtains when A exercises power over B will be enhanced by comparing it to certain dimensions of a relationship in which A exercises authority over B. I wish to say that neither of these concepts is a form of the other and that each is nonetheless important to the understanding of the other.

It is not difficult to see why social scientists have often treated authority as a form of power. Seeking to fit concepts of social inquiry into the grid provided by the descriptive-normative dichotomy, it has seemed plausible to construe power as a normatively neutral master concept covering all means by which A "gets" B to do something B would otherwise not do. If that move is accepted, it then becomes plausible to treat as forms of power the various ways discriminated in everyday language by which we get people to do things they would not otherwise do. Manipulation, coercion, authority, persuasion, influence, identification, conditioning, force, and restraint are then lumped together under this rubric, and the implication is that one can first develop operational tests of power and then worry later about deciding which forms of power the identified relationships assume.

But the fact that all of these relationships share one dimension ("getting" B to do y) tells us very little about other similarities and dissimilarities among them. 'Love' and 'resentment' are both emotion concepts that characterize complex reactive attitudes between persons, and each involves the assumption by one person that the other has set intentions and purposes with respect to him. Yet though understanding each of these ideas is useful to full comprehension of the other, neither is a form of the other in the way that a chair is a form of furniture.

Attention to the way we use the concept of authority, and attention to the *point* of such usage, reveals that authority is not a subcategory, but a coordinate, of those relationships in which A exercises power over B. This can be brought out initially by considering the following statements:

> The Supreme Court has *authority to* order the President to produce evidence in his possession pertinent to a criminal proceeding, but it lacks the *power to* get the evidence from him.

> The President retains significant *power over* members of the House of Representatives, but his *authority over* them has greatly diminished.

> Because the President is *an authority* on world history, a certain physicist (who is not) accepts his analogy between Munich and Vietnam. This acceptance would *lead* ("get") him to support the President's war policy publicly if the antiwar activists who run his department did not have so much *power over* him.

These statements suggest that authority and power, in a variety of ways, can sometimes be in opposition: Authority can provide a motive for conduct that is overridden by power, and vice versa. And the motives are of a different sort in each case. We would hesitate to say, in the third situation, that the antiwar activists *lead* the physicist to withhold public support for the war (though they get him to), but we do naturally speak of the authority of the President *leading* the physicist in that direction. These statements suggest, moreover, that the idea of authority embodies a presumption of legitimacy, while we have already argued that the legitimacy of exercising power over another is something that can be established only after additional arguments and information have been presented. Finally, it seems clear that important shifts in meaning would occur if 'persuasion' were placed in any of the slots where 'power over' and 'authority' now occur. Thus, it would be meaningful to say that the Supreme Court has *persuaded* the President to produce the evidence even though it lacked the *power* to force the evidence from him, but in this case (unlike the original statement) the implication is that the evidence is forthcoming and that the President's reason for compliance is different from the reason he would have had if he had acted on the basis of acknowledging the Court's *authority*.

I take these examples to provide preliminary evidence for Hannah Arendt's view that "if authority is to be defined at all . . . , it must be in contradistinction to both coercive power and persuasion through arguments." [22]

To sustain such a view we need first to sort out two ideas often lumped together under the rubric of authority—the idea of voluntarily obeying a command because one thinks it is the proper thing to do even if it is against one's interests and the idea of responding to coercive pressures that are justifiably applied. When other pertinent conditions are met I shall call a relationship of the first sort a relationship of authority and of the second, a relationship of legitimate power. [23] In each case the claim is advanced that A is justified in getting B to comply and that B is properly obligated to comply; but B's motive for compliance is different in each case, and this difference in motive is important enough to the quality of social life to justify marking it off clearly in the concepts that help to constitute that life.

We have already argued that there is a presumption against the exercise of power over another because such an exercise impairs either the recipient's capacity to exercise choice or his ability to act upon his own choice. But that presumption can of course be overridden. Perhaps the exercise of power is required by the public interest or by considerations of justice. When the presumption against, say, coercion is overridden by other considerations we have a legitimate exercise of power, but identifying the relationship as one of *legiti-*

mate power rather than of *authority* rivets our attention on the nature of the pressures brought to bear on the complying agent and reminds us that pressures of this sort, just because they are coercive, *always stand in need of special justification.*

It is also true that authority, as here construed, can serve both as a resource of power and as a legitimation of power, but that does not touch the distinction between the two ideas. If most of us concur in the view that we are obligated to obey the commands of a given agent, we might for that reason legitimize the exercise of power over recalcitrant minorities to gain their compliance, and we might also voluntarily join in action designed to control or limit them. Authority over *us* contributes to power over *them.* Indeed, if, as many have plausibly argued, authority is in decline in modern society, it follows that one important resource of power is also in decline, but it does not follow that authority is merely a form of power. Wealth and prestige can also serve as power resources, but neither is understood as an idea subordinate to the idea of power.

The validity of the above comments depends upon our ability to make sense of the idea of authority in a way that distinguishes it from both legitimate power and rational persuasion. What, then, is a relationship of "pure" authority like? (I take it for granted that many actual relationships are different mixes of the pure types we seek to isolate.)

When you exercise authority over me I comply voluntarily with your command either (1) because of certain characteristics you and I attribute to the *position* you occupy, or (2) because we agree that you possess a special understanding of the situation facing us that for good reason is not fully or readily available to me. In both of these situations I acknowledge an obligation to obey and act on that obligation; and in neither case is my reason for compliance based on your coercive power or on my necessarily having been persuaded by your arguments about the inherent merits of the course before us.[24] We shall consider (1) and (2) in turn.

Perhaps you have been lawfully elected to a position intended by the electors to coordinate, within a certain sphere, the activities of all of us. It might turn out that others, not holding that position, *persuade* me that there are in fact better policies to follow than the one you have selected, but I might nonetheless voluntarily obey your order. For your position itself justifies a presumption in favor of the requests, decrees, and orders emanating from it; the social benefits to each of all following the same policy in this instance outweigh the benefits of each of us pursuing his own course in opposition to that policy, even if one of those alternative courses would be more beneficial than the official policy were it to be adopted by all.[25] I voluntarily acquiesce not because I am persuaded by your arguments for that policy, but because I am persuaded that a *presumption* in favor of obeying the policy directives of one in your position is essential to effective social coordination. In this case of authority I act in support of the role you perform; I suspend action based upon my own critical judgment while retaining the prerogative of retaining the critical judgment itself. There are occasions, certainly, when this presumption of authority is properly overridden by other considerations, but that is not our present concern. Traffic policemen, university presidents, union leaders, party leaders, and the chief executives of nation-states often exercise authority over people with respect to certain spheres of conduct because of the position they hold and because their constituencies acknowledge the need for such positions to coordinate conduct in social life.

I might, alternatively, accept your judgment with respect to some activity because of the expertise or special knowledge you possess in that sphere and because I trust that you will use that knowledge for the benefit of those around you. You might not, that is, be *in* authority, since you do not hold a position designated to coordinate social activity, but you are *an* authority on, say, the economy. Suppose you convince me to support a policy that will, you say, reduce income inequality without impeding productivity greatly. I am not persuaded by your arguments, for I do not really understand them; I am not coerced by pressures you bring to bear, for you are neither inclined nor in a position to coerce me; I do not accede because you hold a position essential for social coordination, since you are not in such a position. I accede because of my confidence in your judgment in that sphere. If I had the time and training, I say to myself, this expert could show me why that policy is sound. Your influence on my conduct is mediated through an influence on my beliefs. The influence of a person who is *an* authority is always mediated through an influence on the beliefs of the complying agent, while compliance to one who is *in* authority may or may not involve acceptance of his beliefs by the complying agent.

Often, the same individual will both be in a position of social coordination and possess expertise relevant to the problem at hand. Judges often combine these advantages; American Presidents very often seek to bolster their positions in authority with the claim that they are authorities on certain areas of public policy. Sometimes the President will emphasize his training and experience; sometimes he will contend that certain relevant information must be kept secret in the national interest and that his privileged access to such information should lead us to acknowledge him as an authority on foreign policy. The latter example reminds us that the claim to authority can sometimes serve as a vehicle of manipulation, as when one bolsters one's role as an authority by classifying information that could be made public without jeopardizing national security. But this possibility does not erode—it rather underlines—the difference between authority and manipulation.

We still have to consider the situation where a person is in authority and yet some citizens refuse to obey his commands voluntarily. We must distinguish here effective authority from grounded authority. Authority is effective when both parties to the relationship believe that relevant considerations justify the command by A and the voluntary compliance by B. Thus relationships of effective authority are relatively easy for investigators to observe, to "operationalize." For in a complex, stable society the participants themselves will embody these relationships in dress, demeanor, and linguistic forms. These forms will provide the means by which they mutually acknowledge and internally identify the stratified relationships. Thus in medieval Europe the distinction between *thou* and *you* and its equivalent in other languages (*tu* and *vous, tu* and *voi, du* and *Sie*) did not function only to separate the personal from the impersonal salutation. Those in authority used the personal T to subordinates, and the subordinates symbolized their recognition of the authorities by replying with the impersonal V:

> Generally, the nobility said T to the common people and received V; the master of a household said T to his slave, his servant, his squire, and received V. Within the family . . . parents gave T to the children and were given V.[26]

The T form has died completely in the United States and is in decline elsewhere; its eclipse very probably marks the erosion of stable lines of effective authority in our society.

Authority is effective because the parties *believe* it to be grounded, to be justified by relevant considerations. Thus superior knowledge or incumbency in a special position, the parties believe, justifies voluntary obedience by B to A's initiatives as a means of supporting broad social interests and objectives. But central to the idea of authority is the possibility that these beliefs might be mistaken or faulty in particular cases. We can thus have effective authority that is not grounded, and grounded authority that is not effective.[27] Debates over the proper limits of authority, then, can be understood as efforts to establish considerations that warrant or ground authority and to state the limits within which these warrants properly operate. We cannot delve into these important and complex issues here but must rest content to suggest that while mutual consent is sufficient to render authority effective, it is not always sufficient to warrant that relationship, and while failure to gain the consent of potential compliers means that effective authority is abrogated, it still might be possible to argue that authority is warranted.

One additional point before we apply these distinctions to issues in contemporary social theory: While effective authority must be acknowledged reciprocally to operate, effective power need not be. In a complex society this implies that re-

lationships of effective authority must be marked off symboli-
cally to be internally viable, while it might be disadvantageous
for power holders to have their relationships so marked off.
Indeed, those in authority are generally willing to acknowledge
their roles to third parties studying the relationship, while
those in power are often reluctant to acknowledge to third
parties, subordinates, and even themselves the coercive dimensions in their relationships with subordinates. This difference
might lead one to conclude that relationships of effective
power are intrinsically more difficult to establish reliably
through inquiry than are relationships of effective authority.
That assumption is partly correct, for it is probably a *necessary*
condition of complex patterns of effective authority that they
be so symbolized and thus readily observable. But there is an
important reservation that makes such signs insufficient. Because of the very differences in our tacit understanding and
assessment of the two sorts of relationship, power holders are
often inclined to view themselves, and especially to encourage
others to view them, as agents of authority. While such an inclination probably softens the relationships of power somewhat, it also greatly complicates the task of the social scientist
trying to comprehend the structure of these relationships.
Power relationships represented to subordinates and third parties as forms of authority are, I take it, central to Antonio
Gramsci's theory of hegemony.[28] These are among the most
difficult and important judgments a social scientist must make
in seeking to comprehend the structure of relationships in a
particular society.

The pertinence of the multiple distinctions among effective and grounded authority, persuasion, legitimate power, and
unlegitimated power may be brought out by considering the
way in which they illuminate the classic debate between Talcott
Parsons and C. Wright Mills over the "structure of power" in
the United States. Parsons agrees with Mills that corporate
and government elites play a role of consequence in contemporary America, but he thinks that Mills misconstrues their role
in part because his "zero-sum" concept of power compels him
to assume that an increase in the power of these elites requires

a decrease elsewhere in the system—namely, within the "mass society." Against this view Parsons holds that

> power is a generalized facility or resource in the society. It has to be divided or allocated, but it also has to be produced, and it has collective as well as distributive functions. *It is the capacity to mobilize the resources of the society for the attainment of goals for which a general "public" commitment has been made or may be made.*[29]

Parsons' definition of power looks very much like our understanding of 'power to'; it focuses on the ability or capacity of some identified unit to attain desired ends. But, as we have seen, the *relationships among groups* that emerge in the process of "mobilizing societal resources" could include a variety of forms such as persuasion, authority, coercion, and manipulation: To mobilize a unit to pursue specified ends ('power to') may or may not involve relationships in which some members of that unit exercise power over others. The question arises, then, What relationships does Parsons see as obtaining between elites and nonelites in this process of mobilization? Parsons, clearly, is inclined to identify in order of importance authority, persuasion, legitimate power, and unlegitimated power as the sorts of relationship that exist between elites and nonelites and between some elites and others. In other words, for Parsons, elite exercise of power to attain specified objectives involves the minimal exercise of power over nonelites.

Mills shuffles these relationships significantly in his interpretation. The goals for which elites mobilize societal resources reflect only very imperfectly a societal *consensus* (that is, the freely given and informed *consent* of the populace), because the most important issues and alternatives involved in that commitment of resources are not subjected to close public scrutiny and debate. How are the resources mobilized then? The identified elites sometimes and to some extent exercise effective authority over broader publics, but even that authority is often insufficiently warranted. More important than effective authority, though, is elite exercise of unlegitimated power over citizens, power that unnecessarily limits the options available to people without speaking sufficiently to the troubles they have.

Mills and Parsons generally agree that certain elites, identified by each, *play a central role in "getting" citizens to do things they otherwise would not do*. But it is evidence against any definition of power along these lines that the profound differences in their theories of power simply start at this point of general agreement. It is not surprising, moreover, that Mills is accused by many who accept some version of the fact-value dichotomy of offering a condemnation of American elites under the guise of explaining their role in the power system, while Parsons, if less often and by different critics, is charged with justifying the role of established elites while purporting simply to understand it. But the tendency of the first theorist to criticize and the second to justify the role of dominant elites is not, as their critics suppose, the result of their misuse of descriptive concepts in empirical research, but an implication of the central concepts in each theory. These concepts are used in description and explanation but not in a normatively neutral way. The discrepancies in the normative import of the two theories flow from variations in the mix of authority, persuasion, legitimate power, and unlegitimated power that each theory identifies in the relationships between elites and nonelites.

To grasp the variable import of such opposed interpretive systems and to gain some sense of the complex, contestable judgments that must be made to adjudicate between them is to see the point in sorting out the distinctions and connections among authority, persuasion, coercion, manipulation, and associated notions.

THE IDEA OF A POWER STRUCTURE

When one speaks of a power structure one conveys, first, the idea that power in at least some domains is distributed unequally; second, that those with more power in one domain are likely to have it in several important domains as well; third, that such a distribution is relatively persistent; and fourth (but not necessarily), that there is more than a random connection between the distribution of power and the distribution of income, status, privilege, and wealth in the system under scrutiny. While both radicals and conservatives have sometimes purported to see in the United States such a power structure (not always the same one), theorists of a pluralist persuasion have sometimes expressed doubts about the utility of the *idea* itself, at least in countries or communities with multiple interest groups and competing party systems.[30]

Drawing on the argument of the previous sections, I will now explore the idea of a power structure. I will assume that one could have such an idea without necessarily concluding that the society in which one lives fits that idea perfectly.

Consider, first, a hypothetical university where grounded authority is declining, but in which an identifiable hierarchy persists enabling groups at upper status levels to pass some of the burdens they face onto groups at lower status levels. The central administration (group A), holding a strategic position with respect to salaries, appointments, and so on, decides to increase its office space. Since building funds are not available, the members of A agree to commandeer space from a subordinate group of administrators in the graduate program (group B). The members of B do not object too strongly, for they hold joint appointments in academic departments, and they resolve to take over offices in a wing of one of the academic departments where two of them are quite influential. They make their task much easier by selecting a wing populated only by junior faculty members anxiously awaiting tenure decisions (group C). Members of C are not eager to fight (though they certainly do not consider this a legitimate move); anyway, they have located a smaller cluster of offices at present populated by graduate teaching assistants in their department (group D). The graduate students shortly find themselves crowded into one office in the basement, three students to a desk. Doubtless they find ways to shift some of these costs to other groups, but our overview of burden displacement must stop here.

In this minipower structure[31] D's plight is not attributable directly to A, but can only be understood by tracing the series of actions and reactions from A through C. The stages through which burdens are shifted correspond roughly to differences in income and status, and the reaction of each group to the pressures imposed on it is tempered by the realization that it has resources capable of shifting much of this pressure to a level below it. Since each retains its *relative* advantages of privilege and status by shifting burdens to the group below it, the psychological costs of giving in to pressures from above are much less acute. These are the features that make the notion of a power structure such a fertile idea for the study of power in complex, bureaucraticized societies.

The idea of a power structure is converted by Georg Simmel into a theory purporting to explain important dimensions of the politics of large-scale industrial societies. He contends that

> in every hierarchy, a new pressure or imposition moves along the line of least resistance which, though not in its first stage, usually and eventually, runs in a descending direction. This is the tragedy of whoever is lowest in any social order. He not only has to suffer from the deprivations, efforts, and discriminations which, taken together, characterize his position; in addition every new pressure on any point whatever in the superordinate layers is, if technically possible at all, transmitted downward and stops only at him.[32]

One need not conclude that such structural biases must dominate in every complex society to find the model posed by Simmel pregnant with ideas that might have some application to contemporary society. But to pursue this possibility further we must first become more clear about what conditions are required before we can speak correctly of "transmitting pressures" downward and especially before we can describe the transmitters as exercising power over those lower in the social order. And since a power structure involves relationships among groups, institutions, and classes, our question becomes, What criteria must be met before we can speak of one collectivity exercising power over another collectivity? The answer to that question, it should now be apparent, is closely related to the answer we give to questions about the relationship between collective action and collective responsibility. Since I am unable now to formulate formal criteria sufficient to guide judgment in such matters, I will proceed by example, varying in this way the conditions of responsibility while holding constant in the examples the other criteria of exercising power over others.[33]

1. We live in an industrial city where one large corporation is central to the area's economy.[34] To expand employment and tax revenues political leaders encourage corporate growth: lobbyists and political elites support corporate tax exemptions, they de-emphasize enforcement of local laws regulating the corporation, and they deflect or dampen efforts by other interest groups to generate political issues embarrassing to the corporation. While the corporation *intends* to maximize its profits and growth, a by-product of its success is the creation of massive air and water pollution in the area. Health problems and discomfort increase among the citizenry; recreational facilities fall into disuse in the central city; affluent citizens move to the suburbs to find fresh air; and the tax base of the city is eroded through their departure.

The direct and indirect effects of corporate policy fall on all residents, but with unequal force. Those with lowest incomes are hardest hit. They live in the areas where pollution is most severe; they can least afford to escape to the suburbs; nor can they afford vacations during the worst months of pollution. Moreover, erosion of the tax base affects them most severely: Lacking sufficient private resources, they are hurt most by the decline in public transportation services, education, police protection, garbage collection, recreational facilities, and welfare support. All of the effects in turn are intensified by the tendency of local politicians to cut back these services most where residents are at least able to publicize their grievances. Because it is politically feasible to do so, burdens flowing from corporate pollution are shifted disproportionately to the poor.

The poor, in the setting described, *lack power to* redress their grievances, but do the others exercise *power over* them?

A complete analysis would require investigation of the reactions of each group to the burdens imposed on it; to simplify matters we will focus on the corporation. The corporate elite clearly possesses the internal ties and decision procedures needed to formulate policy; its policies, perhaps through oversight and considerations of maximizing profits, have clearly produced a serious pollution problem; it clearly stands in a strategic position whereby it could take action to reduce pollution and thereby alleviate a central cause of the city's decline; finally, it could, but does not, encourage civic groups to convert the pollution problem into a political issue, for if the corporation convinced all involved that it would cooperate fully with stringent pollution control regulations, political officials who had restrained themselves on this issue would now speak out. Pursuing policies with adverse effects on others, capable, first of foreseeing and later of observing these effects, and strategically located to act to reverse them, the corporation exercises power over those whose life chances are limited by its action and inaction.

2. We live in a system where lower middle, middle, and upper income groups are organized into interest groups, most of which are built around occupational categories. One of these groups, a blue-collar union, becomes the focal point of a drive to institute socialized medicine. A union of medical doctors provides the focal point for opposition to the plan. Neither the physicians nor the workers are able to prevail, so each eventually accedes to a compromise in which a portion of health insurance is financed through a national social security system and tax benefits are given to employers who promote group health insurance plans; the physicians, in this compromise, retain the right to set fees privately.

We can speak, roughly, of a balance of power between the workers and physicians with respect to the issue of health insurance. Each group gains or protects what is most dear to it without gaining everything it wants. And, as it turns out, both benefit from the compromise. Blue-collar families receive better and more extensive health care, and because medical costs have been collectivized, physicians and hospitals are able to raise their fees significantly without losing business. Pluralism flourishes.

But the interests of the unemployed, the elderly not covered by social security, and those employed in small nonunionized companies that do not offer group insurance plans are adversely affected by the compromise. Though not really aware of the dynamics that have created this situation, members of these groups soon discover that their medical costs have escalated well beyond their capacity to pay, and, to make matters worse, their former allies in organized labor seem uninterested in efforts to alleviate these new burdens. Unorganized and isolated from former allies, members of the underclass clearly lack power to alter existing arrangements. But have the physicians and blue-collar workers exercised power over them?

This case is both more difficult and more typical because we are dealing with the consequences of a *compromise* between (at least) two disparate groups. We can, though, ascribe at least some degree of responsibility to the compromising parties, even if neither intended the compromise to produce the consequences it has for the underclass. First, neither group was dispensable in this compromise; either group could have altered policy consequences for the third group if it had taken the trouble to weigh those consequences. Second, available economic knowledge made it possible for those implicated in the policy decision to foresee the consequences that would obtain for the excluded groups. Third, it was within the range of understanding of each participant to see that the dynamics of interest-group politics in this setting effectively excluded from the process a segment of the population directly affected by the outcome. Actively promoting their own interests at the expense of others in a setting where alternative directions were available, the compromising parties together have exercised power over the excluded groups. What is a balance of power when only the interests of the participants are considered emerges as an imbalance when the interests of nonparticipants are included.

In the setting described, the *degree* to which the compromising parties are responsible for the plight of the others is surely debatable. Suppose, though, the situation later changes slightly. The underclass and its allies effectively make a public issue of their plight and demand a policy change. If the parties to the initial compromise now successfully *coalesce* to protect a policy advantageous to both, or if one of them accedes passively to the efforts by the other to retain a policy that both now *know* works to the disadvantage of the excluded group, then we have a paradigm case of one coalition exercising power over another. Knowledge about the consequences of action, whether actually possessed or merely readily available, bears a close connection to our willingness to attribute power to those whose actions create the consequences. And thus, as knowledge about the consequences of social policy is broadened and extended, and as it becomes more widely available to strategically located groups, the range of relationships to which the concept of power is potentially applicable expands as well.[35]

3. We live now in a complex industrial system with steep inequalities in the distribution of wealth and income. An objective analysis reveals that although the interests of the bottom strata would be advanced if it were possible to reduce these inequalities significantly, there are no means technically available to implement such changes without undermining the very capacity of the socioeconomic system to meet the elementary needs of the entire population. It is not simply that the privileged classes would pursue every tactic to defeat or sabotage such efforts but that, *given the motivational system workers and consumers have developed within the prevailing system,* changes in income distribution would undermine incentives to work, jeopardize investments, shrink the tax base, and so on. Moreover, a double bind exists here. For given the present mechanisms of production and consumption, the introduction of changes in the motivational system of workers and consumers (who are motivated to work by pay incentives and are dominated by desires to increase commodity consumption) would undermine the system of production. Firm action in either area would produce disaster in the other.

We live in a system, therefore, where structural constraints (or contradictions) make it impossible for any segment of the society to act to redress the *system* of inequality significantly without disrupting the basic capacity of the entire system to provide food, shelter, and security for its members.[36] For every policy mix that is proposed to change the status quo, objective analysis (we shall suppose) reveals that side effects would emerge to undermine the entire system.

To the extent that the accepted explanation is indeed correct, we are confronted with a limiting case. Some segments of society *benefit* disproportionately from the prevailing inequalities, but efforts by the beneficiaries or others to redress the inequalities significantly would work to the disadvantage of all segments of the population. Since no group could redress the situation, the language of power itself cannot get a solid grip within this context. We must speak instead of *structural biases* or constraints that severely limit the range of activity potentially open to those implicated in the system. Marxists, in this setting, might call for revolutionary change and conservatives might counsel an adjustment to the imperatives of social life, but neither would speak easily of some segments exercising power over others with respect to the basic system of income distribution.[37] To make talk about 'power' salient, some dimensions in the explanation of the system of inequality must be altered.

If someone asserted that the Empire State Building was unhappy, we would not simply say he was wrong (for that would imply that the building was actually happy or indifferent), but that he had made the wrong sort of statement in this context. So, too, with talk about power. In some contexts we can ask how tightly it is concentrated or how widely it is dispersed, but we also must ask under what conditions and to what extent the language of power itself is applicable to the phenomena under investigation. Though pluralists and elitists often forget to attend explicitly to this basic question, the position one stakes out with respect to it affects profoundly the theory of power one advances.

C. Wright Mills provides a partial and interesting exception to this tendency. He clearly believed that 'power' applies widely to social relationships in contemporary society because the enhanced ability of those in strategic social positions to foresee the wider consequences of their action and inaction *expands the sphere within which they can be held responsible for "events as decisions."* In this contemporary setting the idea of fate must be displaced by that of power.

> This sociological conception of fate, in brief, has to do with events in history that are beyond the control of any circle or groups of men (1) compact enough to be identifiable, (2) powerful enough to decide with consequence, and (3) in a position to foresee the consequences and so to be held accountable for historical events.[38]

Working in tandem with his argument to attribute power to those in strategic positions, who could, but do not, initiate changes in the interests of broad segments of society, is his judgment that it "is sociologically realistic, morally fair, and politically imperative to hold them responsible for specific courses of events." [39]

Mills contends first, that power is increasingly concentrated, and second, *that it ranges more widely over social relationships than before.* The second claim deserves more attention than it has received. For though it rests, I want to suggest, on a correct understanding of the conceptual connection between power and responsibility, Mills then exaggerates the range of events those very criteria of responsibility actually allow us to include within the ambit of power. His *concept* of power, in short, is sound; it is his *theory* of power that requires emendation.

Criticisms of Mills's theory from the left also acknowledge the conceptual connection we have explored. Thus, Paul Sweezy charges that Mills goes "much too far in the direction of what I may call 'historical voluntarism'." And he goes on to insist that the elites Mills identifies are constrained within tighter limits than he has acknowledged. They have "a *range of choices* which is set by the nature and laws of the social structure under which they live."[40]   As both Mills and Sweezy recognize, at least tacitly, the conceptual connection between power and responsibility forces those who seek to identify the structure of power in any society to explore the limits within which power can be attributed to those classes and elites who benefit from existing arrangements.[41]

Though the idea of a power structure is a complex one, it is often quite pertinent to our understanding of the relationships that exist in modern society across class, generational, racial, and sexual lines.   The idea, indeed, suggests refinements in the "pluralist-elitist" debate about how to interpret the political dimension of these relationships.   For it allows us to see more clearly that the theoretical possibilities include not only the following:

1.   A cohesive elite that effectively exerts power inside and outside of government *to* attain its objectives at the expense of other groups.

2.   A pluralist system in which power *to* attain high priority objectives is widely distributed among many active groups.

A range of other possibilities must be explored to ascertain the extent to which they enter into the system:

3.   Collective A, acting in pursuit of goal x, enacts policies that in their direct and indirect effects severely limit the chances of group B to fulfill its interest y (A may or may not exercise power *to* attain x, but if the condition of responsibility is met, it does exercise power *over* B with respect to y).

4.   Competition and cooperation among elites A, B, and C result in compromises that shift burdens to identifiable minority D, excluded from the balancing system (if the condition of responsibility is met, A, B, and C exercise power *over* D with respect to some z).

5.   Groups A, B, and C, each of which is organized around, say, occupational categories, compromise on issues affecting the occupational interests of each while obstructing the protection of interests *any* member of society might have in his capacity as a citzen, for instance, outcomes in the public inter-

est such as pollution control or resource conservation (if the condition of responsibility is met, A, B, and C exercise power *over* citizens with respect to public interest z).

6.   A set of structural constraints ensure that with respect to goals or interests x, policy alternative b, if instituted by any segment of society, would undermine the system's capacity to meet minimal interests of the population (failure to institute b does not constitute an exercise of power by A over B).[42]

Any adequate theory of power in America will, I think, first specify grounds for ascertaining the extent to which relationships of effective authority and persuasion enter into the system and then emphasize the role played by 3, 4, and 5 within the relatively broad parameters set by 6.   No such theory, of course, will be incontestably established in all respects, but any theory that fails to make explicit judgments with respect to each of these dimensions will be unnecessarily incomplete.

POWER ANALYSIS AND IDEOLOGY

Attention to the grammar of 'power' makes it readily understandable why it is an essentially contested concept.   Since the exercise of power over others limits their range of choice and shifts a degree of responsibility from the recipient to the bidder, the attribution of power to a segment of the society functions more as an accusation than as a normatively neutral description of the political process.   Those who are so accused will either deny the accusation or seek to show that special circumstances intervene to make the exercise of power permissible in this setting.   If they deny the charge, they might try to convince critics that we are all victims of structural constraints that no collectivity could hope to alter ("We're all in this together"), or they might employ forms of power that make identification by recipients and third parties less easy, or they might adopt a mixture of these strategies.   In any event, the denial itself proceeds by getting others to *accept an explanatory theory of power and politics* congenial to the accused and by *deflating the criteria of 'power' itself* so as to minimize the extent to which it applies to the activity and inactivity of the accused. To the extent that the accused fail in their efforts, they allow others to believe that things could be otherwise and encourage them to (try to) hold the accused accountable for events as decisions.

Critics, on the other hand, will typically pursue an opposing strategy, advancing an explanatory theory that *emphasizes* the extent to which consequences harmful to the interests of nonelites are attributable to the power of elites and *inflating* the criteria of 'power' so as to fit activities by the accused more securely within its ambit. Contests over the meaning and interpretation of power are, in this way, part of politics itself.

The difficult question is this: What counts as an *inflation* of 'power' and what as a *deflation?* Part of my purpose in previous sections was to identify broad parameters within which these contests will proceed and outside of which it is reasonable for all parties to identify instances of conceptual deflation and inflation.[43] I want now to emphasize that within these rather broad limits, authoritative argument is insufficient to establish more precise lines that will prove acceptable to every reasonable person. Part of understanding the grammar of 'power' is understanding in what respects and why it is an essentially contested concept.

Thus adversaries might agree that the concept of interests is crucially tied to the concept of power but disagree about what it means to say that something is in someone's interest and about what is *most* in one's interest. When we say that a group has *more* power than other groups, we mean in part to assert that its exercise of power over others touches their most *important* interests. But, as we have already seen, judgments about which interests are most important are, after a point, inherently controversial. As Robert Paul Wolff has emphasized, this means that differences in judgments about power have an "unavoidably evaluative" dimension:

> Radicals and liberals are not so far apart in their values as, say, Bolsheviks and Czarists, but they do genuinely disagree. Hence any dispute between them about the nature and location of

political power will in part be a dispute over what is important, what is worth trying to control, in modern society.[44]

Moreover, since our ideas about power and responsibility are so intimately related, disagreements about the appropriate criteria for holding collectives responsible for consequences will be reflected in disputes about the meaning of 'power'. And since the interpretation of the range of alternative actions open to a collectivity enters crucially into judgments of the direction and extent of its responsibility, different interpretations *about what it is possible to achieve* will be reflected in different assessments of the range of relationships within which power is embodied.

Disputes about the proper concept and interpretation of power, then, are part of larger ideological debates. To convert others to my idea of power is to implicate them to some degree in my political ideology. Power will thereby remain a central concept for students of politics, because attention to the issues swirling around it is essential to understanding the nature and import of conflicts in political life. And investigators who stake out positions on these conceptual and interpretive issues will stake out as well stances on the political and ideological debates of their day. To study power is to implicate oneself in politics.

As debates surrounding the concept and interpretation of power have intensified in political science, as increasing numbers of practitioners have concluded that a neutral, operational definition acceptable to all investigators regardless of ideological "preference" is not forthcoming with respect to *this* concept, some political scientists have suggested that the idea of power itself should be expunged from the scientific study of politics.[45] By breaking this complex and controversial idea down into simple and separable elements we could, it is suggested, circumvent a series of emotional debates that unnecessarily impede the advance of political science.

But such an approach will not dissolve the pertinent issues; at most it will blur and distort them, contributing to the tranquility of political science by inhibiting the intellectual awareness of its practitioners.

For, any concept of power tailored to (even) approach the level of operational rigor desired will be unable to account for exactly those forms power holders are particularly attracted to. By retaining the *term* 'power' but drastically redefining the *concept* for technical purposes, political scientists risk the kind of equivocation that typically emerges when people give new and trivial meanings to important and controversial ideas. It looks as if they are coping with perplexing questions of power while in fact they are dealing with something else.

Second, a science of politics that eschewed all reference to 'power' on the grounds of its vagueness and controversiality would not, for all that, avoid staking out a position concerning the role power plays in contemporary politics: The results of such an inquiry could be translated into its implications for power theory. For example, if the term 'power' found little expression in the theory, the implication would be that power in politics, like phlogiston in combustion, plays little or no role of importance. This is exactly the sort of theory that contemporary functionalists often advance, and it surely deserves a hearing. But they do so, not by arguing that power is an idea unworthy of scientific attention, but by arguing that it is an idea that is at least *clear enough* to allow them to conclude that its role in contemporary politics has been overestimated by social critics. They do not, that is, advance their argument on the grounds of methodological purity but on substantive grounds, and the argument requires them to take a position on contests surrounding the meaning of 'power'. The result, in *effect*, is a conservative version of the structural constraint theory discussed in the last section. People who advance such theories have surely not rejected the idea of power but have taken a position on the debates surrounding the idea and interpretation of power.

Third, proposals to expunge 'power' from our technical vocabularies because *it* is so complex and controversial a concept bypass a larger issue. Political scientists widely recognize the complexity of 'power' today because it has become a focus of disciplinary debates, but many other concepts central to political life and political inquiry share in this complexity and controversiality. To expunge *all* of them successfully would require the formulation of a technical language for political inquiry that is operational, normatively neutral, and uncontroversial in the way the language of political life is not. Such a program has yet to show notable success, and there are, as we have previously seen, grounds for believing that the connection between the concepts adopted by the participants in political life and the structure of that life itself make this general program less feasible in principle than its adherents imagine.[46]

NOTES

1. For these dimensions and others, see Robert Dahl, "Power," in *International Encyclopedia of the Social Sciences* (1968), 12: 405–15.

2. The example comes from Stanley Benn, "Power," in *Encyclopedia of Philosophy* (1967), 6:387.

3. *Thomas Hobbes, Leviathan* (1651; Oxford: Clarendon Press, 1909), p. 66.

4. John Champlin distinguishes among three related senses of 'power' in "On the Study of Power," *Politics and Society* (November 1970): 91–112. Though the distinction emphasized here does not correspond perfectly to the triad he explores, I have profited from his discussion. There may, moreover, be further distinctions pertinent to my purposes; for example, we might speak meaningfully of A having power *against* B. But I will stick with 'power over', with the understanding that my purpose in doing so is to focus attention on those on the receiving end of power relationships.

5. In Flint, Michigan, union officials used to charge that General Motors managers purposely shifted the quitting times at their factories on election day to create traffic jams, thereby making it more difficult for workers to get to the polls. This is a perfect example of power as deterrence.

6. Though sociologists in the classic tradition, such as Karl Mannheim and Gaetano Mosca, recognized the phenomenon of

anticipatory response as an exceedingly effective form of power, contemporary political scientists are indebted to Peter Bachrach and Morton Baratz for forcefully calling attention to this phenomenon and to other dimensions of power as well: "The Two Faces of Power," *American Political Science Review* (December 1962): 947–52. Methodological concerns led Bachrach and Baratz to draw back a bit from their early formulation of this issue in *Power and Poverty* (New York: Oxford University Press, 1970).

7. For the view that application of force signifies that the agent does not have power, see Bachrach and Baratz, *Power and Poverty*, pp. 27–29. I think it is better to say that he lacks power to get B to undertake some positive action.

8. The example is from Robert Nozick, "Coercion," in *Philosophy, Science, and Method*, ed. S. Morgenbesser, P. Suppes, and M. White (New York: St. Martin's Press, 1969), p. 445. I am indebted to him for the following case as well.

9. The term 'responsibility' can refer to many related ideas. I refer here to moral responsibility (in a broad sense of 'moral') in which the bidder is condemned or praised for the act or condition and (some of) its consequences. Among the several other senses is one in which we speak, say, of certain climatic factors as *responsible for* a temperature inversion. That is simply another way of saying the two are causally related, and a causal connection between two events is not a *sufficient* condition to attribute moral responsibility to the precipitant.

10. *New York Times*, February 17, 1973, p. 11.

11. James March, "The Power of Power," in *Varieties of Political Theory*, ed. David Easton (Englewood Cliffs, N. J.: Prentice-Hall, 1966), p. 40.

12. Ibid., p. 70.

13. For more systematic elaboration of these themes, see Peter Winch, *The Idea of a Social Science* (New York: Humanities Press, 1958); and Charles Taylor, "Interpretation and the Sciences of Man," *Review of Metaphysics* (Fall 1971): 4–51. The very possibility of choice, reasoned assessment, deceit, courage, and so on, in response to new elements makes the relation in social life between new factors and resulting behavior quite different than it is, say, when a set of climatic factors create a temperature inversion. Weather systems may be open, but they

do not meet the next two features of human interaction specified above. Arguments, against Winch, that reasons can be causes, do not basically affect these points.

14. Suppose someone argues that when A exercises power over B we can, at least, predict that B's costs or risks are increased in some respect. So we can. We can also "predict" that a bachelor will be unmarried, but that would hardly be a very satisfying result for predictivists. Part of the meaning of 'power over' is the imposition of limiting conditions.

15. Judgments such as those about "normally available" options enter inevitably into our criteria of power. These are, as Stanley Benn puts it, "instances of a class of judgments which cannot be satisfactorily elucidated without using some standard of 'the normal man'. Judgments about freedom, influence, power, and interference are, I believe, of the same class." Benn, "Freedom and Persuasion," *Australian Journal of Philosophy* (December 1967):268. We need only add here that differences in standards of what is "normally available" contribute to the contests surrounding 'power'.

16. Stanley Benn, for similar reasons, presents a paradigm of power in "Power," p. 424. I have used his insightful effort as a touchstone for my own. The differences in emphasis will be brought out shortly.

17. I was very fortunate to receive an early draft by Steven Lukes of *Power: A Radical View* (forthcoming). He cites examples of power analysts who view conflict as a necessary condition of power and gives a thoughtful critique of this requirement. I discuss this issue and others related to it in *Political Science and Ideology* (New York: Atherton Press, 1967), ch. 2.

18. Benn, "Power," p. 426.

19. *Power: A New Social Analysis* (New York: W. W. Norton, 1938), p. 35; my emphasis.

20. Robert Dahl offers a formal definition open to this criticism: "My intuitive idea of power, then, is something like this; A has power over B to the extent that he can get B to do something that B would otherwise not do." Dahl, "The Concept of Power," in *Introductory Readings in Political Behavior*, ed. Sydney Ulmer (Chicago: Rand McNally, 1961), p. 125.

21. The introduction of 'intentionality' into definitions of power

presents problems as well for those who aspire to definitions that are operational in some precise sense. As D. M. White notes, "distinctions, commonplace in discussions of intention, have been almost completely overlooked in discussions of power." White, "Power and Intention," *American Political Science Review* (September 1971):750.

22. Hannah Arendt, "What is Authority?" in *Between Past and Future* (New York: Viking Press, 1954), p. 93. It is true that there are instances where the statement "A has power *to* do x" is compatible with the interpretation that authority is the *form* that such power takes. But our focus is on a comparison of relationships where A has *power over* B to those where A has *authority over* B. For 'power to' does not *necessarily* point to a relationship between two agents A and B but might refer to one between agent A and any objective z. As soon as it is translated into a relationship among agents (persons, groups, classes, and so on), the concerns that control our inquiry are brought into play. Arendt at least tacitly recognizes the distinction pressed here between 'power over' and 'power to' when she distinguishes authority from *coercive* power. We need only add that 'power over' relationships are not restricted to those relationships in which A coerces B.

23. For a thoughtful discussion of such a distinction, see Richard B. Friedman, "On the Concept of Authority in Political Philosophy," in *Concepts in Social and Political Philosophy*, ed. Richard Flathman (New York: Macmillan, 1973), pp. 121–45. I wish to emphasize the above proviso "when other pertinent conditions are met," for while this distinction is essential to an understanding of authority it is not sufficient: We can hold that power is legitimate when it is not and authority can be *effective,* as we shall see, without being *warranted.* It is crucial to both ideas that one could *mistakenly* believe that power is legitimately exercised and authority warranted.

24. There may be elements of persuasion in each of these cases, but their location will be different from that occurring in cases in which we say simply that A persuaded B to do x. Thus you may persuade me in (1) to follow your order because of the special position of social coordination you hold even though I am not persuaded by the substance of your policy. I am persuaded to accept your authority. In (2) you may persuade me

to trust you as a skillful and responsible naturalist, and thereafter I accept your authority in guiding my efforts to save some rare plants.

25. Certain contemporary radicals. I believe, conclude that because it is appropriate to challenge particular claims to authority in oppressive societies and because it is desirable to increase the extent to which the actions of people rest upon rational persuasion in participant groups, the *idea* of authority itself is a bogus one. But this is a confusion. As Friedrich Engels asserts in the process of projecting a future communist society in which workers participate in industrial decision making and in selecting leaders of these units, "wanting to *abolish* authority in large-scale industry is tantamount to wanting to abolish industry itself." See Engels, "On Authority," in *Marx and Engels: Basic Writings on Politics and Philosophy*, ed. Lewis Feuer (Garden City: Anchor Books, 1959), p. 483.

26. Robert Brown and Albert Gilman, "The Pronouns of Power and Solidarity," in *Style in Language*, ed. Thomas Sebeok (Cambridge: MIT Press, 1960), p. 256.

27. This is a distinction drawn and elaborated by Kurt Baier, "The Justification of Governmental Authority," *Journal of Philosophy* (Fall 1972):700–16. The distinction has connections to an older distinction between '*de jure*' and '*de facto*' forms of authority but is not identical to it.

28. Antonio Gramsci, *The Prison Notebooks*, ed. and trans. Quinton Hoare and Geoffrey N. Smith (New York: International Publishers, 1971). That Gramsci acknowledged that not all claims to authority are reducible to efforts to gain hegemony seems to be indicated by the following comment about relationships within his own party: "Unity and discipline cannot be mechanical and coercive; they must be loyal and the result of conviction, and not those of an enemy unit imprisoned or besieged—thinking all the time of how to escape or make an unexpected counterattack." p. lxxxv.

29. Talcott Parsons, "The Distribution of Power in American Society," in *C. Wright Mills and the Power Elite*, ed. G. William Domhoff and Hoyt Ballard (Boston: Beacon Press, 1968), p. 83; my emphasis. The article was originally published in 1957.

30. Raymond Wolfinger, for instance, doubts whether the "*concepts*

of nondecision and power structure contribute anything toward the study of . . . the consequences of different political forms, styles, and processes, the role of myths, the impact of political socialization, etc." Wolfinger, "Rejoinder to Frey's 'Comment'," *American Political Science Review* (December 1971):1104.

31. It is one in which A's *authority* in the eyes of the wider community gives it *power* over B in this instance, and so on through B to C and C to D.

32. Kurt H. Wolff (ed.), *The Sociology of Georg Simmel* (New York: Free Press, 1950), pp. 236–37.

33. My thinking about collective responsibility has been helped by essays by Kurt Baier, R. S. Downie, David Cooper, Virginia Held, and Stanley Bates in Peter French (ed.), *Individual and Collective Responsibility: The Massacre at My Lai* (Cambridge, Mass.: Shenkman Co., 1972). These analysts do not fully agree about the criteria of collective responsibility, but Cooper can help us to establish bearings: "To be condemned (or held responsible in general) a group must be more than a random collection of individuals; it must be a collective of people between whom there are various ties and bonds, whose behavior is partly governed by common rules, conventions, or mores." p. 98. Virginia Held argues effectively that collective responsibility is sometimes attributable to a random collection of people, but these are admittedly exceptional circumstances, involving episodic behavior, and have less applicability to our thinking about structural relationships.

34. This example is not purely fanciful but is inspired by Matthew Crenson's excellent portrait of U. S. Steel in Gary, Indiana, in *The Unpolitics of Air Pollution: A Study of Non-Decisionmaking in the Cities* (Baltimore: Johns Hopkins Press, 1971). I take liberties with his analysis for purposes of pinpointing the conceptual issue.

35. This point is reflected in Robert Paul Wolff's critique of American pluralism when he argues that *not enough* outcomes are attributable to power. The society, he says, "requires an *increase* in power, a transforming into objects of decision of important matters which are now the consequences of uncoordinated acts, rather than merely an alternative to the way in which present power is employed." Wolff, *The Poverty of*

Liberalism (Boston: Beacon Press, 1968), p. 121. For a friendly critique of Wolff's definition of power, see William E. Connolly, "Liberalism Under Pressure," *Polity* (Spring 1970):357–66.

36. Note that in this closed system we can predict with great confidence, but it is exactly the system within which 'power over' has minimal purchase.

37. Both Marxists and conservatives have offered different versions of such an interpretation. Claus Offe suggests that "the welfare state cannot redistribute income to a very great extent because of the constraints built into the economic system," and he quotes the economist Meade to the effect that in the prevailing system income redistribution policies would "affect adversely incentives to work, save, innovate or take risks." Offe, "Advanced Capitalism and the Welfare State," *Politics and Society* (Summer 1972):481. Kingsley Davis and Wilbert Moore give a classic conservative version of the argument in "Some Principles of Stratification," *American Sociological Review* (April 1945): 243–49, in which they argue that power analysis is not needed to explain the *system* of unequal rewards, for such inequalities are *necessary* to ensure work incentives and to filter the most competent into the most important tasks.

38. C. Wright Mills, *The Causes of World War III* (New York: Simon and Schuster, 1958), p. 12.

39. Ibid., p. 95.

40. Paul Sweezy, "C. Wright Mills and the Power Elite," in *C. Wright Mills and the Power Elite*, ed. Domhoff and Ballard, pp. 131–32; his emphasis.

41. I have noted earlier that many pluralists tacitly acknowledge this dimension of 'power' by insisting that only the *intended* results of a person's or group's action can be included with his sphere of power. But as we have already argued, this criterion deflates unjustifiably the sphere over which 'power' ranges.

42. Some of these latter possibilities, especially 3, 4, and 5, are applied to American politics in William E. Connolly (ed.), *The Bias of Pluralism* (New York: Atherton Press, 1969) and Crenson, *The Unpolitics of Air Pollution*.

43. I certainly do not mean to deny that the emphasis of my argument itself is part of the very contests I am now describing, but I do claim that it falls within these broad parameters mentioned.

44. Wolff, *The Poverty of Liberalism*, pp. 94–95.

45. Raymond Wolfinger, for example, once a strong advocate of a pluralist theory of power, is now tired of a "pluralist-elitist" debate, which he finds to be "limited and dull." See p. 1102 of his "Rejoinder to Frey's 'Comment'," *American Political Science Review* (December 1971). He counsels *elimination* of the "nondecision dimension" of power because the problems of operationalism are so difficult and because people with different ideologies interpret this phenomenon differently. He suggests, finally, that it may well be possible to displace the concept of power itself in political inquiry. See Wolfinger, "Nondecisions and the Study of Local Politics," *American Political Science Review* (December 1971):1063–80. I do not criticize here his methodological repudiation of "nondecisions" because I think it is answered very effectively by Lukes, *Power: A Radical View;* and by Crenson, *The Unpolitics of Air Pollution.* Eugene Meehan represents the view I seek to defeat when he says power analysis is no longer scientifically fruitful because "the concept of power is now mainly the property of social critics, and the vagueness and ambiguity that prove such a hardship in explanation are sometimes an advantage in social criticism." Meehan, *Contemporary Political Thought: A Critical Study* (Homewood, Ill.: Dorsey Press, 1967), p. 102.

46. See the arguments in the Chapter 1 of this study as well as Charles Taylor, "Interpretation and the Sciences of Man," *Review of Metaphysics* (Fall 1971):4–51.

4

The Idea of Freedom

FREEDOM AS A
CONTESTED CONCEPT

Freedom is perhaps the most slippery and controversial of the concepts we shall discuss. We can best hope to cope with the notion if we come to terms with just why it is the subject of such intense and continuing controversy. One tradition of conceptual analysis approaches the problem in the following way: The idea of freedom, fairly clear in itself, is today surrounded by positive normative "connotations." These positive connotations encourage advocates of different ideologies to define it persuasively, to advance definitions, that is, that bring the values and goals they favor within the rubric of freedom. As a result, the concept becomes increasingly vague and unclear; misused by competing ideologists, the concept itself threatens to lose its utility in neutral empirical inquiry.

The task of conceptual analysis, according to this view, is first to purge the concept of all normative or value connotations and then to explicate it in ways that enable all investigators, regardless of the ideological orientation they "happen" to adopt, to use it in description and explanation of social and political life. Such an approach will allow us to transcend the current confusions permeating studies in which the concept figures and will in fact make it possible to pinpoint our normative differences. For now all investigators will have access to the same conceptual system, neutral with respect to opposing ideologies, in which they can discuss their differences about the extent to which freedom is properly prized as an ideal of political life. Perhaps the ideological differences will not be fully resolved, it is argued, but at least the factual issues that can be brought to bear on these questions will be stated with clarity in a neutral language. In a book that has contributed valuable insights into the concept of freedom, Felix Oppenheim states this view. "Meaningful disagreement about the value of freedom depends," he contends, "on agreement on that about which one disagrees." To achieve this goal we must "arrive at a system of definitions acceptable to everybody because they do not conflict with anybody's political ideology." [1] Reviewing in a recent article his own efforts to fulfill this objective, he asserts:

> Thus, in the case of the concept of social, political, or inter-personal freedom, the expression we must explicate is, "With respect to B, A is free to do x." This expression can be defined by: "B makes it neither impossible nor punishable for A to do x." Not only does this definition remain close to ordinary usage, it is also descriptive, and in two ways: the defining expression consists exclusively of descriptive terms, and it is "value-free" in the sense that it can be applied to determinate states of affairs by anyone independently of his political convictions. [2]

The concern here expressed for clarity is laudable, but I shall argue, the approach adopted and the presuppositions it embodies are inappropriate to the objective stated. In the ordinary language of political life and in more formal systems of political inquiry the normative dimensions in the idea of freedom are not attached to it as "connotations" that can be eliminated; without the normative point of view from which the concept is formed we would have no basis for deciding what "descriptive terms" to include or exclude in the definition. Debates about the criteria properly governing the concept of freedom are in part debates about the extent to which the proposed criteria fulfill the normative point of the concept and in part about exactly what that point is. To refuse to bring these considerations into one's deliberations about 'freedom' is either to deny oneself access to the very considerations that can inform judgment about the concept or to delude oneself by tacitly invoking the very considerations formally eschewed. That is the charge I shall defend.

The alternative approach pursued here does not promise to issue in a neutral definition couched in criteria acceptable to all regardless of normative commitments; it does promise, though, to clarify the issues underlying conceptual disputes about freedom; and it does purport to help the investigator clarify explicitly the considerations that move him to adopt one formulation over others. [3]

The thesis to be advanced is that 'freedom' is contested

partly because of the way it bridges a positivist dichotomy between "descriptive" and "normative" concepts. Though considerations in support of this thesis will be offered throughout this essay, we will devote the rest of this section to linguistic evidence from ordinary discourse, which provides it with preliminary support.

To capture the grammar of 'free' tacitly accepted in ordinary discourse, Alan Ryan has compared words with the suffix 'free' to others that have the suffix 'less'.[4] We draw subtle distinctions between these ideas, he concludes, that determine which suffix properly applies in particular contexts. Thus a driver might be carefree as he drives down an empty highway just after his car has passed a safety check, but he is careless if he adopts a similar attitude on a crowded thoroughfare with an old car on the way to a safety check. Care*free* motoring and care*less* motoring each call our attention to different aspects of the driver and his situation. We speak of a dustfree room because of our belief that a room without dust is more pleasant and healthy than one with great quantities of dust, but we call a painting worthless (rather than worth*free*) when we conclude that it lacks artistic value. Similarly we speak of being penniless, but not pennyfree when we are out of money. And it would be odd indeed to say that a person without means of defense in the face of a massive attack is defensefree; surely we would describe him as defenseless in that situation. Note that it is proper to say that we would *describe* him as defenseless.

In comparing the circumstances in which these suffixes apply it is clear that in general 'free' applies to situations or outcomes that are advantageous or helpful to the agent involved, while 'less' applies to situations that are deleterious to, involve some deprivation of, or relate to the lack of needed or useful resources to, the agent. The difference between these suffixes, *both* of which typically apply to situations in which something is missing, is not adequately captured by saying they describe the same things, but attach different normative appraisals to those things. A dustfree room, for instance, describes a fairly complex phenomenon: a room without dust, which is, *for that reason,* more comfortable to the inhabitants. As Ryan himself concludes, "Clearly the use of 'free' rather than 'less' implies a good deal about people's wants and purposes, about people's duties, about the uses of objects, and so on. Talking of the so-called fact-value dichotomy here is of little relevance, because there is more to be said." [5]

These two suffixes pick out different elements in situations that refer in the broadest sense to the absence of something; and they pick out different elements *because* each notion bears a different relationship to the wants, interests, and purposes of the agents implicated in those situations. The one suffix, then, does not simply have "value connotations" different from the other; for that choice of words suggests that the use of one suffix rather than the other is determined by the different *feelings* people project onto situations that are *descriptively identical.* But in fact the suffixes pick out different aspects of situations that are only similar in some respects. The choice of "connotation" to capture the difference between 'free' and 'less' is deficient in another respect: Connotations are emotive attitudes that happen to cluster around a word; they can be stripped from the idea itself without altering or emasculating it. The positive normative import of 'free', though, is not attached to it accidentally but flows from its identification of factors pertinent to human well-being in situations where something is absent. And that normative import in turn sets general limits to the sort of situations to which the idea of freedom can be applied. Instead of seeking to strip the idea of its positive "associations," we must ask, Why does 'freedom' carry positive normative significance and what import might the answer have for our shared understanding of, and disputes about, the idea itself?

FREEDOM AS A TRIADIC RELATIONSHIP

When a person just released from prison says he is glad to be free we know well enough what he means. But often the context in which talk about freedom occurs is not so unambiguous; we are sometimes in doubt about what the agent is free to do or become and what restraints have been lifted that make his statement pertinent and allow him now to do those things. In many settings, then, elliptical statements about freedom are misleading. As a preliminary to clarification of the notion of freedom we need to fill out these elliptical statements explicitly, pinpointing the dimensions involved in our use of the idea.

Isaiah Berlin has suggested that no single schema could be devised that would capture all dimensions of 'freedom', for in political thought and action, he contends, two distinct concepts of freedom—two rather different ideas covered by the same term—can be discerned.[6] There is, first, the negative idea of freedom (freedom *from*) in which agents are restrained by others from doing what they want, and second, a positive idea (freedom *to*) in which agents autonomously conceive and pursue their own ends—the positive concept of liberty "derives from the wish on the part of the individual to be his own master."[7] According to Berlin, historically the positive and negative "notions of freedom developed in divergent directions until, in the end, they came into direct conflict with each other."[8] The positive idea is dangerous, for those who accept it often end up compelling people to conform to some standard the people themselves oppose. Any notion of freedom that can so easily be translated into its opposite and used to say that people are "forced to be free," is, in Berlin's view, philosophically and politically dangerous; the negative idea is more consistent with the liberal's principled presumption against forcing others to do what we think they ought to do or would willingly do if only they were autonomous.

Two sorts of objections might be (and have been) brought against Berlin's argument. First, with respect to his denigration of 'positive freedom', it is never in itself a sufficient argument against an idea to say that it can be misused. That is true of all important ideas. The appropriate questions to pose are, How clear and important is the idea when it is properly used? How can its proper use and value be more effectively protected against the dangerous misuses to which it is subject?

Second, several analysts, most notably Felix Oppenheim and Gerald MacCallum, have argued that there are not in fact two discrete concepts of freedom, but one model within which all talk about freedom can be fitted. Each schema, it is claimed, enables us to fill out the ellipses in everyday talk about freedom and to specify and critically examine in this way the exact dimensions of particular claims advanced. Oppenheim proposes the following model:

> With respect to Y, X is unfree to do x, to the extent that Y makes it impossible or punishable for X to do x.[9]

And MacCallum adopts one in which

> x is (is not) free from y to do (not do, become, not become) z.[10]

Although Oppenheim and MacCallum fill out the three variables in somewhat different ways, the formal dimensions of the two models themselves are very similar. Thus in MacCallum's triadic model, x is an agent, y ranges over constraints and limiting conditions, and z covers "actions or conditions of character of circumstance" available or unavailable to the agent.[11] And, MacCallum claims, every statement about freedom refers, if sometimes elliptically, to an agent (x) who is free or unfree *from* constraint (y) to do or be something (z). Put in another way, every instance of freedom has its 'negative' and 'positive' side. Oppenheim's three variables X, Y, and x correspond formally to MacCallum's agents, constraints, and acts, with the qualification that Oppenheim's scheme requires that the constraining agents be identified and implies that constraints cannot be internal to the agent himself. A related difference is that MacCallum leaves the range of each of the term variables relatively open, exploring the various ways in which thinkers have filled them historically, while Oppenheim closes each variable with his own specifications.[12]

For our purposes, MacCallum's open triad will prove more useful, for the conceptual disputes over 'freedom' revolve around the proper limits to impose on one or more of the term variables. Two provisos will circumscribe our use of this model in what follows. First, the model itself does not mean that the competing images of 'positive' and 'negative' freedom described by Berlin are fully convertible into one concept of freedom shared by all; the debates Berlin poses will emerge again in slightly different form within the confines of this triadic scheme. Second, while most important occasions in which the language of freedom is applicable can be fitted neatly into this triadic scheme, it is not clear to me that all statements about 'positive' freedom or autonomy (as we shall label the idea) can be converted without strain into this idiom.

FREEDOM AND AUTONOMY

Debates about the proper meaning of 'freedom' involve disputes over the proper range of the three term variables that enter into the idea. We will explore alternative proposals with an eye toward ascertaining what sorts of considerations are pertinent in deciding among these alternatives and what implications flow from the decision to accept one formulation over others. In this section we will focus attention on views about the characteristics of agents (x) and end states (z); the idea of a constraint (y) will be explored in the next section.

1. What if an agent is able (allowed) to do one, and only one, thing in a particular context? We would not say the person was free from constraint to, say, take the job open to him if he were not also allowed to turn it down. Before the language of freedom applies, at least two opportunities must be open to an agent; he must be free to do or not to do z. One of the reasons talk about freedom carries normative import is that we value highly the opportunity to act upon our own choices, and a choice is exercised only in settings where more than one alternative is available.

2. Suppose, now, that the agent has several options available but none of them is one that he wants or ever will want in the normal course of his life. Suppose he is "free" to torture the child he loves or to speak out against his principles or to steal food from loved ones. In such a context, I think, we respond ambivalently to the question, Does the language of freedom properly apply here? First, though he has several options, none of them are worthwhile or gratifying to him, and

it seems odd to say that someone is free to do things he is and will be opposed to doing.   There is a sense in which Benn and Weinstein are correct when they say that "it is appropriate to discuss whether he is free to do it only if it is a possible object of reasonable choice." [13]   The language of freedom does seem to be bounded by such normative considerations.   But we hesitate to endorse such a stipulation with respect to *any particular act,* partly because the range of actions some agent might choose to take or goals he might consider worthwhile is quite broad. Moreover, even if a person does not and never will choose to do some x, it makes a significant difference whether the decision not to do that x is made by others for him or is open to him to make.   Our very ambivalence about the applicability of talk about freedom in this context is built on conflicting ideas about the grammar of freedom which must be accounted for in any proposed definition of the concept.

3.   To avoid associating freedom with undesired options, many theorists have defined the objects of freedom (x) in terms of the desires or wants of the agent involved.   Thus Bertrand Russell holds that "freedom in its most abstract sense means the absence of external obstacles to realization of desires," and Isaiah Berlin, in a formulation later retracted, once contended, "I am normally said to be free to the degree to which no human being interferes with my activity.   Political liberty in this sense is simply the area within which a man can do what he wants.[14] Suppose, then, we have a situation in which an agent has several options available to him, some of which he wants to pursue.   Surely the language of freedom gains purchase here, but there are also clearly situations when such a situation prevails and yet where the agent is not free.

Before considering examples that challenge this definition consider the kind of theoretical perspective that might be particularly congenial to it.   According to the theory of abstract individualism, underlying and limiting the range of variation in human desires, wants, and aspirations is a fixed set of conative dispositions that will press for release in each and all social settings.[15]   Within this theoretical framework the paradigm case of limiting the freedom of an agent is restraining him from gratifying drives, desires, or instincts that are part of his nature. The primary juncture at which limits to an agent's freedom *can* apply, according to this theory, is at the point where the desire to do some x is translated in the attempt to do it.

Even the theorist of abstract individualism, though, could not accept the Russell-Berlin formulation without qualification. For a person might want, say, food or security and be manipulated to *believe* that he could attain these goals through activity that in fact inhibits their attainment. In such a situation we would have to say that he was unfree from manipulation to get what he wants, though he might be free to act upon his (manipulated) beliefs.

But when fundamental deficiencies in the theory of abstract individualism are exposed, the definition of freedom in terms of the wants persons have is seen to be quite inadequate. For the conative dispositions people have are themselves shaped in part by the concepts, beliefs, and roles they internalize from the society in which they are implicated.[16] Thus slavery is a paradigm of unfreedom. And a slave who is socialized to accept his master's judgment that he is incapable of self-rule is not for that reason more free than a slave who wants to escape his master's rule. If to be free were simply to mean that one could act upon one's desires without constraint, a person could increase his freedom simply by scaling down his desires to match the opportunities available to him. Constraints can operate on one's ability to conceive and formulate wants or projects as well as upon the opportunity to fulfill those projects already formed.

The concern that motivates the formulation criticized here is clear enough. The fear is that if the desires are not recognized in the idea of freedom, it will become definitionally possible to force people to act against their desires under the guise of increasing their real or true freedom. To push the actual desires of concrete individuals into the background of the idea of freedom, it is feared, will allow theorists and political elites to include as part of freedom the very forms of coercion and manipulation the idea is designated to expose. But that fear can be alleviated by insisting that any constraint on an agent's opportunity to do what he wants is a constraint on his freedom.   And then we must add: A person might be released from these constraints and still remain unfree in important respects.

4.   It is rather widely thought that the deficiencies noted in the previous formulations can be corrected by saying an agent is free to the extent that he is unconstrained from doing what he wants or *might* want to do.

> Our freedom of action throughout a field of activity over a period of time is more than the freedom to do whatever we want to do in that field; . . . it is freedom to do whatever we *may* want to do in that field, and, as there is no knowing what we *may* want to do, it is freedom to do everything in that field whether or not we *will* want to do it.[17]

As Scott amplifies his view, "if we do not want to do a thing, the question of freedom does not arise . . ."[18] and so when we ask whether an agent is free with respect to some z it is not necessary that it be presently desired by him but that *if he were to want to do or be that z,* he could do so without constraint.

This formulation advances matters in certain respects. For it now becomes feasible to say that an agent is constrained with respect to some act even though he does not now wish to do it.   Thus, Jews could be unfree to serve in upper management positions of a discriminatory corporation even if no persons of that descent presently desired to become managers in the corporation.   And a slave who adopts his master's image of him as his own could nevertheless be unfree to the extent that *even if he were to try,* he could not escape his slavery. Nevertheless, the definition proposed by Scott is clearly deficient in one respect and contestably defective in another.

The formulation does not adequately explain how constraints can operate on the formation of wants as well as on the ability to do what one wants or might want.   Consider a case in which the agent would be free to do z if he were to come to want to do it, but where there are constraints operating on him that ensure that he will in fact never want to.   On Scott's formulation no question of a constraint of freedom is raised here because he could do it were he to desire to do so. But the proviso is insufficient. Think, for instance, of a woman whose capacities and interests would be well fulfilled were she to serve as an administrative officer in a university. She would be accepted as a candidate were she to prepare herself and press her case through established channels, but she is socialized to role expectations that ensure she never will pursue that path. According to Scott's formulation (and to many views that parallel Scott's), she is *perfectly* free, but once the subtle constraints on the very formation of her goals and projects are recognized we can hardly concur in this judgment. It is undeniably difficult to detect constraints operating at this level. Even those who adopt the same criteria of 'constraint' (a topic we have so far held in abeyance) are likely to disagree in their interpretations of when and to what extent constraints apply to the very formation of wants, but the difficulties surely do not justify an evasion of the question itself through definitional fiat.

It is possible to revise the formulation so as to retain its spirit while meeting the objections raised. But it is further arguable that any definition of freedom in terms of actual and potential *wants* will be deficient in that it will fail to discriminate subtly enough between agents and acts that meet the highest standards of freedom (that is, meet fully appropriate criteria of freedom) and those agents and acts that do not. Subtle distinctions are sometimes profoundly important to the quality of social life, as when we discriminate between an inadvertent and a negligent act or between a civil and servile attitude towards a superior. Such import prevails here.

The very broad and flexible notion of a want incorporates under one rubric ideas best considered separately in our thinking about freedom. A person may want to follow a particular career simply because his parents and friends expect him to pursue this path. He might, however, adopt the same goal after deliberately canvassing the expectations others have of him, reassessing his previous tendency to adopt unreflectively the hopes these others have for him as his own, critically exploring the contours of the profession under consideration in the light of his own capacities, strengths, and weaknesses, and comparing the career in question to other alternatives that might be open to a person with his interests, capacities, and opportunities. Any concept of freedom that takes account only of the content of an agent's actual and potential wants while ignoring the alternative routes by which such wants might be formed is unlikely to foster serious reflection about a contestable view of freedom deeply rooted in idealist political philosophies: the ideal of the autonomous person whose central projects are as nearly as possible "his own," who acts upon choices formed through critical awareness of his situation and the possibilities and constraints that situation provides. We say that a person acts unfreely when he is coerced by a gunman to steal from a grocer; we also hesitate to say that he acts freely when he steals because he is a kleptomaniac. In the former case he does not do what he wants and in the latter he fulfills a want singularly immune to critical self-scrutiny and control. It is this latter situation that those who define freedom in terms of wants fail to account for adequately. Father Zossima, in Dostoevski's *The Brothers Karamazov*, laments this failure when he ridicules the interpretation of "freedom as the multiplication and rapid satisfaction of desires...." We can hardly describe as free, he argues, people who simply act upon whatever "senseless and foolish desires and habits and ridiculous fancies are fostered in them." [19]

A principle is a general rule that places, for its adherents, the onus of justification on those who would break it; to accept a principle is to acknowledge at least a prima facie obligation to abide by it. An ideal is a state of affairs that may or may not be fully attainable but is deemed worthy of aspiration by those who accept it; actions in its pursuit are deemed justifiable unless overriding reasons are given, but they are not typically viewed as obligatory or at least as obligatory as conduct in accord with accepted principles. Most people in our society accept the principle of freedom: Every adult person should be allowed to do as he chooses unless overriding reasons can be advanced that justify limiting him in certain respects. Given this principle, a burden of justification is placed on those who do, or propose to do, the limiting. As Benn and Weinstein have pointed out, the fact that the concept of freedom reflects the principle embodied in it explains why we are not *simply* purporting to describe a state of affairs when we say that some individual or group is not free in some respect; we are also typically advancing a charge or making an accusation that we expect those we advance it against to deny, rebut, or accept.[20] To deny the charge is to argue that the principle is in fact not being infringed; to rebut it is to argue that the infringement is justified by special circumstances; and to accept it is to acknowledge the validity of the charge and concur in efforts to remove the identified constraints. Much of the ideological activity in contemporary society can be understood as a continuing exchange of such charges, rebuttals, denials, and acceptances among various segments of the population.

Among those who accept the principle of freedom are many who accept an ideal of autonomy as well. Acceptance of the ideal affects the assessment of public policies, social arrangements, and political processes. For example, those attached to this ideal are likely to view participation in group decision processes as an essential ingredient in any politics properly described as democratic; for participation, in the right circumstances, both promotes the development of autonomous judgment among citizens and allows that judgment to find expression in the political process. More directly pertinent for our purposes, though, the ideal affects the very meaning of 'freedom' adopted by those attached to it, and in this way the ideal enters into their interpretation of the principle of freedom itself. We can see the ideal of autonomy at work, for instance, in John Dewey's formulation of the role that intelligent deliberation plays in the very idea of freedom:

> Impulses and desires that are not ordered by intelligence are under the control of accidental circumstances. It may be a loss rather than a gain to escape from the control of another person only to find one's conduct dictated by immediate whim and caprice; that is, at the mercy of impulses whose formation intelligent judgment has not entered. A person whose conduct

is controlled in this way has at most only the illusion of freedom.[21]

Dewey's conception of freedom is affected by his understanding of certain capacities peculiar to persons and by the ideal of autonomous judgment and action he accepts. In what follows I will endorse and seek to clarify central ideas in a conception of freedom congruent with these commitments. My strategy will be to elucidate very briefly the ideas of a person and of autonomy and then to propose a paradigm of 'freedom' that reflects this idea of a person and appeals to the ideal of autonomy for nourishment.

Lower animals experience painful and pleasurable sensations, form desires and act upon them, and in many cases are capable of communicating some of their sensations and desires to others. Human beings share these characteristics with animals, but we develop certain of them further, and we also express different ones more or less peculiar to us as persons: We have the capacity to form complex concepts and beliefs, which enter into correspondingly complex desires and plans; we can come to understand the origin and import of some of these desires; we can formulate longer-term projects on the basis of that understanding; we can appraise existing projects in the light of alternative possibilities; and we can reformulate and revise previous concepts, beliefs, desires, roles, customs, and projects in the light of past experience and current comparisons and then act on the basis of such reformulations. Creatures of habit and convention, we are also able to submit particular habits and conventions to critical scrutiny. Capable of understanding our established practices, we are also capable of deliberately charting new paths and of following old ways more reflectively. Capable of some degree of self-understanding, we are thereby capable of changing ourselves to some degree through action based upon that understanding.

It is in the light of these capacities that we recognize each other as responsible agents, and this mutual recognition forms the cement of social life. I do not feel gratitude toward a car that reliably gets me to work every day, though I am glad that it is reliable. Neither do I express gratitude toward a bus driver who does so in the normal course of his duties. But if a neighbor went well out of his way on a cold day to take me to work when I had an important appointment, I would be very grateful to him. My *belief* that his action was intentional and reflected a willingness to sacrifice on my behalf in a context where he could have done otherwise enters into my feeling of gratitude. Without those beliefs (or something like them) about him and his act my *feeling* toward him would have to be described as something else. To express gratitude toward another is to attribute to the other certain capacities to form complex intentions, to carry out those intentions, to act responsibly, and so on; the feeling manifests assumptions about persons that we do not make about things and lower animals. A whole set of complex reactions reflect such presuppositions, and such reciprocal presuppositions enter into a broad range of social relationships that would be impossible without them. To have such presuppositions applied to oneself when another loves, hates, resents, trusts, or respects one is to be treated as a person; to apply them to others is to treat them as persons; and to establish stable relationships that involve reciprocal recognition of these capacities amongst a large number of people is to establish the preconditions of a community.

It is difficult to render this image of a person clear and perhaps to square it with some widely received views about determinism, but it does seem unlikely that anyone could fully and *consistently* repudiate the concept of a person given in this brief sketch. For such a consistent repudiation would force one to deny oneself the opportunity to participate in social practices in which the complex reactive attitudes of love, gratitude, resentment, guilt, respect, and so on, form a constitutive part.[22] Those who adopt the principle of freedom do so because it provides the space in which persons can both develop and express these capacities.

An autonomous person is one in whom these capacities are highly developed and articulated. A person is autonomous to the extent that his conduct is informed by his own reflective assessment of his situation. He realizes that he is enclosed in a system of conventions that shape much of his conduct and tend to limit his self-understanding, and he explores routes to render those habits more amenable to self-conscious scrutiny and possible revision. He seeks to translate those conventions and habits, so far as possible, from forces acting upon him into considerations he can choose to accept or modify in the light of this understanding. In Dewey's language, he encourages intelligent reflection to enter into the desires, projects, and practices he endorses. Knowing that the very concepts and beliefs he brings to a reconsideration of past habits reflect in part those habits themselves, he seeks to expose himself to alternative modes of classification in the interests of identifying new angles of vision from which he can view and evaluate his acquired habits.

As the very statement of the ideal reveals, no one is or can be fully autonomous. It is logically impossible to live up to the ideal in all areas of one's life at once. For internalization of socially received concepts, beliefs, and norms is a necessary precondition for critical reflection into any particular project or practice: The initial system of concepts and beliefs that help to define us provides the materials out of which we define and comprehend our setting. We must always accept some concepts and beliefs in order to isolate others for critical examination; we must therefore follow some practices unreflectively now so that the source and rationale of others can be considered reflectively. It is not that the autonomous person takes nothing for granted, but rather that he is able and willing to question any particular project or practice and to adjust his conduct on the basis of such reconsideration. He *might*, indeed, accept upon examination most of the prevailing practices within his culture, but to the extent that he does so autonomously, reflective judgment and self-understanding enter significantly into his acceptance of these patterns.

While it seems difficult to reject fully and consistently the concept of a person outlined earlier, people can and do disagree significantly on the extent to which autonomy constitutes a worthy standard for individuals and societies. Some argue, with Michael Oakeshott, to qualify or even to reject the ideal.[23] Thus it might be claimed that a highly developed sense of alternative possibilities could undermine the naturalness and rich web of tacit understandings that mark fulfilling social relationships. One who thinks too hard about the rules he has been following in riding a bike is likely to fall off, and one who seeks to probe the subtle dimensions of the bonds that unite him to others is likely to convert them into awkward, self-conscious relationships. A society that seeks such self-consciousness might find that its policies and relationships come to be dominated by a crude "rationalism" that coldly and ruthlessly sweeps aside hopes, considerations, and traditions that do not fit within its formal calculus of rules. Under appropriate conditions, so the argument goes, an entire system could be undermined because some pursue a vision too magnificent for human consumption.

Even those committed to the ideal of autonomy can interpret its implications in radically different ways. Marx, Freud, Durkheim, and Sartre all project some version of the ideal, but since the autonomous person aspires to make decisions in the light of full understanding of relevant circumstances, and since those circumstances include persisting facts about his own nature—about human nature—different theories of human nature will carry different implications for the conduct of the autonomous person.[24] If, for instance, it were true that certain drives or impulses do and must press inexorably for expression in all human beings, the autonomous person, in the process of achieving self-understanding, will acknowledge these drives or inclinations and take them into account *somehow* in his decisions and projects.

Just as it does not count against one's courage to fail to defeat an invincible enemy it does not count against one's autonomy to fail to eliminate an ineradicable drive. It counts against one's autonomy only to fail to identify and acknowledge such facts about oneself in one's deliberations. One might, upon reflection, decide to express, control, sublimate, or deflect such pressures, or if possible, to transcend them, but the autonomous agent will confront them honestly in reflecting on a course of action. But if this is so, judgments about the degree to which some agent or action is autonomous are inherently controversial to some degree: An action that reflects bad faith from Sartre's perspective might emerge as the enlightened response of an autonomous agent from the vantage point of Freudian theory.

I have not introduced these objections and areas of contestability to confront them in detail, though I think the Oakeshottian critique is less applicable to the version of autonomy articulated here than it is to that form of rationalism that emerges from a utilitarian tradition. I have simply sought to indicate, first, that one who rejects the ideal of autonomy as not *one* of the worthy ideals to pursue will be inclined to oppose as well the interpretation of 'freedom' to be offered here; and second, that even acceptance of the ideal (and of the interpretation of 'freedom' attached to it) will not settle a range of deep and persisting issues. But it helps rather than hinders the reflective assessment of social and political practices to identify some of the crucial points around which such controversies pivot and to articulate considerations that might help to inform one's commitments in these contestable areas.

I will advance a formulation of freedom, then, that connects agents (X) and their acts (z) to the ideal of autonomy, while it avoids, I hope, the objections brought against formulations 1 to 4 on pages 145–51. The initial paradigm to be articulated will cover the phrases "X is free with respect to z" and "X acts freely in doing z," and then we shall clarify further the import of the following formulation:

5. X is free with respect to z if (or to the extent that) he is unconstrained from conceiving or choosing z and if (to the extent that), were he to *choose* z, he would not be constrained from doing or becoming z.

X acts freely in doing z when (or to the extent that) he acts without constraint upon his unconstrained and reflective *choice* with respect to z.

a. In this formulation constraints can operate at two levels. There are constraints operating on the character of the agent himself, impeding his ability to conceive and to choose reflectively among alternatives; there are also those operating upon his actual and potential actions, limiting his ability to act upon his choices. While these two levels are not always easy to distinguish in practice, liberals have often emphasized the second and ignored the first.

b.   The phrase "free with respect to z" includes the idea that the agent is unconstrained either from doing z or not doing z. If he could *only do* z, he would not be free with respect to it. In general to be free with respect to some z requires that at least one other option be available to the agent.[25]

c.   The idea of actual and potential *choice* replaces that of actual and potential wants, first, because a choice refers to more than one available course of action (where this is not so necessarily with 'want'); and second, because the notion of a choice embodies more fully a reflective or deliberative dimension. Some of my wants might reflect mere habit, compulsive drive, or simple impulse, but, as Aristotle reminds us, the very paradigm of a choice between options involves "a voluntary act preceded by deliberation." When one says one chooses x *rather* than y, the "rather" indicates that there is a detectable difference between the two and that reasons can be adduced to explain what these differences are and how they enter into the choice itself.[26]

d.   Unlike some proposed definitions this one makes it conceptually impossible to be unfree from constraint with respect to z and still *act freely* in doing z. There are dilemmas here that often promote harmful ambiguity and confusion in debates about the extent to which people are free or unfree in particular settings. Suppose that a dissident is legally unfree to leave a country without a passport and the authorities refuse to give him one because of his political commitments. Suppose, too, he decides, after weighing the alternatives now before him, to leave anyway, knowing that he will face penalties upon his return. He is unfree to leave the country because of legal constraints, but does he nevertheless *act* freely in going? In one sense, of course, he does, because he acts upon his own choice in the setting he faces. But I think it would be less misleading to say that his opportunity to explore alternatives and to choose among the limited ones available has not been limited or impaired, but that his *action* itself is not free, since he faces penalties upon his return. With this sort of situation in mind we can say that a person can be autonomous and still not be allowed to act freely with respect to particular matters.[27]

e. In our formulation of acting freely, the qualification of "acting" by "freely" looks forward to the absence of constraints applied to the action taken, and it also looks back to the agent, considering the extent to which his conscious reflection enters into and informs the action. What do we say, then, when a person merely wants to do something and then does it in a situation where no constraints limit him? Does he really act *unfreely* on this occasion because the action fails to meet one of the conditions specified? No. 'Acting freely' is not a categorical concept, but one that is subject to judgments of degree: A given action (or project) might be more or less congruent with the paradigm of 'acting freely'. The sort of action described above is less fully free (or less perfectly free) than one taken after reflective deliberation. But in many settings we will have no occasion to describe an act in these terms; no point would be served by such a description. It is just that in some settings an important point is served by saying, as we can according to this formulation, that one person or group has acted more freely than another with respect to some project equally open to both of them that both have pursued.

Some examples might help to clarify this last point. If, of two people equally able to attend a baseball game both want to see, one is more clear about why, say, he prefers watching baseball to watching golf, we are hardly likely to notice that difference or to make anything of it. For, as we have seen, not even the autonomous person can or need be reflective about everything; he simply must be reflective in ways that inform his future action about some matters of importance. Suppose, though, a well-socialized consumer unreflectively accepts the consumptive role expected of him and is able to buy the goods he wants, while another citizen, similarly situated, reflectively considers the pressures pushing him into that role, explores alternative styles of life available, and chooses to continue or not continue his previous consumptive habits in light of these reflections. The latter agent, according to the formulation advanced here, acts more freely with respect to that consumptive role than the former; and that judgment might indeed be worth making. Similar points could be made about voters, housewives, adolescents, public officials, blue-collar workers, waiters, and professors. The roles that centrally define our lives are crucially important to us as persons, and it is in exactly these contexts that the distinction we have been pushing provides the most leverage to social thought and action.

CONSTRAINING CONDITIONS

The language of freedom, we have said, involves a triad of agents, constraints, and acts. We must now turn to interpretations of the second variable, those constraints or forms of interference that limit the freedom of agents. We wish to consider alternative views of what counts as a constraint and to explore why the lines around 'constraint' are drawn as they are by the proponents of each alternative. Consider, then, some possible proposals.

1. A blind person cannot see; an elderly person cannot make the Olympics basketball team; and a young child cannot do calculus. Suppose that in each of these cases the agent would choose to engage in the unavailable activity if obstacles to doing so were removed. Could the obstacles of blindness, aging, and an immature mind count in these settings as constraints on the freedom of the agent? Certainly not. They are limits on the agents' abilities but not on their freedoms. With respect to any particular act or goal, the language of freedom does not apply until it is at least generally plausible to assume that it is within the natural capacity of the agent to engage in that act or practice. It would be unnecessarily cruel to say to a blind person, "You are free (from *constraints*) to look out the window—if you can." That these limits do not count as constraints is clear enough, then, but understanding why they do not count helps us to see the point of view from which the idea

of a constraint on freedom is formed. It also helps us to see why disputes persist over the proper range of the idea of a constraint.

To say that an object or arrangement poses a constraint on the freedom of an individual or group is typically to state a grievance against those responsible for it; it is to make an accusation to be *refuted, denied* or *overridden* by the parties against whom it is tendered. But we can't hold any individuals or groups responsible for obstacles and barriers to human action that are not subject to human intervention or control. Stanley Benn and William Weinstein make this point well: "Since Freedom is a principle, whatever interferes with it demands to be justified; consequently only those determining conditions for which rational agents (God or man) can be held responsible can qualify as interfering with it." [28]

Our agreement that obstacles not subject to human control do not count as constraints reflects our tacit agreement that statements about freedom involve judgments about responsibility. The shared rationale behind this agreement provides us with clues about the nature of debates over the appropriate criteria of 'constraints' in talk about freedom. We can now restate the issue before us to include more explicitly considerations that typically play a background role in debates over the meaning of freedom: Among those obstacles and limits to human action that are potentially subject to human (or superhuman) control, what further conditions must be met before an obstacle counts as a constraint of freedom? If the notion of a constraint (y) involves the idea of agents responsible for limiting the range of options (z) available to persons (x), what are the criteria of responsibility appropriate in the triadic relationship of freedom?

2. It might be argued that a limit counts as a constraint only when it is imposed deliberately and intentionally by others. Scott, for example, endorses this view, which he attributes to everyday usage, when he says that "inability does not raise the question of freedom except where the inability is the result of a conscious human intention to render us unfree." [29]

Others adopt a rather similar approach in which it is clear that they seek to keep "impersonal social forces" (Scott) outside the idea of constraint. Berlin, for instance, says

> if I am prevented by other persons from doing what I want I am to that degree unfree; and if the area within which I can do what I want is contracted by other men beyond a certain minimum, I can be described as being coerced.[30]

But what does "preventive action" mean to Berlin? We get a clue about the limits he has in mind when he tells us that coercion, the paradigm form which a constraint on liberty takes, "implies the *deliberate* interference of other human beings within the area in which I want to act."[31]

Oppenheim adopts a similar view. Under the heading "Not Enabling Is Not an Instance of Unfreedom" he asserts that "Y makes X unfree to do x if Y *prevents* X from doing x, but not if Y merely *fails to make it possible* for X to do x."[32] Two stipulations are posed here, one dealing with preventive action and the other with omitted acts described as failures to enable. Some sense of the intended limits to the meaning of preventive action is gained through Oppenheim's proviso that those obstacles to X's action resulting from "prevailing social practices and theories *rather* than to the actions of any particular group" do not constitute constraints of X's freedom. And the intent behind the second stipulation is clarified by an implication Oppenheim draws from it for the understanding of poverty. Even if the government "failed to make it possible for them" to escape poverty in a setting where such enabling policies were feasible, we could not properly describe the poor as unfree with respect to government policy to escape poverty.[33]

The three formulations by Scott, Berlin, and Oppenheim vary in certain respects. But they share an inclination, first, to describe those limits to action imposed by impersonal social forces as mere obstacles rather than as constraints on freedom; and second, to place deliberate acts of coercion or restraint (for instance, imprisoning a person, passing laws against abortion) within the ambit of 'constraint' while pushing outside its rubric limits on the options available to agents flowing from possible but omitted actions by others and from the unintended consequences of the actions others take. We shall consider each of these stipulations in turn.

The line separating those impersonal social forces that reflect "prevailing practices and theories" from the "action of any particular group" is much more difficult to locate than proponents of this view acknowledge. Our actions are constituted in part, as we have seen, by the concepts, beliefs, and theories that enter into them. A ruling class might, for instance, accept a prevailing theory (say, of laissez-faire capitalism) that explains poverty as the result of necessary and irremediable arrangements and then act within that frame of reference to outlaw trade unions. *Its own description of its action* includes "restraining trade union organization to leave the individual free to contract with the employer of his choice" and "keeping the economic system open and competitive." Anyone implicated in prevailing practices *and* accepting prevailing social theory would not understand the members of this class to be imposing new constraints against those in poverty. From within that vantage point the poor have not been made less free to escape poverty, though the workers (for reasons justified within the theory) have been made unfree from legal sanctions to organize unions. But why should *we* always accept the understanding that enters into such practices and that is manifested in such a prevailing theory as the guide to our assessment of the situation? To accept such a stipulation consistently is to accept the conclusion that the more successful a group is in gaining ideological hegemony the less liable it is to the charge that it has limited the freedom of other groups. If an enslaved population falsely accepts the belief, promulgated and believed by its masters, that it is naturally docile and in need of guidance, we would properly say, I think, that the theory itself operates as a constraint on the slaves. The masters, in this setting, are the constraining agents, even if they honestly but mistakenly act in terms of this prevailing social theory. Introduction of this consideration means that the assessment of constraints of freedom necessarily involves us in the assessment of the beliefs and theories within which the social practices under scrutiny proceed. But it would be surprising if a reasonable definition of 'constraint' could avoid that implication.

This conclusion receives support from another direction. One of the points of the accusation that an individual or group is unfree in some respect is to get those against whom the charge is made to reassess the import of their own conduct. When feminists charge that men have imprisoned women in roles that reflect male fantasies more than female needs, part of the point of that statement is to pressure those accused of repression to look again at the consequences for women of these theories, role expectations, and fantasies about them. It is not necessary to conclude that every such charge is always warranted to see that the charge itself is perfectly coherent and comprehensible in exactly those contexts in which the target group has not consciously intended to constrain those in whose name the charge is made. The charge encourages the accused to review the assumptions upon which they have acted, to look at their conduct from the vantage point of those making the accusation, to confront the possibility that an element of self-deception intrudes into their acceptance of dominant theories and practices. But the charge and accompanying pressures for reappraisal could gain no foothold at all if Y could not be said to constrain X's freedom except by acts deliberately intended to do so. Parents, capitalists, males, teachers, and political elites might well feel uncomfortable with a notion of constraint that encourages them (us) to reappraise the import of their conduct for others, while those others find enhanced conceptual space within which to issue the charges and accusations that prod that reappraisal. The unease, though, reflects more a sense of strategic disadvantage than a recognition of linguistic impropriety.

The second restriction suggested in the foregoing formulations flows from the distinction between restraining someone from doing something and failing to enable him to do it. Oppenheim correctly points to a risk in any view that includes the failure to enable as a constraint: If we were to say that a person is unfree to do something with respect to all those who do not help him to do it, we would have to include "practically everybody" as agents of constraint.[34]   But the conceptual possibilities before us are not restricted to including all such omissions as forms of constraint or including none.

We must observe in passing that the distinction between restraining someone and failing to enable that person to do something is not all that clear.   Conduct that appears under one description as failing to make it possible for X to do z can, under another description, be seen as preventing X from doing z.   A President of the United States refusing to sign a reform bill to establish an income floor might be described as failing to support a new law that would enable the poor to escape poverty or as supporting old laws that prevent the poor from escaping that plight.   If the formulations advanced here aim to exclude only those failures to enable that cannot be redescribed in terms of preventive interference, then the formulations themselves recede in importance.   For in many contexts it is possible to redescribe the pertinent conduct in ways that fit the prescribed formula.

But the formula itself is too restrictive.   While it is inappropriate to describe the poor as unfree with respect to everyone who could but does not act to relieve their poverty (consider the marginal member of the middle class who would be impoverished by such an individual effort), certain individuals like the President and members of Congress, and certain groups like the middle class and corporate elites, stand in a particularly strategic position with respect to enabling the poor to escape poverty.   If a government stood in a strategic position to remove impediments against those striving to escape poverty "but failed to make it possible for them to do so," the government's failure, in my view, would properly be seen as a constraint on the freedom of the impoverished.

3.   Ignorance, poverty, and the internalization of oppressive social roles are not, along the continuum we are considering, equivalent either to obstacles such as hereditary blindness and the inability to fly like a bird or to those such as imprisonment and enslavement.   Poverty, for instance, is not a natural necessity in modern society nor is it always imposed deliber-

ately on its victims. *Contests over which end of the continuum such intermediate obstacles are to be assimilated to are at root contests over the extent to which a presumption of social responsibility should obtain for the obstacles themselves.* Within this grey area, the idea of a constraint is an essentially contestable component of the larger idea of freedom, and arguments that seek to extend or restrict its range of application within this space are inherently open to reply and objection. Since no conclusive arguments are available here, the space itself, we might say, is irreducibly political. It is in this spirit that I shall support a formulation that includes as constraints on freedom certain obstacles potentially subject to social remedy even though not deliberately imposed. In capsule form, the case to be argued is this: The extent to which such an obstacle interferes with the interests or autonomy of persons properly plays a role in our assessment of its conceptual status.

If an inexpensive operation were discovered that could restore sight to the blind, those who were denied such treatment would be considered unfree from (socially remediable) blindness to live a more satisfying life. Our standards of what counts as a natural limitation can be altered in this way by improvements in medical knowledge and technology. But if the operation were extremely expensive and terribly dangerous for those performing it (for instance, the surgeon would have to be exposed to radioactive materials), we would not be willing to describe refusal to perform the operation as a constraint on the freedom of the blind person. The notion of a constraint, then, involves the idea of a normal range of conduct people can be expected to undertake or forgo when doing so restricts the options of others.

Similarly, if massive social expenditures could make it possible for motorists to drive 5 miles an hour faster on expressways with the same safety as they now have at the current limit, we would not say that failure to enact that policy is a constraint on our freedom as motorists to drive faster. Or rather, one could say that without being incoherent. But it would be straining or extending the grammar of 'constraint', and the statement would invite special questions and answers. For the notion of a constraint also involves the idea that the options it limits are in some sense *important* to the agents involved by comparison to the costs and risks required for its elimination.

These two judgments enter into our decision whether to call a limit a constraint, and the criteria of importance accepted are in turn partly shaped by the conception of persons and actions one accepts in the triadic scheme of freedom. Each of the variables in the triadic scheme of freedom in this way helps to shape the contours of the other two.

The point can be stated in another way. If a government bureaucrat claims he was unfree to expose corrupt practices in the White House because he would be fired for doing so, a rejoinder might be: You were *free* enough; you were simply *unwilling* to accept a lower-paying job to expose these practices. We refuse in this context to count the penalty as a *sufficient* constraint to justify the employee's silence because of the importance of his failure to expose the activity. To assert that a claimed constraint is unimportant by comparison to the action forgone "is to insist on the agent's responsibility for what he does . . . and perhaps to charge him with lack of will or faith." [35]

With this as background I want to suggest that no formula can be advanced that precisely and abstractly distinguishes between a constraint on freedom and other sorts of limits to conduct. One can at most propose a flexible set of considerations deemed to be pertinent in particular contexts. My proposal, then is this: y is a constraint if (1) the limit is imposed deliberately or negligently by individuals or groups, and/or (2) if the agents are limited with respect to important actions or goals by circumstances potentially alterable at a less than prohibitive cost through individual or social action. And, as noted earlier, the more important the end the higher the cost must be before it is prohibitive in that context. The undefined terms 'negligent', 'important', 'remediable', and 'prohibitive cost' play a central role in this statement; they must be interpreted in specific contexts, and the interpretation will be influenced by the conception of agents and actions accepted by those who are assessing the situation. A final stipulation applies to 'important'. Others cannot say an agent is "really free" from constraint simply because they construe the goals he is prohibited from fulfilling to be unimportant. On the other hand, outside observers (or agitators) can, on this formulation, claim that an agent is really *unfree* from certain constraints on the grounds that his failure to recognize a range of goals as important flows from the very coercive pressures that imprison him. This is not to say that such claims are necessarily correct just because they are articulated. But acceptance of the legitimacy of advancing them, and of offering reasons in their support, is necessary if we intend to adhere to our intuition that happy slaves (and others in less extreme situations) are unfree.

In many contexts most participants and observers will agree in their judgment of what counts as a constraint. In some instances of disagreement, the source will be straightforwardly empirical in the sense that, say, two persons might agree about the meaning and importance of autonomy but disagree about the extent to which the lack of certain educational facilities limits the chances of some segments of society for developing their capacities for autonomous judgment. In other contexts a conceptual dimension will enter into the dispute; the dispute itself will pivot around contests over the range of criteria appropriate to 'important' and 'prohibitive costs'.

The proposal advanced here not only has the advantage of identifying those junctures at which contests emerge in this essentially contestable idea but it also includes as a standard case within its rubric obstacles that we typically sanction as constraints in ordinary language but that other explicit definitions would exclude. Poverty and ignorance, for instance, do limit profoundly the ability of those afflicted with them to formulate social options knowledgeably and to act upon those formulations. Where potential remedies are available that would not impoverish the entire society, the obstacles confronting the poor count as constraints on their freedom. And given the importance and range of the limits imposed, this is so even in social settings where dominant ideologies construe poverty to be an incorrigible feature of social life.

To endorse the ideal of autonomy is also to endorse the view that constraints can operate either on an agent's opportunity to act upon his own choice among possible alternatives or, at a prior level, on the agent's very opportunity or capacity to conceive and explore possible options themselves. Liberal analyses of freedom, following Hobbes, have often focused attention on constraints of the first sort while ignoring or discounting those which apply at the second, more fundamental, level.[36] The lingering effects of the doctrines of abstract individualism and operationalism probably help to explain this tendency, but it does result in a superficial approach to the study of freedom.

A young woman, for instance, may prefer upon reflection to remain single, but after exploring systemic biases against single people, decide to marry anyway. Here we have a constraint applied at the first level—it limits the availability of a course of action she might otherwise choose. Suppose, though, the woman has internalized a complex of self-images and role expectations characteristic of the authoritarian personality. She cannot conceive or realistically explore any alternative other than marriage to an authority figure; these internalized constraints bear on her very capacity to explore and carve out alternative styles of life.

Those constraints operating on the character of persons can be profoundly restrictive. A stratified educational system might induce role expectations among lower-class students that fall well below their potential capacities; an empty, routinized work life might deaden the mind and blunt the capacity for reflective choice among those subjected to its daily regimen; a family might transmit contradictory messages to a child, stunting the very development of the confused and disoriented child's capacity for choice.[37] Constraints operating at this second level are likely to be embedded in the very fabric of the social order; the constraints themselves flow out of the structure of work life, the nature of educational systems, the nuclear family's response to broad social pressures, the dynamics of class relationships. The dimensions of such constraints are notoriously difficult to identify, and any theory that purports to comprehend them adequately will draw upon assumptions and ideals that are inherently controversial at some points or along particular dimensions. Thus Marxists and Freudians both take such constraints seriously, but their respective efforts to identify their location and import vary significantly. Controversial as they are, though, such questions should not be legislated away by definitional fiat. The freedom to act on one's own choice is hollow if one has had a marginal chance to develop the very capacities presupposed by that freedom. Free action involves free persons, and constraints against the development of the capacity for autonomous judgment inhibit freedom of action as well.

ASSESSMENTS OF OVERALL FREEDOM

A person is never free from all constraints to do anything he might upon reflection choose to do. Indeed, freedom in certain respects requires the limitation of freedom in others; often what is from one perspective a constraint is, from another, something I am free to do. There are, first, those recurring situations in which the freedom of one agent in one sphere requires the constraint of others in other spheres. To make reporters free from the threat of subpoenas to publish newsworthy information from secret sources often requires that defendants facing trial be unfree through legal restraints to gain pertinent information from these sources. There are, second, those occasions in which the agent can legitimately see the situation before himself as both one of constraint and freedom. Thus the union shop might render the worker more free from corporate constraint to advance his grievances publicly and to receive due process in adjudicating them, while it makes him unfree through legal restraints to work for the corporation without joining a union. There are, third, situations where freedom with respect to a particular agent in one area means that freedom with regard to that same agent in other areas must be curtailed. The market system makes employees free to bargain with employers individually for their wages, but those same processes make employees unfree to supplant the employer-employee relationship itself with one that involves worker participation in management. Finally, it often happens that freedom at one time must be curtailed so that freedom at a later time is possible or more fully possible. Restraint on young children, according to most theories of child development, is necessary to development of their critical skills later. Given such complex and complicating circumstances, how are we to judge whether persons are more free in one setting or circumstance than they are in another?

It is tempting to say that when the *severity* of pertinent constraints are held constant,[38] agent A is more free than agent B to the extent that the former has more options available. But difficulties immediately arise. Suppose A is free to choose among thirty-five brands of new automobiles to provide him with transportation, while B is limited to three options: a used Chevrolet, a new Buick, and use of a mass transit system. Intuitively we would conclude, I suppose, that B is more free in this sphere even though he apparently has fewer options. We would say that the options available to B are real options while A's more numerous alternatives exist within more restrictive limits. The underlying problem here is to distinguish among 'options' themselves: Options or alternatives do not just stand there in quite the way that bricks do; they are constituted in part by the standards of importance we bring to the process of differentiating among them. Are there *really* only two options available in this example—transportation by car or by mass transit? If so, B is obviously more free in that respect. Or are there, perhaps, 1,500 options in fact potentially available, since each brand of car has a large variety of motors, styles, and color options? If so, A is obviously more free, since he has 1,500 options to a mere 45 for B.[39] As this example illustrates, no simple quantitative list of options will suffice in comparisons of freedom. Normative or qualitative considerations enter, first, into the very judgment of what counts as an option, and second, into assessments of how different or distinct particular options are from one another. A person cannot be said to act freely if he can only pursue one path, but there is no simple relationship between the number of paths open to him and the extent or degree to which he is free.

The judgment that A is more free than B necessarily invokes normative considerations. The judgment itself sometimes (or in part) appeals to an ideal internally related to freedom, such as the ideal of autonomy, and sometimes to a standard that is at least in part external to that ideal. Consider the latter first. Among several options available to an agent, if at least one of them corresponds to what he wants or is in his interests, we will say he is more free than if he had several options, none of which promoted his wants or interests very effectively. A person who is free to choose among four job offers, none of which he wants very much, is less free than one who is free to choose among three, two of which are very attractive to him. Since judgments about what is in one's best interest are often contestable, these controversies will enter into competing comparisons of freedom.

Consider, now, appeal to an ideal internal to freedom. A classical economist might construe a worker who can choose among four specialized jobs graded according to pay to be more free in that respect than a worker who can choose between only two jobs of equal pay, one of which allows play for his creative capacities. One who accepts the Marxist theory of alienation, though, would surely reverse that judgment. For, from the standpoint of the ideal of autonomy central to the theory of alienation, the *distance* between the latter two options is greater than that among the first four. Both the Marxist and the classical economist favor 'freedom'. But different conceptions of persons and constraints in the triadic scheme of freedom enter into their divergent assessments of what counts as an option and which array of options makes one comparatively more free.

In pointing to these sources of difference in conceptions and assessments of freedom I do not mean to imply that we lack that preliminary common ground that makes communication possible. Our shared starting points in this sphere provide the base from which disagreement proceeds and sometimes the standards to which initial disagreements are referred for adjudication. Our use of the language of freedom itself embodies areas of common agreement in comparative assessments of freedom. We do not, for example, always use the word 'constraint' in our everyday discourse about obstacles to freedom. We speak variously of people being confined, deprived, restrained, oppressed, repressed, dominated, and coerced; differences within this family of concepts embody in part differences in their severity and importance as constraints. Similarly, when people are freed from certain limits, it is not always appropriate to say that they have been liberated or emancipated, for these latter ideas are also graded by standards of importance. Neither a Marxist nor a classical economist would ever say that X is *emancipated* from legal *oppression* to drive his car 5 miles an hour faster, though each might say that he is *free* from legal *restraint* to do so. People are *emancipated* from *slavery* and *oppressive* rules; they are *liberated* from *stifling role expectations,* but not from distasteful chores.

The varied language we share to cover situations of constraint and freedom is graded by partly shared standards of severity and importance; to the extent we adopt common conventions governing the use of these notions we share as well judgments about more or less freedom. The fact that we universally apply certain of these terms in some settings and exclude them in others signifies that we share to some degree common principles and ideals of freedom. Our disagreements, important and profound as they are, are grounded in these preliminary areas of partial agreement. Our disputes about freedom are in fact more important and intense *because* we share certain ideas about the criteria of 'freedom' and the point of discourse about it.

NOTES

1. Felix Oppenheim, *Dimensions of Freedom* (New York: St. Martin's Press, 1961), p. 9.

2. Felix Oppenheim, " 'Facts' and 'Values' in Politics," *Political Theory* (February 1973), p. 56. The issue, though, is not simply whether anyone can apply it to determinate states of affairs, but whether everyone will find it equally worthwhile to do so.

3. It should be noted that the approach adopted here does not, simply because it has recourse to normative considerations, *reduce* 'freedom' to "anybody's moral or political ends," making the concept thereby "vacuous." The alternatives are not as Oppenheim would suggest, between formulating a neutral, descriptive definition or making freedom "cover whatever actions, policies, or institutions may be deemed valuable." The criteria of a concept might have fairly definite limits that specify for those who accept them a definite range within which it applies even while those criteria themselves are influenced by normative considerations. We don't hold people responsible, for instance, for acts they could not avoid: The criteria governing that concept are clearly influenced by normative considerations, yet we don't conclude that it is therefore vacuous. Only those who equate moral judgment somehow with emotive expression could rest easy with this statement of alternatives. The quotations are from Felix Oppenheim, "Freedom," in *International Encyclopedia of the Social Sciences* (1968), 554 and 558.

4. Alan Ryan, "Freedom," *Philosophy* 5 (April 1965):93–112.

5. Ibid., p. 102. Ryan offers more evidence in support of this thesis, but that noted above is sufficient for our purposes.

6. Isaiah Berlin, *Two Concepts of Liberty* (Oxford: Clarendon Press, 1958). A revised version of these arguments is included in Berlin, *Four Essays on Liberty* (New York: Oxford University Press, 1969).

7. Ibid., p. 16.

8. Ibid.

9. Oppenheim, *Dimensions of Freedom*, p. 81.

10. Gerald MacCallum, "Negative and Positive Liberty," in *Contemporary Political Theory*, ed. A. de Crespigny and A. Wertheimer (New York: Atherton Press, 1970), p. 109.

11. Ibid., p. 109.

12. Indeed, MacCallum, while indebted to Oppenheim, holds that he "limits the range of the term variables so sharply as to cut one off from many issues. . . ." Ibid., p. 123. I share such a debt and also concur in this judgment. Pertinent here is Oppenheim's assertion that "freedom of choice" is quite different from "social freedom"; only the latter can be analyzed within the triadic scheme. "Freedom of choice" simply means X *can do* x; it makes no reference to other agents who might constrain X; and it is neither a necessary or sufficient condition of "social freedom" (which does make such a reference). Many analysts, he contends, have failed to make this distinction and have hence implied that X is constrained by others with respect to some x when in fact X merely lacks the ability to get or do x. Better to eliminate "freedom of choice" from the vocabulary. But then Oppenheim, I think, overplays his hand: he sometimes sees others *confusing* the two ideas he has separated when, in my view, they actually *disagree* with him about the proper criteria of constraint in the triadic scheme of ("social") freedom. Thus, he says, "Unemployment during a recession is an instance of *lack of freedom of choice, not of lack of social freedom,* unless the recession itself can be causally linked, e.g., to *specific* governmental policies." Oppenheim, "Freedom," p. 556; my emphasis. Accepting, as I do, a broader interpretation of the constraint condition, it seems likely to me that the lack of freedom involved here does fall within the triadic scheme posed by MacCallum.

13. Stanley Benn and William Weinstein, "Being Free to Act, and Being a Free Man," *Mind* (April 1971): 195.

14. Bertrand Russell, *Sceptical Essays* (London: George Allen and Unwin, 1952), p. 169; Berlin, *Two Concepts of Liberty,* p. 7.

15. For a lucid discussion of this perspective and its connection to other forms of individualism, see Steven Lukes, *Individualism* (New York: Oxford University Press, 1973).

16. See the discussion in Chapter 1 of this book.

17. K. J. Scott, "Liberty, License and Not Being Free," in *Contemporary Political Theory,* ed. de Crispigny and Wertheimer, p. 105.

18. Ibid.

19. *The Brothers Karamazov* (1880; New York: Modern Library, 1945), pp. 328–29. There are in fact three ideas in competition

here: linking freedom only to doing what one pleases or might be pleased to do; to what one chooses or might choose to do upon reflection; and to what one ought to do according to an external normative standard accepted by the observer. I will support inclusion of the second idea.

20. Benn and Weinstein, "Being Free to Act, and Being a Free Man," pp. 198–99.

21. John Dewey, *Experience and Education* (1938; New York: Macmillan, 1950), pp. 75–76.

22. These themes will be discussed further in Chapter 5. My presentation of them is particularly indebted to P. F. Strawson, "Freedom and Resentment," in *Studies in the Philosophy of Thought and Action,* ed. P. F. Strawson (New York: Oxford University Press, 1968), pp. 71–96.

23. Michael Oakeshott, *Rationalism in Politics* (New York: Basic Books, 1962). In my view his contentions count against making autonomy the only ideal worthy of pursuit and count as well against certain "individualist" interpretations of it, but I do not think they undermine the version advanced here.

24. It might surprise some to see Durkheim's name on this list, but he claims that we who come to accept and follow existing practices should have "as clear and complete an awareness as possible of the reasons for our conduct. For it is this awareness that confers on our action that autonomy which the public conscience henceforth requires of every truly and fully moral being." Quoted from Steven Lukes, *Emile Durkheim: His Life and Work* (New York: Harper and Row, 1972), p. 115. My own interpretation of autonomy is indebted especially to Karl Marx's discussion of species life in his theory of alienation, and to Stuart Hampshire. See T. B. Bottomore (trans. and ed.), *Karl Marx: Early Writings* (New York: McGraw-Hill, 1963); and Stuart Hampshire, *Thought and Action* (New York: Viking Press, 1959).

25. See Oppenheim, *Dimensions of Freedom,* p. 119.

26. "If a person takes a cigarette from a pack of cigarettes, an unknown card from a deck, or a drink from a tray when he does not care which kind of drink he gets, he does not choose a particular item. . . . If one chooses, there is a basis for choice, and if there is a basis for choice, there is a reason why one does x rather than y." Andrew Oldenquist, "Choosing, Deciding and

Doing," in *Encyclopedia of Philosophy* (1967), 2:98. The quotation from Aristotle also comes from this essay, p. 99.

27. To adopt the opposing view, as Hobbes and apparently Oppenheim do, has pernicious results. Oppenheim says, "One may do freely what one is socially unfree to do." *Dimensions of Freedom*, p. 151. This means that a slave who sits down in protest against his enslavement in the face of expected punishment from his master acts freely, even though the most serious constraints limit the availability of the course he takes; it means that an employee who quits his job rather than engaging in a fraud required by his employer acts freely. Descriptions of such acts as "free" trade upon the positive normative import of that description while deflecting political attention from the fact that neither the slave nor the employee can exercise his choice without facing serious consequences.

28. Benn and Weinstein, "Being Free to Act, and Being a Free Man," p. 200.

29. "Liberty, License and Not Being Free," p. 103.

30. *Two Concepts of Liberty*, p. 7.

31. Ibid.; my emphasis.

32. *Dimensions of Freedom*, p. 71; my emphasis.

33. Ibid. I press for a more precise demarcation of the unit ideas "preventing X" and "failing to enable X" in Oppenheim's formulation, because such precision is essential to the model of conceptual analysis he supports. If *these* ideas are left open-ended, so is the concept of freedom in which they figure, and the acceptance of these *terms* by those advancing opposing ideologies could easily mask divergent construals of their range of application. Open-textured concepts create room for variable interpretations; and such room for maneuver is at odds with the objective of constructing a neutral conceptual system acceptable to all. The other side of my argument, of course, is that any proposed *precise demarcation* is contestable at some points by those who accept different ideologies. It is this double bind that exposes the unviability of the model of analysis itself.

34. Ibid. Oppenheim, it should be noted, qualifies his initial formulation that "not enabling is not an instance of unfreedom" by acknowledging that inaction making it *impossible* for someone to act in a certain way is to make him unfree in that respect.

p. 72. This qualification moves in the right direction but does not proceed far enough.

35. Benn and Weinstein, "Being Free to Act, and Being a Free Man," p. 208.

36. "Liberty, or freedom, signifies properly the absence of opposition—by opposition I mean *external impediments* to motion." Thomas Hobbes, *Leviathan* (1651; New York: Bobbs-Merrill, 1958), p. 170; my emphasis.

37. For thoughtful discussions of constraints operating on the character of persons, see Christian Bay, *The Structure of Freedom* (Stanford, Calif.: Stanford University Press, 1958); and R. D. Laing, *The Politics of the Family* (New York: Vintage Books, 1969).

38. Constraints can be graded according to the *severity* of the penalties they impose for transgression and according to the *number* or *importance* of the options they foreclose. The constraint against driving 75 miles an hour is more severe if the penalty is 30 days in jail than if it is a $5 fine; a constraint against criticizing political leaders is more important than one against watering the lawn on weekends. See Oppenheim, *Dimensions of Freedom*, ch. 8, for a discussion of such questions.

39. Divide brands (35) into styles (1,500) = 43. Add one used car and one transit system to get 45.

5

Conceptual Revision and Political Reform

ON THOUGHT AND ACTION
(IN GAMES AND POLITICS)

The concepts of politics do not simply provide a lens through which to observe a process that is independent of them. As we have seen, they are themselves part of that political life—they help to constitute it, to make it what it is. It follows that changes in those concepts, once accepted by a significant number of participants, contribute to changes in political life itself. It follows further that *proposals* for revision in some dimensions of our concepts carry similar import for political practice. This connection between conceptual revision and political change, once grasped, can deepen our understanding of the intimate relationship between thought and action in politics.

When an agent probes the settled usage and practices of a quiescent community, he can, if he chooses, adopt what Henry Kariel has called the indicative mode. Working within this mode, he tries to move "as close to the phenomena under study as (he) can, . . . to embrace the prevailing definitions of 'event', 'problem', 'fact', 'cause', and 'decision' ".[1] Even then the lines of emphasis one selects inevitably operate to support the orientations of some of the participants over those of others; the analysis itself affects, if it is heard by the participants, the world that it merely seeks to describe. But when that is acknowledged, it still remains true that in such contexts the spirit of work done in the indicative mode is passive and receptive: He sanctions the internal understandings he describes not by actively celebrating them but by suspending critical judgment with respect to them.

Alternatively, he might decide that life in a stable community needs to be jostled or shaken up; he might seek to challenge, revise, reinterpret established practices because of the idea that the quiescent atmosphere confines and oppresses the inhabitants. He adopts, under those circumstances, the transactional mode, seeking "to confront the present state of things—himself included—but not accepting it as it appears to be, as complete, as having ended."[2]

The choice among alternative modes, clear enough when a person explores a harmonious, settled milieu, becomes blurred and restricted when he confronts a complex political process in which many of the concepts that help to form political practice are themselves contested by the participants. It seems less possible to confront such contest-imbued practices in a purely indicative mode; there is a tendency to take sides, to applaud some of the practices of some of the participants, to identify dark areas in prevailing practice that might, if illuminated, allow a transcendent view to gain ascendancy. If conceptual contests play a peculiarly important role in *political* life, then a person who seeks to comprehend the depth grammar of concepts that enter into that life will find that the mode he adopts is more transactional than indicative. Provided only that he is heard and heeded or heard and opposed, he will find that he has entered into the stream of politics itself, affecting (in some large or small way) the flow and force of the current. The impact an agent and those with whom he identifies have is more likely to correspond to his purposes and ideals if he comes to understand just how and by what means reflection into the concepts and practices of politics can affect the practices themselves.

Consider such connections, first, in a nonpolitical context. Suppose a friendly group of Americans compete together each week in a game something like our game of basketball. The rules governing the game vary from ours in one significant respect: It is permissible for the offense to block, tackle, or push members of the defense while trying to score a basket, and the defense can reply in kind. In fact, short of conformity to generally understood norms against maiming or injuring opposing players, "anything goes" in this game of basketball— as long as each team limits itself to five players, players dribble the ball when advancing it, the ball is turned over when it goes out of bounds, and so on. While the number of players, court size, boundary lines, scoring rules, and length of the game remain as they are in our game of basketball, the game itself is radically different from the one we know and play. The offensive tactics, defensive strategies, and standards of excellent performance are quite different from their counterparts in our game of basketball.

Suppose, now, a British gentleman of high character and charismatic personality, invited to join the weekly game, begins to describe as "foul play" various practices of holding, hacking, bumping, and pushing opposing players. Overwhelmed by his character and reasonableness—he himself never indulges in "foul play"—the American players gradually begin to reciprocate. They incorporate into their play the precept, "Try to avoid bumping, pushing, . . . opposing players," and they characterize a player as indulging in "foul play" when he stoops to such conduct.

The term 'foul play' gradually comes to be a means of describing a certain open-ended range of behavior within the game *and* an expression of reproach in the light of that description. Gradually the concept is refined and sharpened through the accumulation of shared experience. (Even in the highly organized game as we know it the standards of what counts as a foul are continually evolving.)

Suppose that as part of that process of refinement it is eventually found convenient to push the intentional component in the idea of 'foul play' into the background. The *consequences* of certain actions, such as blocking the opponent's path to the basket, now become more central to the idea than the intentions and purposes of the agent who produces those results. It is no longer so important to know whether he bumped the other on purpose. The pertinent question becomes, Did that action impede the flow of the game as the game is *now* understood and appreciated by the participants?

As one component in the idea of a foul changes, adjustments in other dimensions also come to be seen as warranted. It seems less appropriate to accuse someone of "foul play" now, since a foul can be committed accidentally. So the players hit upon the idea of assessing penalties for "committing a foul," giving the opposing player a "free throw" or two when that happens. Now to "call a foul" is to assert that an act in the game meets certain conditions in light of which a prescribed penalty is warranted. Since the purpose of calling fouls is now to maintain the flow of the game as it has come to be understood, to call a foul on a player signifies a judgment less of the player's character and more of the character of his play.

The evolution of the idea of a foul and of the norms it embodies is part of the evolution of the game itself. Because certain actions are now fouls the game is radically changed from its original form. The strategies and plays open to the offense change significantly, the responses of the defense now move in different channels, and the standards of excellence in play are transformed. Thus, a player who blatantly tackles another or holds his arms in the new game "doesn't know how to play basketball." And a smart player might commit a "strategic foul" against a poor "foul shooter" when his team needs the ball near the end of the game; this latter *action* itself, it should be noted, could not have been performed prior to the entry of the idea of a foul into the game.

The point of 'calling a foul' (to assess a penalty) now remains constant in the revised game, but the conditions that must be met before the point applies continue to be relatively open-ended and contestable; the open texture and stable function of the idea in the game combine to create both the room and the motivation for disagreements among players that were not possible before the idea was introduced. And as players and referees (the latter introduced to call fouls and award penalties) debate and settle these issues the game itself continues to evolve. If, for instance, participants were to decide that it is a foul to block a shot, the strategies available to the players, the relative importance of a player's height in the game, and the standards of excellent play would all shift significantly. Similar results would follow if it became a foul to "set a pick," an offensive tactic currently effective only because it is a foul to knock a player over who has set a pick on you.

This hypothetical history of the progressive insinuation of the idea of a foul into our game of basketball illustrates several themes about concepts and the practices into which they enter. First, 'foul' is neither a 'descriptive' nor an 'emotive' or 'normative' concept as mainstream social scientists understand those categories. For to "call a foul" is to *assess a penalty* in the light of certain *specified conditions* that an action meets in the game. Second, the entry of the idea (the concept) of a foul into the game does not only affect the way we see the game but also helps to reconstitute the game itself. Certain acts are now available that were not available earlier, and the entire array of strategies and standards of excellence change as a result of the entry of this idea into the game (practice) of basketball. Third, journalists, spectators, referees, and players have different relationships to the game and to the practices that make it up. Players and referees (and eventually owners) do not just report or apply established rules in their discussions, debates, and decisions with respect to the game; they play an active role in refining, adjusting, modifying the concepts and practices that make up the game in the very process of interpreting those arrangements. Journalists and spectators might adopt something more of an indicative mode in these settings, but they too debate whether some act "really" counts as a foul; and their judgments and decisions about this open-ended concept affect the direction of its evolution. To stake out a position on contests surrounding the idea of a foul is to express a judgment about how the game of basketball is properly to be understood and played; the cumulative weight of such debates and judgments over a period of years can have a massive effect on the very structure of the game. Finally, those who enter into such contests must usually have some sense of the historical development of the concept and the function it plays in the game if they are to be in a good position to reinterpret the rather open-ended criteria of a foul in the light of new and unanticipated situations that arise.[3]

The idea of a boycott plays a role in our political and social life resembling in certain respects that played by 'foul' in the game of basketball. Captain Charles Boycott, a nineteenth-century land agent for English landlords with holdings in Ireland, was deliberately and systematically isolated by peasant members of the Irish Land League because of the exorbitant rents he charged and the ruthless collection procedures he followed.   As this strategy became more refined and widespread among the peasantry in Ireland, leaders of the peasant movement began to call concerted actions of this sort Boycotts in the memory of the Captain and of the energy, coordination, and group commitment expressed in that early and locally celebrated effort to punish him through systematic and publicized isolation.   It is noteworthy that the term 'boycott' was coined by peasant strategists to capture in the public mind subtle differences between this particular form of ostracism and other forms practiced for somewhat different purposes against persons in different social positions.   This is exactly what James Redpath and Father John O'Malley, two Irish organizers of the peasantry, had in mind in choosing this word to cover the idea. As Redpath himself recalled,

> I said, "I am bothered about a word." "What is it?," asked Father John. "Well," said I, "when a people ostracize a *land-grabber* we call it *social excommunication,* but we ought to have an *entirely different word* to signify ostracism of a *landlord or a land agent like Boycott.* Ostracism won't do. The peasantry would not know the meaning of the word...." "No," said Father John, "ostracism wouldn't do." He looked down, tapped his big forehead, and said, "How would it do to call it " 'to boycott him.' " [4]

As the notion of a boycott has evolved, it has retained for many something of the initial idea of (1) an organized and (2) economically disadvantaged group, (3) refusing and calling upon others to refuse to associate with or use the products of (4) an employer or other agent (5) whose policies are deemed unduly harsh in order to (6) punish him or coerce him into abandoning those policies.   Others (particularly those who identify less with goals of organized labor) extend the idea to include the concerted effort of any identifiable group to coerce for almost any purpose any other individual or group by means of such refusals.

A political society that employs the idea of a boycott has actions, strategies, judgments, and problems available to it that would be lacking in a society without any such idea in its traditions. When the participants with such an *idea* use one *word* (or phrase) to capture it, the idea itself is likely to become more sharply defined and widely understood: It becomes more convenient to plan mass strategies with or around the shared idea, allowing leaders to coordinate the actions of the membership and to alert and enlist third parties whose cooperation is often essential for its success; it becomes more feasible, when new situations not quite anticipated in the original formulation are faced, to revise the idea in the light of a shared understanding of its point and historical development; and finally, laws can now more readily be formulated to regulate such acts in ways readily understood by the populace.

Because of the role played by boycotts in politics and because a boycott involves a restraint imposed by one group on the activities of others, participants in the system are likely to find that some dimensions of the idea itself are subject to dispute by opposing parties. What, exactly, is to count as a "concerted action" in such cases? Is the possible distinction between pressure applied directly to the principal target ("primary boycotts") and pressure applied to others who could harm the target if they would ("secondary boycotts") worth drawing? If so, how is that difference to be more finely developed, and what differences in legal regulation are called for once the distinction is drawn? Is a "lockout," a "blacklist," a "blackball," or "social excommunication" importantly different from a "boycott"? What is the point of marking off such differences? What of refusing to draw such lines? Members of labor groups, management, political protest groups, state authorities, and professional associations find themselves contesting the internal grammar of 'boycott'. Thus, given our present legal arrangements and the broadly shared presumption against harming *innocent* parties in labor-management disputes, it is important for labor to construe the criteria of a primary boycott (which is legal) broadly and that of a secondary boycott (which is illegal) narrowly, while management typically acquires opposing interests in this respect.

The idea of a boycott helps to constitute a new form of strategy available in our politics, and contests about its proper range of application and the restrictions to which actions within its ambit are properly subject become foci around which some of our political conflicts themselves are built. In such a setting, one who explores the idea and practice of boycotting finds himself adopting the transactional mode in the process of sorting and organizing the issues themselves.

The notion of a boycott in politics, then, is in some respects analogous to that of a foul in basektball. Each notion helps to constitute the practice into which it enters; conflicts within each of these practices often pivot around the criteria appropriate to 'foul' and 'boycott'; and the evolution of each notion contributes to the evolution of the practice of which it is a part. Nonetheless, the analogy is incomplete; the differences deserve some attention.

First, the "games" within which these two ideas are respectively located vary significantly. The relative scope and stakes of basketball and politics are so profoundly different that to push the similarities between them very far is to mock politics. To put it briefly, people playing basketball rarely suffer miserably or face violent death during the game; they seldom find themselves reduced irrevocably to a brutish existence because the game is played one way rather than another. Though conceptual contests and the transactional mode are central to each, persistent losers in politics derive slight comfort from "playing the game."

Second, the participants in basketball *debate* (within certain limits) what acts count as a foul but they *agree* that the point of describing an act as a foul is to assess a penalty. Participants in our politics, though, disagree (within certain limits) both about which acts count as boycotting and what the point of including those elements within that idea properly is. For the interested parties adopt partly opposed *theories* of economics, and supposing for now that the more restricted criteria of 'boycott' offered earlier will suffice, the *consequences* for the economic and social system of workers organizing against employers in this way look different from the vantage point of each theory. It is not simply that 'boycott' has positive connotations for employees and negative connotations for employers, but each views the propriety of acts meeting these conditions differently *because of* differential assessments of the consequences such action will entail over the long run for the entire society.

It is a bit misleading to say that each party has a vested interest in protecting its assessment of boycotts, for it is only as long as his theory seems at least plausible to him that each participant finds warrant for his negative or positive assessment of these actions. One is inclined to say, then, that each party has a vested interest in the theory itself, since the theory is needed to justify the judgment he seeks to sustain about boycotts.[5] But that won't quite do either, for such a judgment is relative to the theoretical orientation from which *it* issues. If I as a laborer came to accept a managerial interpretation of the economy, I would no longer see myself as having a vested interest either in organized labor's justification of boycotts or in convincing a larger public to accept labor's interpretation of the political-economic process. For I would now be strongly motivated to oppose these orientations on the grounds that laborers like me will eventually be victimized by the practices they sanction. Each of the parties, we can say, has historically intelligible *predispositions* in favor of one interpretation or the other. But these predispositions themselves in part explain one's commitment to a particular theory and in part are explicable in terms of the theory one accepts. There are clearly connections between one's social position and one's inclination to accept a set of political judgments, but efforts to *reduce* a group's theoretical commitments to the vested interests it has in them grossly underplay the extent to which the theories people accept help to shape their assessments of what is in their interests.

We can see the clashes over the meaning and point of 'boycott' as one among those many ambiguous and unsettled points of conceptual disharmony that provide the grist of politics. The parties share certain perspectives, but imperfectly, and neither feels obliged by the constraints of available evidence or the import of partly shared standards to concede further ground to the other. The proliferation of such contests within partly shared systems of social interpretation is one of the manifestations of an open polity. But here, too, we must resist the temptation to convert an insight into the connection between conceptual contests and politics into a transcendent claim that we have reached The Criterion of the open polity. For to say that a polity is relatively open or relatively closed is to appeal to a standard of the range within which contests over partly shared concepts can rationally proceed. A polity is judged open or closed relative to that standard, and the accepted standard itself will not be neutral between opposed theories of social and political life. A Marxist would view contests over the idea of a boycott as marginal; the fact that politics flourishes here and languishes with respect to more basic categories of thought and action such as 'class', 'power', and 'freedom' is itself an index of the hegemony of the ruling class over the ideas of the laboring classes. Michael Oakeshott, by contrast, would almost certainly view contests over 'boycott' as a healthy sign of open discourse within shared traditions of civility; to contest more basic ideas would be to convert politics as a limited, adjustive process of mutual accommodation into a grand ideological struggle between parties gripped by mutually illusory ideas. Though both interpretive schemes would converge in their assessment of limiting cases where terrorist control by state officials freezes the terms of public discourse, more solid agreement about the openness or closure of a policy must await agreement about the proper theory within which to interpret political arrangements.[6]

These last considerations relate to a final difference between 'foul' and 'boycott' pertinent to our understanding of the nature of conceptual disputes in politics and of the resources we can potentially draw upon to subject these contests to a measure of rational control. Unlike 'boycott' in its "game," the idea of a foul is evidently *fundamental to* the game of basketball as we now understand it. If the notion of goal-tending or even of playing a zone defense were dropped out of our game of basketball, discernible changes would emerge in the game, but it would still be recognizable as basketball. If the idea of a foul were eliminated, though, the game itself would be radically transformed—we would hardly recognize a similarity between that new game and our former game of basketball. There is, then, a rough hierarchy among those concepts that enter into the game of basketball; and they can be graded in terms of their relative importance to the very constitution of the game.

Ludwig Wittgenstein has suggested that the concepts entering into and helping to shape the way of life of a society can also be graded roughly along a hierarchy of importance and permanence within that life. The internal relationships among such concepts are analogous to those among the current of a river, the more solid bed of sand upon which it rests, and the bank of hard rock that directs its flow along a certain route:

> But I distinguish between the movement of the waters on the riverbed and the shift of the bed itself; though there is not a sharp division of the one from the other.... And the bank of that river consists partly of hard rock, subject to no alteration or only to an imperceptible one, partly of sand, which now in one place now in another gets washed away or deposited.[7]

In the context of our discussion such a hierarchy might be viewed in the following way: Our politics would alter in slight but discernible ways if the distinction between primary and secondary boycotts were to be lost by the participants. If the idea of a boycott itself were to disappear from our politics, a more notable change in the flow of political life would emerge, but the stream itself would not be profoundly affected. Now expunge those ideas to which 'boycott' has close conceptual ties such as 'striking', 'picketing', 'negotiating', 'bargaining', and (perhaps) 'compromise'. Wouldn't we now have to say that the politics of this new society is quite unlike that of our "bargaining culture"? It would be almost as difficult for us to comprehend the political life of that society as it would be for a fourteenth-century priest to grasp the moral life of a society in which the notions of sin, penitence, blasphemy, and soul were absent. Suppose now we confront a society in which the ideas of power, interest, freedom, public, and private are only present in the most vague and casual way. Where these ideas gain no foothold we might say that a society or community exists, but we could not say that it is a community with a developed *political* process. Such communities, apparently, have existed, and the social ties that bind them together are often subtle and deep—so deep, in fact, that they do not need politics to arrive at collective judgments binding on all the members. (But I suppose some idea of *authority* must remain intact in such communities). Finally, imagine what it would be like to confront a population in which our ideas of person and responsibility were completely eliminated from their interactions. Surely we could no longer speak of a society here. For these people would lack the ability to establish relationships that express those complex reactive attitudes of love, trust, hate, resentment, gratitude, indignation, remorse, and contempt; they would lack the very capacities and understanding that form the basis of *social* ties and relationships.

If we can (roughly) order the concepts that enter into social and political life in terms of their comparative importance in constituting that life, it might also be possible to improve our understanding of the sorts of appeals available to one who adopts the transactional mode in probing and exploring those contestable concepts so important to political life. Such conceptual disputes typically involve, of course, a strong component of special pleading on the part of the disputants—each seeks to capture certain elements of an idea for partisan purposes. But in such settings each party also accepts, though often not in *exactly* the same way, a more basic set of understandings pertinent to the contest in question. They confront, say, a new situation that provides the *occasion* for conflict over the grammar of 'power' or 'freedom', but the occasion itself can arise because they disagree about the import of more basic and partly shared ideas for this new, unanticipated setting. When the notion at issue is conceptually connected to shared ideas about persons and responsibility, the shared, more fundamental ideas provide a common court of appeal to which the conflict can be brought and within the confines of which the disagreement can be subjected to a measure of rational control. There are, I want to suggest, limits of rationality within which conceptual contests in politics proceed, though the availability of these limits does not ensure that each party will recognize them nor that all who do acknowledge them will be forced to accept a *single* interpretation of each contested concept.

Again, to say that partly shared rules at one level can help to set limits to conceptual contests at other levels, does not mean that these rules are always sufficient to dissolve such contests completely. Thus the connection between our notion of freedom and our ideas about responsibility ensures that no one who reflects on that connection will argue seriously that a person is unfree if he is physically unable to fly. Different readings of the criteria of responsibility might support different readings of 'freedom', but the connection nevertheless establishes outer limits to the contests. If this connection between freedom and responsibility were somehow to be abrogated completely, there would no longer be any *point* in drawing such a line between unfreedom and natural inability—*there would neither be appeals available to cope with contests about 'freedom' nor a point or occasion for the contests in the first place.*

But if our shared ideas about persons and responsibility play such an important role in conceptual contests, what status do these basic ideas have? Surely they are not singularly immune to challenge, revision, contests. We know, for instance, that such ideas vary somewhat across societies and even from person to person and class to class within the same society. We also know that some contemporary thinkers would completely eliminate these ideas from social science and social life; behaviorists treat such commitments as superstitions to be transcended by the advance of contemporary science. B. F. Skinner has argued, for instance, that we are no more justified in holding a person responsible for whispering in church than we are for coughing in church: "There are variables which are responsible for whispering as well as coughing, and these may be just as inexorable. When we recognize this, we are likely to drop the notion of responsibility altogether. . . ." [8] Are these ideas so variable and so inherently contestable, then, that they cannot provide any foothold of the sort we seek? I think not. In what follows I will not seek to establish my position in detail. My purpose, rather, is to specify my assumptions with respect to the relevant issues and to identify and endorse a contemporary literature that provides them with philosophical support.

Though the standards of responsibility vary within society and across societies, there is a central core to the idea, which seems to be embodied to some degree and *in some spheres* in the life of every society. Some societies, by comparison to ours, exhibit a strong propensity to hold collectives responsible where we would attribute responsibility instead to an individual. Some invoke strict liability over a broad sphere of conduct, and some attribute responsibility to inanimate objects (animism) in a manner we reserve for persons. But some aspects of these variations are explicable by the fact that they attribute characteristics to collectives and things that we attribute most fully to persons, less strictly to collectives, and never to things. In these cases, it is less that we disagree on the criteria of responsibility (though that is involved to some degree) than that we disagree on the extent to which the behavior of things and collectives meet those criteria. It is generally agreed that any agents capable of forming intentions, of deliberately shaping their conduct to rules, of appreciating the significance of their actions for others, and of exercising self-restraint are the sorts of agents worthy of being held responsible for conduct that fails to live up to expected standards. The inhabitants of all societies tacitly distinguish at some point between a reflex action and a purposive action and between having something happen to one and doing something; and all embody in their institutions the view that persons are capable of acting purposively and worthy thereby of being held responsible for a range of conduct. The variations, important as they are, build upon this common understanding.[9]

Similarly, within contemporary industrial society, that participants tacitly share these assumptions to some great extent is manifested in our common propensities to love, resent, trust, hate, and respect other persons. For it is because we hold persons to share this range of capacities and potentialities that we view each other as able to enter into such relationships and to express such reactive attitudes. I resent you because I believe that you deliberately or thoughtlessly have said things to my friend that lower me in his esteem; my resentment grows as I decide that nothing I have done to you in the past justifies your action. These beliefs about your conduct, and thus about your capacities, enter into my very feeling of resentment; if someone were to convince me either that you were not the kind of being who possesses the requisite capacities (perhaps you are a parrot) or that in this particular case you could not have known the import of your comments, my feeling of resentment itself would dissipate. I might still feel dismayed by the result, but would no longer *resent* you because certain beliefs about your intentions and capacity for restraint are essential to the reactive attitude of resentment itself; they are part of its meaning. And this is true of a vast range of reactive attitudes. To establish social relationships and to express reactive attitudes is to adopt such a set of assumptions about the capacities of the agents who enter into them. It is to treat them as agents capable of acting responsibly and of being held responsible for activities that fall below (or rise above) an expected norm.

We do disagree to some extent about the boundaries of these ideas and to a greater extent about the spheres of life in which they appropriately apply. Thus certain psychiatrists may treat a mental patient falling within a particular classification as if he lacked some of these characteristics. The patient is handled, managed, and controlled, and perhaps one feels pity for him; but he is not thought of as an agent capable of being befriended, respected, loved, hated, or resented. To resent the conduct of a schizophrenic would be, on this view, to reflect faulty assumptions about his capacities to formulate objectives and to control his feelings; it would be to treat him as a responsible agent when he lacks the requisite capacities.

Critics of such an orientation, though, argue that schizophrenia is a *rational* response by the patient to an intolerable and inescapable set of pressures to which he has been subjected. The staff's treatment of patients in mental institutions, according to these critics, is part of the patient's problem, for it embodies a view of him, and of the therapy appropriate to him, that further alienates him from social life. In R. D. Laing's view, the treatment of patients implied by orthodox definitions of schizophrenia contributes to "the illness one is purporting to cure." [10]

These proponents of different theories of psychiatry generally agree, at least tacitly, in their assumptions about the characteristics of persons and the standards of responsibility appropriate in the daily life of healthy persons, but they disagree about the propriety of those assumptions and standards with respect to a range of mental patients. When such a condition exists, the contests over ideas such as 'paranoia', 'schizophrenia', and 'psychosis' have a texture very much like that we have identified with respect to key concepts in politics. To revise assumptions about the characteristics of these mental patients would be to require changes in a whole set of concepts by which these patients have been understood and through which the staff has established relationships with them. I want to say, to overschematize the point, that these conceptual debates reflect tacit agreement over the norms of responsibility appropriate to ordinary persons in ordinary contexts but disagreement over the extent to which those norms are applicable to another sphere of life, that of relationships between staff and mental patients. And that latent agreement in the first sphere provides some common ground, I will suggest, for the critical assessment of alternative commitments in the second." [11]

Some contemporary philosophers contest in an interesting way the view that such partly shared norms can provide a justifiable court of common appeal. Recent work in linguistic philosophy, they concede, has exposed the extent to which this shared understanding of persons and responsibility is deeply embedded in our language and relationships. They concede as well that behaviorists like B. F. Skinner implicitly embody in their everyday relationships some of the very norms of responsibility their theories explicitly lead them to repudiate. Such behaviorists do not consistently adhere to their own theories.

These critics agree, in effect, that deep and persistent dimensions of our social relationships have been brought to a point of awareness through recent work in linguistic philosophy and that previous efforts to formulate a language for social relationships or social inquiry that eliminates these presuppositions have simply failed. But, the critics then claim, the practitioners of "ordinary language" analysis ultimately claim too much for their work; they unjustifiably assume that commitments persistently embodied in the "common idioms" of everyday life are thereby true. The anthropomorphic assumptions of one era can be displaced by the advance of science in the next. And our current assumptions about persons and responsibility could, and probably will, be displaced by a better theory in the future. Because this is true, these shared judgments stand as mere conventions that happen to be accepted tacitly by most people in our society. P. K. Feyerabend can stand as a strong proponent of such a view:

> Such idioms are adapted not to *facts* but to *beliefs*. If these beliefs are widely accepted; if they are intimately connected with fears and hopes of the community in which they occur; if they are defended and reinforced with the help of powerful institutions; if one's whole life is somehow carried out in accordance with them—then the language representing them will be regarded as most successful. At the same time it is clear that the question of the truth of the beliefs has not been touched.[12]

According to Feyerabend, our shared distinction between the actions of persons and the movements of things, thoroughly embedded as it is in our social life, may well be displaced by a materialistic theory that shows the former to be assimilable to the latter.

I wish to endorse P. F. Strawson's view that such a displacement is not to be expected. Contests over the exact dimensions of these ideas can be anticipated, but these are, nonetheless, "categories and concepts which in their most fundamental character, change not at all."[13] Such commitments must remain intact in at least some spheres of social life, not simply because people happen to internalize them but because they are essential to social life as such. Without a range of relationships and reactive attitudes such as resentment and gratitude, trust and friendship, indignation and respect, guilt and remorse, social life itself could not persist. And without something like our basic ideas about persons and responsibility those relationships and attitudes could find no grounding. In Strawson's words, our "human commitment to participation in ordinary interpersonal relationships is, I think, too thoroughgoing and deeply rooted for us to take seriously the thought that a general theoretical conviction might so change our world that in it, there were no longer any such things as interpersonal relationships as we normally understand them." [14]

Perhaps this gloss and endorsement of Strawson's argument is sufficient to clarify at least the sorts of considerations that incline me to view our imperfectly shared ideas about persons and responsibility as more than mere conventions susceptible to radical change. These are not commitments we know to be true but postulates we necessarily accept in at least some spheres of daily life.

In our society, I wish to say, those who disagree about the grammar of key political concepts also share, if tacitly, a range of commitments about persons and responsibility. Some aspects of those shared commitments reflect conventions relative to our social life, while the central core reflects conventions relative to social life as such. A variety of factors intervene between our shared acceptance of these general commitments and our exploration of their implications for various dimensions of social life such as the family, the workplace, penal institutions, mental institutions, and political life. One must take into account, for instance, differences in the purposes and functions of each sphere, possible differences in the characteristics of the agents involved in each, differences in the extent to which each shapes the practices of the others, and so on. Nonetheless, some of the notions that enter into these latter dimensions of social life bear close conceptual connections to our shared ideas about persons and responsibility. In political life this is true of such notions as 'interest', 'power', 'freedom', and 'politics' itself. It is partly because we share the pertinent norms of responsibility *imperfectly* that contests arise with respect to such political concepts, and it is because we *share* these norms imperfectly that we are provided with some common leverage for limiting the range within which these contests can rationally proceed. Finally, it is because we acknowledge these basic ideas that we are so interested in the outcomes of the conceptual contests in politics; *for to revise one of these latter concepts significantly is to reformulate the standards of responsibility participants in politics are expected to meet.* It is to this last claim that we shall now turn.

POLITICS AND RESPONSIBILITY

Consider two societies inhabiting the same geographic area but separated by 150 years of history. In one the rifle is the ultimate weapon, the farm and the small shop constitute the typical economic units, and the local community is the hub around which social and political life is organized. Here many decisions that carry consequences for the lives of individuals are quite readily identifiable by the persons themselves. Sometimes it is difficult to get the shopkeeper or the local sheriff to *assume* responsibility for the effects of his decisions on others, but it is typically not too difficult to identify agents as responsible for the benefits or burdens received by others.

In the second, more familiar, society the nuclear device is the ultimate weapon; to produce it, to guard the secrets of its design, and to regulate its use, a complex organization is required. The large corporation is the economic unit of consequence; its internal and external transactions, international in scope, are also coordinated through a vast bureaucratic complex. The nation-state is the fundamental political unit; it too is highly centralized, with multiple bureaucratic organizations that mediate the web of relationships between it and its citizens. In such a society the troubles people have, except for those rooted simply in the idiosyncracies of their *personal* biographies, are connected by complex chains to institutional policies and practices beyond the individual's reach and easy comprehension. Since the troubled ones often cannot locate the structural sources of their problems, potential political grievances and public issues remain unstated and undebated. For one can have *grievances* only against some individual, group, or institution; if no viable target can be identified, the grievance itself dissipates into vague anxiety or unfocused discontent. Thus a breadwinner wonders why he cannot find a job; a white-collar worker struggles to control a "drinking problem"; a consumer incomprehensibly fails to find satisfaction in the expansion of his consumptive opportunities; a housewife feels vaguely depressed much of the time. When the connections between such troubles and the practices of public and private institutions go undetected by the victim or unperceived by the relevant institutional elites, the political life of the society itself misfires. We encounter a politics of crisis or a politics of resignation, but we do not find sustained debate and conflict over issues that might connect these troubles to their sources in the practices of our dominant institutions.

Many will recognize the above as a highly abbreviated gloss of the characterization by C. Wright Mills of political life in modern American society.[15] The terms of comparison between the society of scattered shops and communities and modern bureaucratic society are his as well.[16] I wish only to add (or perhaps to emphasize) that a lag in conceptual development in the historical transition from the first society to the second contributes to the contemporary gap between the troubles people have and the paucity of political movements and publicly debated issues that speak to them.

It is quite true that a certain discrepancy between private troubles and public issues must inevitably emerge in the course of a modern, bureaucratic, stratified society's development. But it is also true, I believe, that in our society the conceptual lag accompanying that development, while itself in need of explanation,[17] has made its own contribution to our current loss of political moorings. Concepts of power, interests, freedom, politics, public, and private, which may have been tolerably pertinent to one era, can create disorientation when carried into another with only minimal change. This is particularly true of those notions bearing close conceptual connections to our norms of responsibility. If part of the point in saying that A has power over B is to *charge* A with closing B's options unnecessarily, it may turn out that the *criteria* appropriate to establishing such a charge in the society of the local shopkeeper are rather different from those appropriate to the society of the corporate manager.

To reform successfully a notion embedded in our political life that bears close conceptual ties to our basic ideas of responsibility is to infuse the norms of responsibility themselves more deeply into the political practices of modern society. Debates over the grammar appropriate to such concepts are at root debates over the extent to which such infusions are justified. Such debates, certainly, are difficult enough to resolve. But a mind stuck in the grooves of a bankrupt positivism is unlikely to grasp the import of these debates; the intense commitment and passion expressed by the partisans to such conflict must remain vaguely mysterious to it. By moving beyond such confining presuppositions we have already seen how conceptual revision can contribute to change in the structure of a game or a political system. We must now exemplify more closely how revision of a concept with close links to our basic norms of responsibility can insinuate these norms themselves more deeply into the fiber of our politics.

In the society of small shopkeepers, we shall suppose, racism meant an attitude of superiority over another group built upon the false belief that the group had markedly inferior biological capacities. To charge a person with racism in this setting is to say that his conduct manifests such assumptions, that he is in a position to know that these assumptions are false, and that his failure to revise his assumptions and conduct is culpable. Suppose this idea of racism is introduced in unrevised form into the life of a stratified, bureaucratic society. And suppose it turns out that most white managerial elites do not personally hold these exact views, but that, in ways unintended and only vaguely noted by them, the policies of their organizations significantly freeze blacks out of job opportunities, promotion chances, educational possibilities, lines of credit, access to the cultural life of the dominant society, and so on. Since these whites are not "racist," since, that is, their policies are not informed by personal hatred of blacks deemed to be inferior, the effects of these policies are seen to be remote or impersonal; they stand (to the elites) as *facts* first to be ignored and then to be labeled "unfortunate," not as the *consequences* of policy decisions for which the elites themselves are collectively responsible. And for a time many blacks may vaguely share this understanding.

Suppose that a militant group of black activists accuses the elites of these organizations of "institutional racism." Their intent, of course, is to retain the culpability already attached to 'racism', to revise the old requirement that 'racist' actions with adverse consequences for blacks must reflect personal prejudices, and to apply the culpability for such consequences to bureaucratic organizations rather than merely to individuals. To adopt this idea is to hold managerial elites responsible for the discriminatory consequences of their institutional policies. When such consequences are so pervasive and so profoundly injurious to the victims, when the pertinent elites are in a position to comprehend these consequences if they would only strive to do so, and when alternative policies open to them could rectify this situation significantly, failure to reassess these consequences and to revise policies in the light of the reassessment constitutes institutional negligence—hence institutional racism. That is the argument. Moreover, those individuals who passively acquiesce in roles that sustain such policies of institutional racism are culpable until they reassess the implications of adhering to such role expectations and until they advance criticism and pressure within their organizations to revise the policies. Responsibility, it is charged, applies in some degree to the individual's role acceptance in the workplace as well as to the more personalized thought and action he takes outside of bureaucratic structures.

Those who accept this reasoning will charge the pertinent organizations with institutional racism, and because the charge bears a purported relation to larger ideas of responsibility accepted by all, the elites find themselves, provided the pressure against them is maintained and publicized, in a situation where they must defeat the claim or be convicted of hypocrisy.

Their immediate response is one of incomprehension: They act as though the blacks are misapplying the old concept of racism to a new and different situation. "We are not prejudiced," they say. But as the charge is reiterated forcefully and backed by militant actions that ensure that the message will be received by wider publics, the message itself becomes more clear. And now the defensive elites argue that it is inappropriate to hold an *organization* responsible for policy consequences *unintended* by its members and only marginally subject to their control.

At this stage an interesting shift in the terms of discourse emerges. While debates can reasonably continue about the legitimacy of holding elites collectively responsible for past oversights ("no group could reasonably be expected to take these considerations into account," and so on), *the very introduction of the idea of institutional racism into political life makes these pleas less and less defensible for present and future policies.* For now the connections between the policies and the consequences are sharply and publicly drawn; the oversights that might have excused the elites in the past are no longer possible; and if current elites continue to acquiesce passively in old roles and patterns of policy, they are now clearly guilty of bad faith. The introduction of the idea into public discourse has shifted the burden of evidence away from the blacks and toward the elites, and thus the balance of political pressures has shifted perceptibly too. 'Institutional racism' remains a contested concept—its exact lines of demarcation are open to intense dispute—but there are now circumstances in which all of those who do not remain (or do not want to be considered) old-fashioned racists must agree that an institution's failure to revise former policies with respect to blacks properly subjects it to public control and constraint.

I do not wish to say that the introduction of this concept resolves the pertinent issues in favor of the challenging group. It does, though, require challenged elites, previously immune to critical surveillance of their performance on this score, to respond in some way to new pressures and expectations created by the revision. Depending on a variety of circumstances, a challenged elite may respond by reforming its hiring practices, by giving symbolic assurances to the aggrieved groups and to (especially) its allies while resisting significant policy change,[18] by seeking to undermine the public credibility of leading critics, by intimidating and repressing leading challengers, or by instituting any combination of these responses. Indeed, anyone familiar with the history of repression against dissident movements in the United States must anticipate that movements that massively challenge prevailing practices and expectations will be met by a variety of repressive responses.[19]

Conceptual revision is not, then, a sufficient condition of political change, but it is indispensable to significant political change. It is part of that process by which events once considered mere facts come to be seen as the outcomes of a political process and thereby as properly subject to public debate and the play of pressure. In our example of the progressive, if incomplete, incorporation of the idea of institutional racism into political life, a conceptual contest was apparent at the beginning and the end of the process. But the contours of that contest were modified as the debate continued, and shifts in the distribution of political pressures and public expectations accompanied this development. Without the militance of activists this idea could not have forced its way into the system, but without the introduction of the idea, connected as it is to more basic norms of responsibility, the militants could not have exerted effective pressure on established elites.

The new concept, as it were, embodies a new argument built in part upon old and familiar ideas of racism and responsibility. To *employ* the new concept in political life is to accept the argument it expresses; to be the institutional *recipient* of the argument is to find certain pleas and excuses available in the past foreclosed in the future.

Conceptual revision is involved in any political strategy that aims at reconstituting social life in modest or in radical ways. Without forgetting that the process of conceptual revision does not work in isolation from other factors it is nevertheless a profoundly important dimension of politics itself. More generally, without a proliferation of conceptual contests, politics, with its complex blend of pressure bounded by civility, its tensions, and its relatively open horizons, would wither or dissipate.

When these points are established we can comprehend more thoroughly the political implications of those conceptual disputes that mark disciplinary debates within and among the academic professions of political science, sociology, and economics.

Social scientists are not so influential that their conceptual decisions inevitably affect the practices of the polity. But the social scientist's limited influence does not justify his lack of attention to the political import of the conceptual contours commonly accepted within his profession and his society. If the understanding of conceptual contests in politics elaborated here is at all correct, then the social scientist has an obligation to *endorse* those ideas that he thinks would help to nourish a politics of responsibility were they to be incorporated into the practices of our polity. One can and must debate just what interpretations of key social and political concepts are worthy of such endorsement, but to deny any intellectual responsibility in this area is to falsify the connection between such contests and the constitution of social and political life.

I would like to have the formulations of 'power', 'interests', 'freedom', and 'politics' offered in this volume assessed in the light of this understanding of conceptual contests and of the linkages between conceptual revision and political change. If one agrees that there are such connections, it is not sufficient, when an interpretation of a concept is offered, to ask, Does this proposal correctly capture prevailing usage? Other questions become pertinent. For example: What if a large group of social scientists and journalists insisted publicly upon interpreting our political life within the frame of these concepts? How would the self-images and the conduct of privileged elites, ordinary citizens, and social outcasts then be affected? What if certain segments of the population began to act as if these proposed revisions were actually warranted? Would a shift in the system of pressures and mutual expectations emerge? What if most segments of society eventually came to accept such conceptual revisions and the arguments they embody?

My commitment to particular positions on the various conceptual contests we have explored rests finally on the belief, to state it with some brevity, that the successful incorporation of these revisions would help to weave authentic norms of responsibility and a respect for persons more tightly into the fabric of the politics of a modern, bureaucratic, stratified society.

These judgments, as I understand and advance them, are inherently controversial responses to unavoidable issues of political thought and action. Such a judgment is inherently *controversial*, because, first, it projects outcomes into a hypothetical future and second, it appeals for support to more basic standards of responsibility that are imperfectly shared by the disputants. We are dealing here with controversies, though, and not merely with differences unsusceptible to reconsideration and possible revision through debate and deliberation. For those involved do have some common ground to stand on, even if the footing is insecure. Those committed to probing the limits of reasoned discourse have ample room for exploration.

The controversies, moreover, are *unavoidable* for anyone who seeks to comprehend our politics and who is willing to announce his findings to us. For one can hardly study our politics without staking out a position on some of these contested concepts, and the position one endorses will not be neutral in its political import.[20] To enunciate a public position on these issues is to implicate oneself to some degree in our politics.

In the political sphere, intellectual work and political work, embodying somewhat different standards of craftsmanship and excellence, are nevertheless bound intimately together. One devoted to either enterprise will benefit from an enhanced understanding of his essential involvement in the other.

NOTES

1. Henry Kariel, "Neither Sticks Nor Stones," *Politics and Society* (Winter 1973):183.

2. Ibid., p. 189.

3. Think of an 8-foot-tall player who is strong and very agile. If new understandings are not reached about permissible ways to guard him, the game will soon become a one-man game. Debates will now concern the extent to which that outcome is acceptable, and people will take up sides. The example is not fanciful, for basketball buffs know that the permissible defenses one could adopt against a center were tacitly broadened after Wilt Chamberlain joined the professional ranks. Here the effort was to change the criteria of a foul so as to *preserve* the strategies and necessity for team effort that had evolved over the years. Spectators played an important role in this revision, for they might not have remained so interested in a game in which one figure became so dominant.

4. The conversation as reported by Redpath to Harry Laidler in *Boycotts and the Labor Struggle* (New York: Russell and Russell, 1913), p. 23; my emphasis.

5. One of the points in our earlier discussion of the breakdown of the analytic-synthetic dichotomy was to show that there is no sharp demarcation between those elements that are part of a concept and those that are part of the theory in which it moves. Why, then, don't we interpret the opposing views about the extent to which boycotts are justifiable simply as conceptual contests? Such an interpretation would miss the fact, I think, that while labor would doubtless prefer a formulation of 'boycott' that sets sufficient qualifying conditions around the practice to *justify* it in most circumstances in which those conditions were met, it *accepts* a broader formulation of the notion today. In that broader formulation some boycotts, justifiable within labor's interpretation of the economic system, are not justified given the interpretation of other groups. This result will not help those who wish to conclude that 'boycott' is *simply* a descriptive concept. For part of the point in gathering these elements together in the broad idea is to offer prima facie reasons against such acts of *restraint* by one group against another. Labor, to

put it briefly, advances a theory of the economy which goes some distance toward overriding this initial presumption in many instances while the groups opposing it offer theories that tighten and extend the presumption. The example, though, does help us to see why social theorists have been tempted to categorize concepts contested along these lines simply as "descriptive" notions.

6. The connection between conceptual contests and politics is explored insightfully by J. G. A. Pocock, "Verbalizing a Political Act," *Political Theory* (February 1973):27–45. He thinks "language is an effective medium for political communication and action . . . , not because it is neutral but because it is relatively uncontrollable and so hard to monopolize." p. 35. I would only add that the language of our politics seems to me to be less open and more controlled than Pocock imagines. The illusory quest within the social sciences for a neutral, antiseptic language of politics makes its contribution to that closure, but its influence is outstripped in effectiveness by the periodic recurrence of official repression against those dissident ideological movements that threaten to gain a foothold within the society. Pocock and I agree, I think, about the connection between language and politics but disagree about the appropriate theoretical framework within which to appreciate this connection. For a useful corrective, see Herbert Marcuse, "Repressive Tolerance," in Robert Paul Wolff, Barrington Moore, and Herbert Marcuse, *A Critique of Pure Tolerance* (Boston: Beacon Press, 1965), pp. 81–118. The limiting case, in which public discourse is frozen through terroristic control, is explored by Alasdair MacIntyre, "A Mistake About Causality in Social Science," in *Philosophy, Politics, and Society,* eds. Peter Laslett and W. G. Runciman (Oxford: Basil Blackwell, 1967), pp. 48–70.

7. Ludwig Wittgenstein, *On Certainty* (1922; New York: Harper Torchbooks, 1969), p. 15e. This metaphor suggests that Wittgenstein might be critical of the extreme conventionalism Peter Winch advances in his name. Underneath the shifting sands of convention is a hard rock that changes very slowly and sets limits to these shifts. For an insightful discussion of Wittgenstein's elucidation of 'convention' and a resultant critique of Winch, see Hannah Pitkin, *Wittgenstein and Justice* (Berkeley: University of California Press, 1972), especially chs. 6, 11, 12.

8. B. F. Skinner, *Science and Human Behavior* (New York: Free Press, 1953), pp. 115–16.

9. Perhaps the single best statement of what these core ideas involve is offered by Herbert Morris, "Persons and Punishment," *The Monist* (Fall 1968):471–501. See Joel Feinberg, "Action and Responsibility," in *The Philosophy of Action*, ed. Alan White (New York: Oxford University Press, 1968), pp. 95–119, for discussion of differences among such related ideas as "being responsible for" and "being liable for."

10. R. D. Laing, *The Politics of the Family* (New York: Vintage Books, 1969), p. 42. Erving Goffman examines the dehumanizing treatment of such patients in *Asylums* (New York: Anchor Books, 1961). Bruno Bettelheim shows how the dehumanizing treatment of ordinary people in concentration camps can induce 'schizophrenia' in *The Informed Heart* (Glencoe, Ill.: Free Press, 1960). And George Kateb explores the import of extending such attitudes to new dimensions of modern life in "The Next Stage of Nihilism," *Social Research* (Autumn 1973):468–80.

11. Laing, certainly, would not contend that we should hold people who have been trapped in a "double bind" (for instance, schizophrenics) responsible in exactly the same way we do people who have not, but that the former should not be treated as though they have lost those characteristics most central to persons. We always make adjustments for special circumstances, even with ordinary people living through ordinary experiences. Our use of 'mistake' and 'accident' as excuse words symbolizes this shared understanding. His point is that one caught within a double bind can be understood to have responded rationally to an impossible situation, and that therapists can start to help him by comprehending his situation as he does. The patient's family setting, say, has created binds similar to those Bettelheim sees generated by Nazi concentration camps; and his response is similar to that of a prisoner in such a camp.

12. P. K. Feyerabend, "Materialism and the Mind-Body Problem," *The Review of Metaphysics* (June 1963):51–52. For a very thoughtful critique of Feyerabend's view, see Richard Bernstein, *Praxis and Action* (Philadelphia: University of Pennsylvania Press, 1971). That book in turn is subjected to an illuminating, if friendly, critique in Alasdair MacIntyre, "Praxis and Action," *Review of Metaphysics* (June 1972):737–44.

13. *Individuals: An Essay in Descriptive Metaphysics* (New York: Anchor Books, 1959), xiv.

14. P. F. Strawson, "Freedom and Resentment," in *Studies in the Philosophy of Thought and Action,* ed. P. F. Strawson (New York: Oxford University Press, 1968), p. 82. Much more must be said to connect these considerations to something called "the moral point of view," but I agree with Strawson's view that it is barely more than a "conceptual possibility" for one to manifest the personal reactive attitudes toward others to a high degree (for example, resentment) while showing no inclination to manifest their "vicarious analogues" (for instance, indignation) or to apply similar standards to one's own conduct (say, sense of obligation, guilt). For an argument that does connect such considerations to a broader statement about the moral point of view, see Stuart Hampshire, *Morality and Pessimism* (Cambridge: Cambridge University Press, 1973). If I had to pick one study that best reflects my views about the moral point of view, it would be Hampshire's.

15. This thesis permeates all of Mills's work, but a representative statement can be found in his *The Sociological Imagination* (New York: Oxford University Press, 1959).

16. One could fruitfully pose other terms of comparison as well, such as that between (some version of) a capitalist society and (some version of) a socialist system. Some of Mills's radical critics have suggested his analysis is less profound than it could be because he selected the former terms and ignored the latter. There is something to that position, but let me say something in defense of this contrast model. It gives some aid in trying to capture the historical evolution of central concepts of politics *within* a given culture. Moreover, there is insight in Mills's argument that modern capitalist and socialist regimes share some of the same deficiencies in identifying "responsibility for events as decisions." For interesting comparisons between market and command economies that move toward rectifying the restrictions flowing from the terms of comparison adopted here, see Frank Parkin, *Class Inequality and Political Order: Social Stratification in Capitalist and Communist Societies* (New York: Praeger, 1971).

17. For the sort of explanation I have in mind, see Ernest Gellner, "Concepts and Society," in *Rationality,* ed. Bryan Wilson (New York: Harper Torchbooks, 1970), 18–49.

18. For an illuminating statement of how symbolic reassurance can serve as a cover for refusal to implement policy changes, see Murray Edelman, *The Symbolic Uses of Politics* (Urbana: University of Illinois Press, 1967).

19. For a valuable case study of the use of legal instruments to repress dissent within a university, see Harry Blaine and David Kettler, "Law as a Political Weapon," *Politics and Society* (August 1971):479–526. With respect to our example of "institutional racism' it is relevant to point out that between May 2, 1967, and the end of 1969, 768 Black Panther members were arrested in the United States. See Alan Wolfe, *The Seamy Side of Democracy* (New York: David McKay, 1973) for a history of officially sanctioned repression in America.

20. It should be noted that nothing I have said denies that two investigators who share a set of concepts completely might not reach somewhat different conclusions about the same topic of study. That is an obvious possibility and numerous studies of research methodology seek to devise neutral tests to resolve such disagreements. We are concerned, though, with situations in which two investigators accept somewhat different boundaries for a set of concepts brought to study "the same" social phenomena. I discuss this and related matters further in "Theoretical Self-Consciousness," *Polity* (Fall 1973):5–35.

6

The Politics of Discourse

POLITICS AND COUNTER-EXAMPLES

The desire to expunge contestability from the terms of political inquiry expresses a wish to escape politics. It emerges either as a desire to rationalize public life, placing a set of ambiguities and contestable orientations under the control of a settled system of understandings and priorities, or as a quest to moralize public life thoroughly, bringing all citizens under the control of a consensus which makes politics marginal and unimportant. Since neither of these orientations is easy to support explicitly today, they typically emerge as methodological themes disconnected from an account of their political implications. By depreciating politics at the level of theory, a politics of depoliticization is covertly endorsed in public life.

This book was designed to dissolve the appearance of neutrality in conceptual analysis, to help render political discourse more self-reflective by bringing out contestable moral and political perspectives lodged in the language of politics. It is a text on the language of politics and the politics of language. There are adjustments I would now make in the readings of "power", "interests", and "freedom" presented in this text, but they are revisions which continue to reflect its basic thesis. Rather than concentrating on those marginal changes, I will here defend, clarify and revise modestly the larger perspective which informs the text itself.

Consider "power". My account of the concept power moves within an expressivist philosophy of language. That is, rather than treating concepts merely as vehicles to designate objects or represent the world as it is in itself, I have tried to delineate the point of view from which power is formed in our way of life, the standards and judgments, presumptions and prohibitions, expressed in the language of power. If we examine the concepts of persuasion, coercion, force, offer, bribe, deterrence, terror, etc., we see that this family of concepts is rooted in a more basic set of ideas about ourselves as agents capable of autonomous action, self-restraint and coherence, and worthy, because of these capacities, to be treated as responsible agents. In a society where such a conception of

213

self and responsibility has achieved hegemony, the language of social relations will express these deeper conceptions; it will specify their meanings in particular contexts; it will differentiate relationships and actions which honor these standards from those which do not. Its criteria of differentiation will be shaped, in part, by standards of agency and responsibility. Relations, for instance, which inhibit the capacity for autonomous judgment will be differentiated from those which foster it, and those which limit the opportunity to act upon one's own judgment will be distinguished from those which encourage such action. Thus, we distinguish between persuasion and manipulation and between an offer and a threat. Unless our discourse included discriminations of this sort (of course, it houses discriminations along many other dimensions as well), we could not articulate the conception of self and responsibility inscribed in our social practices. More pertinently, if those differentiations were thoroughly absent from the terms of our discourse the conception of self and responsibility they express would be absent from our lives as well.

The language of power in modern life doubtless has more than one use, but it is intimately linked to the conception of self and responsibility operative in that life. Contests over the grammar of power involve debates over the best way to specify these root conceptions or, more fundamentally, the defensibility of the root conceptions themselves. In bringing out linkages between the concept 'power over' and responsibility, I am trying to bring out a rationale implicit in the distinctions we make between relations of power and other social relations. I am also trying to explain why, constituted as we are, we concentrate on a particular set of distinctions in this domain and ignore a much larger set which might be appropriate to us if we were constituted differently. I have suggested, therefore, that the exercise of power over another involves the limiting or impairing of the recipient's capacity for choice or action in some respect and that before such effects are seen as the "manifestation of some person's or collectivity's power over the recipient, there must be some reasons to hold the bidder responsible for the limitation" (p. 97). I have challenged those who claim that there is no linkage between our conception of power and our assessments of responsibility to offer an account of the forms of power (manipulation, coercion, deterrence, etc.) which accounts for their shape and moral import without appealing to our underlying conceptions of agency and responsibility.

Andrew Reeve, in a thought provoking essay, has challenged this interpretation.[1] He agrees that conceptions of power built around the *intentions* of the bidder are too restrictive to capture the actual and proper grammar of the concept; he believes as well that proposals merely to drop the intentionality criterion generate a concept of power so broad that it loses its ability to do serious work. He does not indicate, however, *why* intention is too restrictive or the alternative too broad. He then goes on to argue that the criterion of responsibility neither captures the range of relations covered by concept of 'power over' nor allows us to discern the rationale implicit within the criteria of inclusion and exclusion constituting the concept 'power over'.

Reeve proceeds by counter-example, delineating cases which seem intuitively to fall inside or outside the orbit of 'power over', in ways which contradict the judgment sustained by the criterion of responsibility. An examination of his counter-examples will help to bring out presuppositions, strengths and limits residing in this mode of argumentation.

First, Reeve believes that I restrict power (I will usually avoid the term 'power over', even though it is the concept to be examined) to those cases where A in some way limits B's ability to form or act upon B's desires, wishes or obligations. "This has the rather odd consequence, however, that to introduce or fail to remove a constraint will act as evidence of the existence of power, but actually to remove a constraint which B faces, will not."[2] But the conception I have offered does not have that implication at all. It is clear (I hope) that the term 'power to' covers the ability to achieve some outcome even against difficult odds and even in situations where power over others is essential to the achievement. But can one, on my reading, exercise power over another by removing a constraint? Certainly. A might limit B's capacity for action in one respect and in doing so remove burdens or limits facing B in another. A might, for instance, obstruct B's desires and thereby enhance B's ability to realize particular interests. Moreover, in some of these instances we may conclude that A's exercise of power over B is legitimate. Hence the discussion of legitimate power in the text.[3]

The connections among agency, power and responsibility do not mean that the exercise of power over agents is never justified, merely that our commitment to treat persons as agents introduces a presumption, expressed in the grammar of 'power', against the imposition of limits or constraints on others. The initial presumption might be overridden, most importantly, perhaps, when a set of limitations help to foster the capacity for agency itself. The "oddness" Reeve discerns in my characterization of power dissolves when this dimension is included, but another question remains unanswered: what rationale or set of standards does Reeve invoke when he assessed a reading of power as odd, inappropriate or confused? Is ordinary language assumed to provide rational and sufficient criteria as it now stands or is it to be supplemented by some other court of appeal?

Reeve's second counter-example speaks to the connection between assessments of responsibility and assessments of harm to the recipient. Some undesired effects are normally not judged to be harmful and some harmful effects are not normally judged to be the responsibility of agents knowingly entangled in the processes which generate them. For example:

> If A is taking an examination in which the top 10 percent pass, and does as well as he can, knowing that this will impose a disbenefit on weaker candidates, he is Connolly-responsible for a restriction on them, and has power over them.[4]

This judgment, Reeve adds, goes against our normal intuitions.

Consider a counter to the counter-example. Suppose that A is a member of a privileged minority, that he is taking an examination especially geared to his background and training, that the examination is designed to select a small number of employees from a larger candidate pool, that the examination questions are not linked closely to the skills actually appropriate to the job assignment, and that the favored examinees are, or easily could be, aware of these conditions. I would say that the examinees (along with the authors of the examination) share responsibility for a limitation imposed upon those excluded and that they exercise power over the excluded members (as long as the other specified conditions of responsibility are operative). In the example developed by Reeve, I would say that the successful examinee is neither responsible for B's limitation nor exercising power over B.

The two examples are distinguished by particular differences in the contexts in which the agents act. The point in establishing connections among the conceptions of agency, responsibility and power, is to bring out how implicit considerations which help to shape one of these concepts enters in to the constitution of the others as well. Their relations cannot be exhaustively captured in a couple of definitions. That is why I refuse to offer a *definition* of power or responsibility and insist on articulating a *paradigm* of each (p. 103) which allows us to fit the elements of the paradigm to a variety of specific circumstances.

We do not, for instance, say that a change in someone's conduct is the result of coercion if an acquaintance threatened to ignore him in the future should he continue to act on his most fundamental principles. We do not because the threat is trivial by comparison to the importance of the action. In my paradigm of power I say that the agent of power must have access to resources which can limit the range of options "normally available" to the recipient (p. 102 and footnote, 132). What counts as normally available depends on the norms accepted within a way of life. If, for instance, the ends of growth, productivity and efficiency, which have played a prominent role in our civilization, were to undergo fundamental devaluation, we would assess Reeve's example differently. We might, as some now do, construe the examination as a selection procedure to to be a mechanism of power. Such an invocation of implicit norms is inevitably involved in assessments of power and this is so because the concept is closely linked to context-dependent norms of responsibility. If those implicit norms themselves were subjected to a thorough critique, the range of contests over the composition of 'power' would be extended radically. A paradigm of power helps us to discern the complex relations between its grammar and those norms, but it cannot exhaustively detail them. It also helps us to identify points of attack for those who would disconnect 'power' from these associations.

As we shall see later, theories in which the norms of agency and responsibility are treated as arbitrary mechanisms of disciplinary control must also transform the concept of power lodged in our discourse. These alternative theories signify the internal connection in our discourse between power and responsibility.

A further objection to the conceptual link between responsibility and power has been posed by John Gray.[5] Gray contends that sometimes those whose actions severely limit the life chances of others are themselves locked into patterns of "socialization" or, perhaps more credibly stated, structural determinations which restrict their range of choice and action. Thus, their actions are linked to constraints imposed on others, but they are not responsible for them.

> Since those who exercise power, no less than those upon whom power is exercised, have their preferences determined by the culture in which they are immersed and the institutions by which they are surrounded, how can it be justified to impute responsibility to the former but not to the latter?[6]

If this is an objection to themes presented in this book, something has gone amiss. It is actually a restatement of a thesis argued here. I argue (pages 122 – 5) that when agents in superordinate positions are themselves locked into a set of structural contradictions, where action in either of two directions available will necessarily impose burdens on others, the language of power itself begins to lose its grip. It is not just that we cannot locate responsibility: we cannot specify the agents who could be said to exercise power. We might, in these circumstances, stretch the language to say that power is exercised without being able to identify agents who exercise it, but in this book I have concluded that, in an instance of this sort, structural determination should be seen to have superseded the exercise of power. I have done so to endorse the view that power is intrinsically connected to individual or collective agents who exercise it. One could proceed in a different direction, as Michel Foucault has done, by articulating a conception of power which is invested in institutions and divested from agents, but I see no sign that Gray is prepared to follow this path. Foucault's concept of power without agents is bound up with his theory of the agent as an artificial production without moral or epistemic privilege. The counter-example designed to break the connection between power and responsibility has the undesired effect of severing power from agency.[7]

Since I now endorse a theory of the subject (or agent) as an essentially ambiguous *achievement* of modernity, it is incumbent upon me to endorse at least some of the connections among agency, responsibility and power operative in modernity which express such a theory of the subject. I thereby reserve the concept 'power' for those contexts in which power can be said to be *exercised;* I adopt the vocabulary of structural constraints to characterize the parameters within which the exercise of power can occur and the vocabulary of structural determination to characterize those (if there are any) in which the constraints are so tight that there is no space for the exercise of power.

But what can one say in those intermediate conditions where one collectivity, with options available to it, is regularly implicated in transactions which limit the interests, desires or obligations of other collectivities? How do we move from consideration of individual relations of power, agency, and responsibility to those involving collectivities such as organizations, classes, ethnic groups, and regions. It may be that the reach of the traditional language of power, coming from an era in which the web of social institutions was less tightly drawn, is now insufficient to characterize the conditions in which we live. In affirming connections among agency, responsibility and power I intend not merely to *unfold* those already intact in our discourse; it is also necessary to *revise* the language of power to fit more closely the circumstances in which we now live. That is the topic of Chapter 5 of this text (especially pp. 198 – 205). "If part of the point in saying that A has power over B is to charge A with closing B's options unnecessarily it may turn out that the criteria appropriate to establishing such a charge in the society of the local shopkeeper are rather different from those appropriate to the society of the corporate manager" (p 200).

This lag between inherited terms of discourse and changing constellations of social life contributes both to the contestability of core concepts and the inherently creative dimension of political conceptualization. We may not be able to *discover* within the inherited web of meanings unambiguous answers to the questions we pose to it. Creativity is required in these instances, but it is a mode of political creativity which must advance on several fronts together if it is to advance securely at all. We might see recent constructions such as "institutional racism", "affirmative action," "bureaucratic responsibility," "non-decision", and "citizen entitlement," as elements in a broad, precarious movement to root the concepts of agency/responsibility/power more firmly in the organizational matrix of contemporary life. These political advances in turn help to generate the conceptual space—to generate, if you will, a new fund of examples and counter-examples—in which a conception of power linked to agency and responsibility can be adapted to the conditions of modernity.

These innovations, though creatively linked to conceptions of responsibility within our discourse (pp. 191 – 205), are not immune to counter-examples; if they succeed it will be because we become convinced first, that the ideals of agency and responsibility are worth retention, and second, that to prize these ideals today is to seek ways to weave them more fully into the fabric of organizational society.

The counter-example, given royal status as a testing procedure in philosophies which pretend that established concepts are in order as they are or claim that a reconstructed system of concepts can impose a rational order on the loose texture of natural language, must play a more modest role when the established terms of political discourse are understood to house heterogeneous standards of conduct. In these circumstances, counter-examples selected by one party in a debate might provide considerations which modify the initial reading or identify anomalies in need of assimilation; but it is always necessary to *decide* whether the counter-example will be allowed to override the thesis or the thesis to override the counter-example. Ordinary language, as a repository of conflicting examples, cannot suffice to govern such judgments, for the question revolves around ascertaining which of the multiple tendencies within it should be given primacy in the instance at issue.

The fetish of the counter-example in contemporary analytic philosophy is a ghostly legacy of defunct philosophies which promised to save philosophy from political engagement by endowing it with a neutral method to adjudicate between competing perspectives. Many who have overtly acknowledged the failure of this latter quest continue to evade the political dimensions of their own enterprise and to treat the counter-example as if it could be a definitive testing devise. The fetish of the counter-example allows analysts to occlude the intimate connection between the discourse of politics and the politics of discourse.

The counter-example plays its most constructive role when it is deployed not only to counter a thesis but to sustain an alternative thesis. For in a debate between articulated alternatives, in which each side offers putative counter-examples with some foundation in established discourse, the contestants will be driven to a deeper question, What considerations can be invoked to ascertain which example should be given primacy?

Felix Oppenheim has not only criticized the conception of power defended in this text, he has formulated an alternative conception to replace it. By exploring the contest between these two conceptions, we will be able to discern more clearly why 'power' is a locus of persistent turbulence in contemporary political thought and why each rival party strives to impose its particular order on it. For these debates are indispensable elements within larger debates over the ideals and standards to be given hegemony in modern life.

Oppenheim opposes the view that certain concepts of politics describe from a normative point of view and the claim that some of these latter concepts are essentially contestable. He promises to explicate a set of neutral, descriptive concepts which all rational social scientists must accept, regardless of their moral or ideological convictions. The quest is important to Oppenheim. For, unless it can succeed, we cannot hope to have a science of politics and unless we have a science of politics we cannot, he thinks, hope to bring reason to political and moral debates. Oppenheim treats ordinary language as only one test of a good conceptualization. We must be willing to repudiate its guidance whenever it contains ambiguities or surrounds descriptive concepts with moral connotations. The goal is to reconstruct the language of political inquiry to make it a suitable medium for a science of politics.

To relieve power of the normative "connotations" which persistently cling to it, Oppenheim defines authority and persuasion as forms of power. This move, if it succeeds, clearly divorces 'power' from a moral point of view. For it lumps modes of determining conduct which are presumptively legitimate in our discourse with those which are presumptively illegitimate. Why are persuasion and authority to be treated as instances of power?

> From the point of view of an *effective* language of political inquiry, the decisive question is, What is more *important*, the differences between rational persuasion and deception/ deterrence/coercion or the similarities between all these relationships of interaction? Different political scientists may give different answers, depending mainly on their research topic. But all will *agree* that we *need* a single concept tying together all methods by which one actor determines another actor's conduct . . . .[8]

Why do we need a single concept tying together all methods by which one actor determines anothers conduct?

Oppenheim is vague at this point. He says such a general concept will be more "fruitful" for inquiry, that this demand corresponds with similar judgments he has made for other concepts in political inquiry, that the overarching concept of power recommended will be free of normative entanglements, and that, because of its purely descriptive character and generality, it will establish essential preconditions for the formation of a science of politics. The last contention assumes, I think, overriding importance for Oppenheim; but it also contradicts his promise to develop one definition of each political concept suitable for use by theorists supporting alternative theoretical orientations. This characterization of power is, on Oppenheim's own reading, incompatible with an interpretive approach to political inquiry because the latter approach only makes sense when couched within an expressivist philosophy of language, and an expressivist philosophy contends that the web of concepts a populace shares expresses in its network of differentiations their most fundamental ideals, standards, and conflicts. The science Oppenheim's definitions serve is not neutral between competing conceptions of political inquiry and I will contend further that the understanding of social life implicit in Oppenheim's concept of power (and associated concepts) supports a specifiable and contestable set of political prescriptions.

The purposes governing differentiations among alternative ways to get people to do what they would otherwise not do might vary in significant ways. We might seek to know the extent to which alternative modes respect and treat the self as a responsible agent. If that were the purpose, conceptions of persuasion, authority, coercion, bribery, etc. residing in our practices could provide a valuable launching pad from which to articulate the desired differentiations. Alternatively, the objective might be to assess techniques for controlling behavior according to their relative effectiveness, range of applicability, efficiency, cost, and completeness. When these latter priorities are given hegemony, the set of differentiations listed above loses much of its pertinence. Another set is needed which gives primacy to the reliability, scope, and efficiency of various modes of control. If we interpret Oppenheim's account to be governed by this latter purpose, we can see why he thinks it "important", "fruitful", and "effective" to draw authority and persuasion into the concept of power and why he construes power to be a master concept into which "all methods of determining behavior" should be absorbed. The differentiations built around standards of agency and responsibility must be reshuffled and subjected to a new calculus of differentiation when these ends are given priority.

Oppenheim's "reconstruction" of 'power' and associated concepts does not represent a neutral language of political inquiry, it expresses a technocratic ideal of politics. One could, of course, elaborate this set of distinctions and identities to show how it subverts a conception of self and societal ends worthy of endorsement. But Oppenheim never provides such a reading of the conception of power he presents. Intentionally or unintentionally, the differentiations he affirms subjugate the norms of agency and responsibility to a technocratic conception of social life. This ideal is so compelling to Oppenheim that he believes it to describe the world as it is fundamentally beneath the rhetoric and normative connotations of everyday discourse. He convinces himself that his concepts describe fundamental realities when they in fact describe an ideal to which he is wedded.

Oppenheim's reconstruction of political concepts constantly runs into two dilemmas. The rationale guiding his constructions can be discerned once the technocratic conception they express is articulated, but that very specification undermines his claim to construct a neutral system of political concepts. He must remain close to ordinary language if his reconstructed language is to influence the audience he strives to reach, but he must deviate it from it significantly if he is to disconnect the terms of political discourse from normative ideals and standards they express in everyday life. If he moves far away, he loses contact with the community to which he speaks, and if he stays close the appearance of normative neutrality dissolves. Thus, the necessity for conceptual revision supported by vague justifications. When we discern the links between Oppenheim's 'explication' of power and a technocratic ideal of politics, we can see more clearly why the language of power in our discourse does not mesh perfectly with the criteria of responsibility. We can also see why it is unlikely that a concept of power could be articulated today which incorporates smoothly all the elements now competing for space within this frame. The concept 'power' is composed of heterogenous elements standing in unstable relations to one another. It is one of the sites of a struggle between rival ideals of the good life competing—though not on equal terms—for hegemony in our civilization. If modernity is marked by rivalries in which efficiency and community, democratic citizenship and the imperative of economic growth, utility and autonomy, rights and interests, domination and appreciation of nature all compete for primacy, it is not surprising—at least to those who accept an expressivist philosophy of language— to see microcosms of this rivalry inside the concepts which help to constitute that way of life. As long as modernity continues to house debates over the character of the good life, the terms of political discourse will provide sites upon which the debates are pursued.

The central terms of political discourse, then, are *contestable* and they are more likely to be *contested* overtly when modes of conceptual analysis which pretend to transcend or neutralize these contests are demystified. The neutralists do not transcend the politics of discourse. They practice an academic politics of depoliticization through reification of the terms of political discourse.

ESSENTIALLY CONTESTABLE CONCEPTS

To say that a particular network of concepts is contestable is to say that standards and criteria of judgment it expresses are open to contestation. To say that such a network is *essentially* contestable is to contend that the universal criteria of reason, as we can now understand them, do not *suffice* to settle these contests definitively. The proponent of essentially contestable concepts charges those who construe the standards operative in their own way of life to be fully expressive of God's will or reason or nature with transcendental provincialism; they treat the standards with which they are intimately familiar as universal criteria against which all other theories, practices, and ideals are to be assessed. They use universalist rhetoric to protect provincial practices.

The thesis of essentially contested concepts (i.e. concepts which are contested or open to contest) has been challenged from several directions. The charge most commonly launched within the Anglo-American tradition of analysis is that the doctrine is too radical: it overlooks resources of reason or logic or tradition or neutral representation which can legitimately dissolve the definitional disputes persistently operative in moral and political philosophy. The Continental tradition of genealogy and deconstruction would criticize the thesis, as it has been developed by Hampshire, Gallie, Lukes, Montefiore, MacIntyre and myself, from the opposite direction. On this view, the proponents of the contestability thesis continue to erect barricades—such as the conception of the self as an agent—which arbitrarily confine the space in which the contests can legitimately move. I will consider the Anglo-American strategy of containment first, saving consideration of the continental charge that a residue of transcendental provincialism still clings to the contestability thesis until the last section of this chapter.

The first charge is that the doctrine is internally contradictory.[9] It is contradictory to say first that a concept is essentially contestable and second that the particular reading one endorses is superior. Yet the thesis as I endorse it does not include the latter claim; it does not pretend to show that the reading it prefers is demonstrably superior to every other reading it opposes. The thesis claims (1) that a conceptual contest involves rival parties who accept some elements of the concept in common;[10] (2) that the common resources of reason and evidence available can illuminate these debates but are insufficient to reduce the number of interpretations rationally defensible to one; (3) that a strong case can sometimes be made within this remaining area of contestability in support of a particular reading. One argues for one's reading within this space but does not claim to demonstrate its validity. One of the points in emphasizing the contestability of concepts which enter into a way of life is to establish rational space for debate over the terms of discourse. The thesis expresses an appreciation for politics by encouraging opposing parties to discern a possible element of rationality in the reading they contest.

Why should the parties not merely suspend judgment in the circumstances we have characterized? Sometimes that might be appropriate, and surely advocates of this thesis often do hold their position on particular issues in a different and more open way once they have acknowledged an element of rationality in opposing orientations. The concepts of politics, however, also help to constitute the standards and priorities of political life. Politics is the sphere of the unsettled, the locus of those issues not fully governed now by the unconscious play of tradition or the conscious control of administrative rationality; it is also the sphere in which collectively binding decisions sometimes must be made even though the available resources of reason and tradition are insufficient to determine the outcome. Politics is, at its best, simultaneously a medium in which unsettled dimensions of the common life find expression and a mode by which a temporary or permanent settlement is sometimes achieved. In these circumstances, to endorse a particular set of standards is to support criteria for decision where decision is imperative, and to acknowledge that the decision endorsed is contestable is to endorse the case for keeping dissident perspectives alive even after a political settlement has been achieved. There is no contradition in first affirming the essential contestability of a concept and then making the strongest case available for one of the positions within that range. That's politics.

A second objection rests on the charge that the doctrine of essential contestability is by its own premises essentially contestable. The doctrine is therefore alleged to be self-refuting. For if its premises allow *it* to be essentially contested then it is quite permissible for people to contest it. Let us look at the logic of arguments of this sort more closely.

The argument is located on the same plane as the following questions. To what does the correspondence of truth correspond? Are the criteria of rationality rational? Is the empiricist theory of knowledge empirically established? Hegel used a version of this argument to refute the primacy of epistemology presupposed in empiricist and rationalist philosophies. He argued that the importation of an external criterion of knowledge (e.g. clear and distinct ideas, falsifiability, or verification through observation), to test the truth of an operative mode of consciousness not committed to that criterion, must run up against one of two unwanted implications. Either the defense of the criterion imposed invokes the criterion again (e.g. the doctrine of clear and distinct ideas is known to be true by the character of its clarity and distinctness) or it appeals to another criterion itself in need of grounding. The first argument is viciously circular and the second draws itself into an infinite regress. I think this is a powerful argument and it is probably at the base of those contemporary continental philosophies which deny the primacy of epistemology continuing to govern Anglo-American analytic philosophy. An argument of this sort can be powerful against doctrines which purport to reveal some demonstrative truth, then, and the argument concerning the dilemma of epistemology helps to launch the contestability thesis.

The most promising way to avoid this dilemma is to present and defend some form of transcendental argument. Such an argument begins by identifying a sphere of experience taken to be undeniable, and it then indicates what capacities the subject of that experience must have for it to be possible. The argument in effect establishes a privileged level of presuppositions at one level to explain undeniable experience at another, and it uses these presuppositions (about the self or reason) to support a larger set of conclusions. The doctrine of essentially contested concepts is incompatible with transcendental arguments of the strongest type, though I have supported a weaker version in this text (pp. 192 – 8). If one were established to secure a particular moral doctrine specific enough to guide practical judgment in concrete contexts, the thesis of contestability would be refuted.

The affirmation of essential contestability is not self-refuting because it is not presented as a necessary or demonstratable truth. It does not even claim that its counter-thesis cannot be pursued. First, it claims that no previous or current philosophy has been able to secure a set of basic concepts both specific enough to guide practical judgment and immune to reasoned contestability. Second, it anticipates that future attempts to do so will falter unless they establish closure artificially through the exercise of power. Third, it promises to offer internal critiques of current and future doctrines which purport to eliminate rational contestability. We do not *know* that achievements unavailable to us now will necessarily be unavailable in the future. It is therefore not irrational for someone to deny *essential* contestability. But the denial does not have much bite until it is linked to articulation of one theory capable of withstanding the charge of contestability.

I concur with John Gray's reminder that what is open to contestation now may be susceptible to rational resolution later.

> My claim that rival positions in political philosophy can be shown to hinge on differing answers to substantive questions of philosophy leaves open, however, the possibility that these questions are susceptible of a conclusive rational resolution . . . Obviously there is no assurance that there will be sufficient progress in other areas of philosophy to permit the central problems of political philosophy to be resolved conclusively. . . .[11]

The history of political discourse and our best current understanding of language supports the belief that space for contestability will persist in the future, even though that space may be closed politically and/or difficult to recognize by those drawn into a particular practice of discourse. This expectation about the future, however, cannot be demonstrated to be true, for a future populace may generate discursive forms not now conceivable to us.[12]

Ambiguities lodged within the predicate "essential" are probably responsible for several misreadings of the thesis advanced here. Not only does the predicate signal that these disputes are central rather than trivial or peripheral, some have interpreted it to mean that they are *demonstrably* interminable rather than reasonably expected to be so and that there are no rational grounds whatsoever to guide and inform these debates. I wish to affirm the disputes to be centrally important, to deny that it is demonstrable that they are in principle irresolvable, and to deny that there are no criteria at all to illuminate these contests. Let us consider this last issue.

To say that a contest is essential is not necessarily to affirm the radical relativism several critics have read into the thesis. It may be to contend, as I have done explicitly, that the universal criteria of rationality available to us limit and inform such debates but are insufficient to resolve them determinately. "It is partly because we share the pertinent norms of responsibility *imperfectly* that contests arise with respect to such political concepts, and it is because we *share* these norms imperfectly that we are provided with some common leverage for limiting the range within which these contests can rationally proceed" (pp. 197 – 8). The limits recognized in the text flow from an endorsement of Strawson's view that, though the conception of agency and responsibility inscribed in our practices is not identical to those affirmed in other times and places, these are nonetheless "categories and concepts which in their most fundamental character change not at all" (Strawson, quoted on p. 197). I will contend later in this chapter that the Strawson thesis is too strong, but neither the initial formulation nor the revised account endorses radical relativism. If that were the thesis we might be able to speak of conceptual differences, but not of contests.

The phrase "essentially contestable concepts", properly interpreted, calls attention to the internal connection between conceptual debates and debates over the form of the good life, to the reasonable grounds we now have to believe that rational space for such contestation will persist into the future, to the value of keeping such contests alive even in settings where a determinate orientation to action is required, and to the incumbent task for those who accept the first three themes to expose conceptual closure where it has been imposed artificially. The thesis refers to essentially contestable *concepts* to focus attention on the locus of space for contestation, not in some abstract space in which language is deployed as a neutral medium of communication, but in the fine meshes of social and political vocabularies themselves. I would happily accept a retitlement of this thesis as long as it properly accentuated the internal connection between the concepts imperfectly shared in a way of life and the contestable standards, judgments and priorities which help to constitute that life.

CONTESTABILITY AND DECONSTRUCTION

The thesis of essentially contestable concepts, developed within the Anglo-American world, is both a precursor of continental philosophies of genealogy and deconstruction and a potential target of their assault. Deconstructionists show how every social construction of the self, truth, reason, or morality, endowed by philosophy with a coherent unity and invested with a privileged epistemic status, is actually composed of an arbitrary constellation of elements held together by powers and metaphors which are not inherently rational. To deconstruct these established unities is to reveal their constructed character and to divest them of epistemic privilege. Genealogy is a mode designed to expose the motives, institutional pressures, and human anxieties which coalesce to give these unities the appearance of rationality or necessity. Some forms of deconstruction/genealogy seem to be in the service of nihilism, while others, by bringing out the constructed character of our most basic categories, aim at opening up new possibilities of reflection, evaluation and action.

Michel Foucault, after defining his early project as an archaeology exposing the underlying elements holding together the institutional forms and epistemological constructions of past eras, now characterizes himself as a genealogist of the present. The shift is merely one of emphasis, since his studies of the history of epistemes, medicalization, madness, punishment, and sexuality have consistently aimed at distancing contemporaries from the unities which govern our way of life by bringing out the artificial and constructed character of these forms. Genealogy is a radicalization of the earlier project, concentrating on the "strategies" of power which establish and maintain the most basic unities of modernity while suspending any appeal to rationality or truth to understand these constructions.

Foucault's genealogies represent a reversal of the project of interpretation. While interpretation seeks to bring out the rationale implicit in the practices, say, of tribal society, partly to allow us to come to grips more reflectively with the underlying priorities and standards in our own way of life, genealogy strives to distance us from the rationale implicit in past and present practices. Our modes of rationality, morality, agency, sexuality, and responsibility, through a genealogy of the elements from which they are constructed and the forces which bind the constructions together, become experienced as arbitrary impositions to be opposed, evaded and resisted. The genealogies appeal to the aspect of our experience which is contained, subjugated or excluded by these constructions. Genealogy thus totalizes the project of politicization modestly pursued in the thesis of essentially contested concepts. It is uncertain (to me) just how far Foucault himself would push this process of politicization. There are many occasions where he seems to endorse a politicization complete enough to break up modernity itself, thereby enabling perhaps a new set of artificial constructions to emerge in its place. At other times it seems possible that Foucault, believing that the forces of order are always well represented and armed in the bureaucracies and academies, has decided to focus exclusively on the genealogical project to provide a counterpoint to the forces of order and unity. Foucault may see himself as "the other" (or fool) of modernity, exposing artificialities it congeals or conceals in the hope of enhancing space for politics. To redress the current imbalance in favor of ordered constructs he puts all his weight on the other side of the scale. We cannot explore these alternative possibilities here; we will examine those aspects of Foucauldian genealogy which make critical contact with the thesis of essentially contestable concepts.[13]

Three Foucauldian themes are particularly pertinent: (1) the thesis that the modern agent or subject is an artificial production of modernity rather than a rational achievement which establishes standards through which to assess modernity; (2) the contention that a social practice construed by interpretationists to be constituted partly by concepts which express its norms and standards is better seen as a "discursive practice" in which heterogeneous elements such as architectural design, available instruments, concepts, and rules of evidence congeal into a particular structure of mutual determinations; (3) the view of 'power', not as a possession of agents who exercise it to define the options of others, but as a set of pressures lodged in institutional mechanisms which *produce* and *maintain* such privileged norms as the subject or the primacy of epistemology. The key to the last two themes resides in the credibility of the Foucauldian view of the subject. If the subject, for instance, is construed to be an artifact of power rather than an agent who, among other things, exercises power, then clearly the modern tendency to link power closely to agents would have to be revised. And if the concept of the self as subject endorsed in this text were undermined completely, the limits within which contestation can proceed rationally would be broken too. The thesis of essential contestation would give way to the practice of total deconstruction. We will concentrate, therefore, on the Foucauldian account of the subject.

This book endorses the idea of the self as agent and the agent as a center of responsibility. We are seen here as "agents, capable of forming intentions, of deliberately shaping . . . conduct to rules, of appreciating the significance of actions for other . . ., of exercising self-restraint;" and we are therefore said to be "worthy of being held responsible for conduct that fails to live up to expected standards" (p. 193). The most basic norms of agency and responsibility, because they are unavoidably presupposed in our daily transactions, are treated here as criteria to guide and limit conceptual contestation: "those who disagree about the grammar of key political concepts also share, if tacitly, a range of commitments about persons and responsibility . . . some aspects of these shared commitments reflect conventions relative to our social life, while the central core reflect conventions relative to social life as such" (p. 197).

Foucault challenges any such attempt to privilege the norms of agency and responsibility. He does not say that the inhabitants of modernity are not subjects or that the modern subject is a mere fiction; he presents the subject as a real arti-fact of modernity, as an artificially engendered unity which becomes a vehicle for the extension of disciplinary control over the self. The subject, on this reading, is neither a universal phenomenon, nor a historical achievement which, once at-tained, allows us to come closer to rationality, truth, and autonomy.

Foucault does not seek to refute the idea of the subject directly, for that would implicate him in standards of truth and rationality bound up with the notion of a subject who recognizes them. His approach is indirect. He constructs genealogies of modern formations which engender the sub-ject, seeking to disconnect us thereby from the standards of reason and truth which presuppose subjectivity. He thus studies the formation of modern forms of reason, sanity, responsibility, and sexuality by linking these constructions to the forms of unreason, sanity, irrationality, and perversity they simultaneously engender and subjugate.

Foucault deconstructs the modern subject by connecting the norms and institutions which form it to the elements of unreason, madness, delinquency, and perversity it thinks it transcends in itself and treats humanely in others. The genealogies typically begin with an era in which these dualities are not yet perfected and proceeds to modernity where they emerge together. The subject is a modern artifact and these institutionally engendered dualities provide its con-ditions of existence. Thus, if the late middle ages confronted ambiguities in madness by treating the mad as the fallen bearers of truths too deep for human articulation and yet susceptible through madness to some dark manifestation, modernity subdues the ambiguity in madness. It contains, confines and treats unreason to protect itself from that which does not fit into its affirmative constructs. That which escapes the control of subjectivity, rationality and responsibility must either be brought back into the fold through modern confessionals (therapy, rehabilitation, and the dialectic of self-consciousness) or confined and controlled by disciplinary mechanisms. The disciplinary mechanisms and the confessionals together produce us as subjects and function to maintain the production from disruption. The mad are today treated as victims of an illness to be cured, never as *signs* that the norms of subjectivity, reason, and responsibility are too demanding of the self to which they are applied. The criminal is either immoral (to be punished) or delinquent (and in need of treatment); he is seldom seen as evidence of the arbitrary character of the norms which produce him. The epistemic privilege invested in the subject is sustained by constituting that which is differentiated from it as a deviation in need of treatment or containment.

These genealogies of the self and its other are buttressed by a genealogy of three epistemes which have taken turns in providing the site upon which theories of the self, language, reason, and knowledge can be articulated and contested. The epistemes of the late middle ages and of the classical age did not create space for the modern subject; the conceptions of language, knowledge, and truth they allowed did not articulate with the self as a subject. The modern episteme does support this conception of the self, but since no episteme contains the resources to establish or justify itself, to prove the truth of its governing rules and norms, these artifacts of modernity are not proven to embody truth merely because they fill the space available to them. No transcendental argument can be constructed without deploying resources within the modern episteme and no argument deploying those resources can deduce the truth of the episteme itself. What we can do through genealogy is to glimpse limits set by the modern episteme, and this is particularly possible today because the elements it has held together are beginning to break up.

The genealogies at these two levels are together sup-posed to generate a reversal of the modern orientation to sub-jectivity and responsibility. Instead of viewing them as univer-sal norms or modern achievements, we glimpse how they are artificially engendered and how the maintenance of the affirmative side constantly requires the production of the other which denies and resists it. The dualities of reason/unreason, rationality/irrationality, responsibility/irresponsi-bility, normality/abnormality, sanity/insanity constantly engender and sustain each other. Our treatment of deviations and deviants are not unfortunate necessities required to main-tain norms transcendentally established, but the institutional means (imprisonment, rehabilitation, confessional, therapy, confinement) by which we protect the dualities themselves from the deconstruction to which they would otherwise succumb.

The power of Foucault's genealogies resides partly in the detail of the account and partly in the metaphors he deploys to unsettle our confidence in metaphors we ordinarily apply in similar contexts. The disruptive use of unsettling metaphors is particularly important in these genealogies, I think, because it draws our attention to ways in which the position we endorse is sustained not by argument or logic, but by the power of a dominant metaphor insinuated into our discourse.

Out of this deconstruction of the subject emerges an alter-native picture of (as I shall call it) the bifurcated self of disciplinary society. One part of this self is the free, rational, and responsible agent capable of consenting freely to rules, of being guided by long-term interests and principles, and of being punished for deviation from those norms to which it has voluntarily consented. This side of the self is susceptible to social control by appeal to its virtue or responsibility or by threats of coercion or by the introduction of incentive systems which make it in its interests to behave in certain ways. This first side of the self is the site of self-discipline, and part of the pressure to accept self-discipline flows from its desire to avoid official definition as "the other" which can no longer be treated as a subject. The second dimension of the self is the other (the double or the shadow) which does not fit neatly into the first construction. It is the site of impulses, desires, feelings and pressures which are not subjected to rationality and self-control. When this side achieves hegemony the self is officially defined to be insane or delinquent or mentally unstable. And these official judgments license therapy to draw the loose elements more fully into the control of the subject or they license disciplinary controls to intimidate the self into conformity. This second site of the self is the object of institutional mechanisms of confinement, treatment, rehabilitation, confessional therapy and drug therapy.

If the self remains unsusceptible to control through one of these sites the mechanisms of disciplinary society turn to the other. The choice is not governed by knowledge or truth but by strategic considerations of relative effectiveness in control. "Individualization" itself is a process by which the self is rendered susceptible to dual strategies of bureaucratic control.

> In a system of discipline, the child is more individualized than the adult, the patient more than the healthy man, the madman and the delinquent more than the normal and non-delinquent. In each case, it is towards the first of these pairs that all the individualizing mechanisms are turned in our civilization; and when we wish to individualize the healthy, moral and law-abiding adult, it is always by asking how much of the child he has in him, what fundamental crime he has dreamt of committing. . . . All of the sciences, analyses or practices employing the root 'psycho' have their origin in this historical reversal of the procedures of individualization.[14]

So both sides of the bifurcated self are sites of control, and those humanists who oppose bureaucrats, technocracy, harsh punishment, and incentive systems to the norms of responsibility, self-consciousness, civic virtue, therapy or rehabilitation, function as the disciplinary twins of those they oppose. The two philosophies of politics complement one another. Those who celebrate the agent as a center of self-discipline, rationality, freedom and self-consciousness are thereby unwitting vehicles of disciplinary society. To seek to dismantle the modern subject, along with its shadow which grows longer the more it is perfected, is to oppose the hegemony of disciplinary society. Anything else plays into its hands.

How does one assess such a genealogy with its charge that modern humanism is a vehicle of disciplinary control? One can try to argue that Foucauldian politics is self-refuting.[15] One can try to show that the genealogies draw inevitably upon norms of rationality they seek to deconstruct and are thus self-reflecting.[16] One can criticize the detail of Foucault's histories. I doubt, however, that any of these strategies would suffice by itself. We need to confront the Foucauldian reversal of the theory of the subject directly to ascertain which elements from this account are compelling and which are not. This tactic, at least, is essential to a doctrine which has asserted that there is an essential sphere of contestability in the political discourse of modernity *and* that conceptions of agency, reason, and responsibility presupposed in those discourses help to set limits within which these contests legitimately proceed.

It appears that a strong case can be made in support of the view that the subject is a modern formation. Hegel, for instance, concurs with Foucault on this point, though he tries to construe the mutually constitutive forms of civil society, the state and the subject to be *achievements* of modernity. And A. H. Adkins has developed persuasive support of the view that the Homeric Greeks construed themselves in ways which deviate sharply from the modern conception of the subject (and from the associated categories of morality and responsibility).

Adkin's interpretation is drawn from a reading of "ordinary language" in the Homeric myths; it thus coincides nicely with the expressivist view of language I have adopted while challenging a central presupposition within my original account of conceptual disputes. The concepts of the Homeric age, he contends, reveal a self interpreted by participants to house a plurality of "little selves", each little self functioning as a quasi-independent center of emotion, consciousness, and action. This plurality is only occasionally and "lightly" organized into a coherent unity.

We are accustomed to emphasize the 'I' which "takes decisions" and ideas such as 'will' or 'intention'. In Homer there is much less emphasis on the 'I' or decisions. Men frequently act as *kradie* or *thumos* bid them.[17]

Thumos, kradie, ker and *etor* each function within the self as centers of feeling and action; the self is thus experienced as a constellation of "separate springs capable of impulse, emotion and thought; the existence of, so to speak, separate 'little people' within the individual seems natural in the light of Homeric psychology and . . . physiology."[18]

This conception of self as a multiplicity governed sporadically and loosely by unifying pressures is articulated within a world of multiple gods which intervene competitively in the life of the self; it also emerges within a small, vulnerable social form which is continually susceptible to fate and to the threat of enemy invasion. These forms in turn are associated with norms of responsibility and merit which depreciate intention, motivation, or effort as criteria of assessment and appreciate failure or success in protecting the community.

The terms of discourse in this setting express conceptions of self, responsibility, merit, and worth which are alien to modernity, or better, emerge as minor chords within our lives barely audible within the modes of expression available to us. If Adkins' account is correct, then Strawson has overplayed the hand of rationality in contending, after a careful account of the conception of self and responsibility inscribed in *our* language and *our* reactive attitudes, that these are "concepts which their most fundamental character, change not at all". Any argument seeking to defend modern postulates of agency and responsibility must retreat from the claim that these are universal orientations presupposed in all human societies and merely lifted to a peak of realization in modernity.

The work of disparate thinkers such as Hegel, Adkins, and Foucault requires a loosening of the standards of self and responsibility taken in this text to provide the indispensable background to discourse and the criteria for assessing it. Do these studies, though, after the disappearance of Hegelian Geist, deconstruct arguments for agency and responsibility altogether? I believe this latter implication is not required and I will close by sketching a set of considerations which might, when properly developed and integrated, sustain a defense of the subject as a precarious and ambiguous achievement of modernity.

Amidst the differences detected by Adkins and others between the modern and a variety of pre-modern conceptions of self, there are also notable continuities. These aliens are recognizably human even if they are unlike us in significant ways. The multiplicity which the pre-Platonic Greeks experienced heavily is also experienced by us occasionally, though we contain and organize it in different vocabularies (e.g. the concept of the unconscious and romantic images of the self which continue to haunt the official understandings of modernity). And this similarity is reversible. The Greeks, after all, experienced the unity of the self lightly.

Moreover we and they are essentially *embodied* selves, and the nature of that embodiment itself helps to shape the form of perception available to us, our spatial and temporal experience, and the experience of the self as implicated in a cycle of birth, maturation through dependence on adults, and death. These experiences, variable to be sure, but containing a universal dimension, help to give a sense of unity to a single life. They allow the self to experience itself to have continuity through time, to have a past and a future. We are also essentially language users, and we bestow a name upon each individual which individuates one and draws one into the discourse of the community as an active, identifiable participant with a past and a future. These are materials from which a loosely bounded transcendental argument concerning the structure of the self can be launched.

There are additional considerations, more particular to our own age, but capable of defense from a variety of directions. The gods, for instance, have retreated from the world, and we could not seriously endorse a conception of self and responsibility which presupposed their competitive intervention in our world and lives. Similarly, the sciences of modernity make it extremely improbable that we could once again endorse a cosmology in which the universe is filled with purpose and meanings to be acknowledged by us. We might develop, partly through a deeper recognition of ourselves as *embodied* selves necessarily implicated in nature, a deeper appreciation of the integrity and complexity of nature than we now manifest, but it is unlikely that we could again invest nature with agency and purpose. We, finally, have access to historical and anthropological accounts capable of making us more aware of the distance between us and other worlds and thus more self-conscious of presuppositions built into our practices and conduct. This developed capacity for self-consciousness is itself one of the elements which enhances our capacity for coherence and agency; it allows us, though incompletely and imperfectly, first, to convert preconscious and unconscious elements of conduct into conscious premises and then to assess these premises for their internal coherence.

Universal characteristics humans share as essentially embodied selves, and premises deeply rooted in modernity, together provide materials from which a conception of the subject as an achievement can be defended. The elements particular to modernity may in principle be contestable, but these are contests we are not now in a position to open.

This combination, then, might support a conception of the subject as an inherently ambiguous achievement. We take it to be an achievement because we know that those who have experienced the affirmative side of modern freedom, self-consciousness and citizenship (the subject at the level of political life), invariably seek to retain and extend this experience. Even Foucault's genealogies become exercises in self-consciousness particularly available to the modern self as subject. The subject is arguably an achievement in a second sense as well. Every way of life imposes some sort of order on the chaos and multiplicity which would otherwise prevail, and every way of life must therefore develop some means of setting and enforcing limits. The development of a subject-centered morality may turn out, when compared to other conceivable alternatives, to be the most salutary way to foster order through the consent and endorsement of participants. Democracy is an achievement of citizenship. It requires the subject, capable of adjusting conduct to norms, willing to assume responsibility for commitments, and willing to take the common good into account in its public life when assured that others will too.[19]

After confronting the challenge of Foucauldian genealogy I would, however, also contend that the subject is an *ambiguous* achievement of modernity; the most basic agenda is to ascertain how to reconstitute the achievement to enable us to acknowledge the ambiguities within it, to find ways to temper some of them, and to develop compensatory mechanisms for dealing with others. The subject is an ambiguous achievement because the history of its formation has been marked by a corollary history of the perfection of instruments, enclosures, therapies, and medications to control and contain the other which does not fit into officially designated norms of agency. The formation of the modern self correlates with the modern imperative to coordinate more and more aspects of public and private life. To confront the ambiguities in the modern subject is to explore those pressures in modernity to bring more of the self into the orbit of social control through incentive systems, civic virtue, morality, observation, confessional therapies, medical treatment and criminal punishment.

We can recognize and relieve ambiguities in the modern achievement of subjectivity by finding ways to loosen these imperatives which simultaneously require modernity to draw more and more of the self into the orbit of social control and encourage many participants to find ways to elude, resist, and subvert those controls. To loosen the imperatives of social coordination would be to relax pressures on both sides of the bifurcated self; it would allow a wider range of conduct to *be* untouched by normative assessment; and it would allow a larger portion of that conduct which must be normatively appraised to be housed within categories such as the eccentric, the odd, the weird, and the wayward rather than concepts of the irrational, delinquent, sick, obsolete, illegal, or abnormal. For the latter judgments license bureaucratic modes of correction through confessional therapies or disciplinary controls. The way to loosen the reins of social coordination is to relax those expansionary imperatives of the civilization of productivity which, to be met, must treat the subject and its shadow as dual sites of strategic control.

I do not claim of course to have presented an adequate theory of the subject here, let alone to have shown how the ambiguities within this achievement could be more fully acknowledged and relieved in our civilization.[20] I merely wish to suggest, first, that the frame in which essentially contested concepts was initially enclosed was too narrowly defined and, second, that even after confronting attempts to deconstruct the modern subject, considerations remain available from which an appreciation of the subject as an ambiguous achievement of modernity can be articulated. To show the subject to be a construction is not to render its deconstruction imperative.

NOTES

1. Andrew Reeve, "Power Without Responsibility," See also Alan Ware, "The Concept of Manipulation and Its Relation to Democracy and Power," *British Journal of Political Science* (Spring, 1981), 163–81.
2. *Ibid*, p. 83.
3. In general, Reeve ignores the discussion of legitimate power in Chapter 3, Power and Responsibility. This allows him to suggest that I think power is immoral or wrong. "Connolly . . . thinks of power itself as something unpleasant" (p. 85). As the presentation of legitimate power makes clear, I think, in fact, that power one exercises *over* another is always in need of legitimation, not that power in a good society would be unnecessary or that it must be illegitimate in existing societies. I believe, in fact, that no order could sustain itself without power, though that will not be the *principle* basis of order in a well-ordered polity. It is crucial to recall that, on my reading, while a presumption against exercising power *over* another is operative, it does not apply in exercising power to achieve an end, unless *that* involves power over another.

4. Reeve, *op cit.*, p. 84.
5. Gray, "Political Power, Social Theory and Essential Contestability," in *The Nature of Political Theory*, ed. D. Miller and L. Siedentop (forthcoming). Gray has illuminating things to say about the scope and limits of the thesis of essentially contested concepts, and I will consider that topic shortly. But his discussion of my concept of power contains misreadings of themes advanced in the text. He treats the "Connolly/Lukes" concepts of power as if the two were one. There are in fact notable differences in our accounts amidst the significant similarities. Gray interprets me to say (with Lukes) that to exercise power over another is to limit the other's *interests*. I do not, however, restrict power so tightly; I speak of constraints on the interests, desires, or obligations of another and even then leave that which is restricted open-ended. This would be an innocent enough misreading if Gray did not then conclude that the exercise of power for me always limits the capacity for agency. It is, though, on my reading, quite possible for A to restrict B's *desires* in ways which support the realization of B's interests or autonomy. Hence, one of the reasons for the discussion of legitimate power in the text—a topic ignored by Gray. My argument, it will be recalled, is that because the exercise of power over another limits the other in some respect, and because we generally endow persons with the presumptive right to act according to their own judgment, there is a presumption against "power over" which needs to be overcome if it is to be made legitimate. It is this presumption which helps to account for contests between those who try to extend the conventional criteria of power and those who try to contract it. The first is trying to extend the sphere of presumption and the second to contract it. Finally, partly because of these preliminary misinterpretations, Gray concludes that I look forward to a possible polity in which power is inoperative. That apparently would be a fully legitimate polity for me. But I do not. It is not just that I think full consensus is unrealizable, I think the attempt to realize it is always a form of tyranny. The thesis of essentially contested concepts *is* a thesis about the unrealizability of rational consensus and it supports efforts to help keep the terms of discourse open. In a society of this sort there will be power and, especially, politics.
6. Gray, *Ibid.*

7. Gray may intend to argue that, since I think subordinate constituencies in our civilization are systematically indoctrinated, I should argue that putative agents of power are similarly constrained. Hence no responsibility and no power. I do not adopt, however, the first premise. One can have a concept of real interests without concluding that everyone is in fact unconscious of his or her real interests.

8. Felix Oppenheim. *Political Concepts: A Reconstruction* (Chicago: University of Chicago Press, 1981), p. 39.

9. Since the effort in this text to resurrect the thesis of essentially contested concepts developed initially by Gallie and Hampshire, a series of texts on the topic has emerged. They include: Steven Lukes, *Power: A Radical View* (London: Macmillan, 1974); Alan Montefiore, "The Concept of Politics," in *Neutrality and Impartiality* (Cambridge: Cambridge University Press, 1975); John Gray, "On the Contestability of Social and Political Concepts," *Political Theory* (August, 1977), pp. 331 – 48; Gray, "On Negative and Positive Liberty", *Political Studies* (December, 1980): 507 – 26; Gray, "On Liberty, Liberalism and Essential Contestability," *British Journal of Political Science* (October, 1978): 385 – 402; Gray, "Political Power, Social Theory and Essential Contestability" *op. cit.*; Michael Shapiro, *Language and Political Understanding* (New Haven: Yale University Press, 1981), ch. 7; K. I. Macdonald, "Is 'Power' Essentially Contested?" *British Journal of Political Science* (July, 1976): 380 – 2; Steven Lukes, "Reply to K. I. Macdonald," *British Journal of Political Science*, (July, 1977): 418 – 19; Barry Clarke, "Eccentrically Contested Concepts," *British Journal of Political Science* (January, 1979): 122 – 6; Fred Frohock, "The Structures of 'Politics' ", *American Political Science Review* (September, 1978): 859 – 70; Amy Gutmann, "Moral Philosophy and Political Problems," *Political Theory* (February, 1982): 33 – 48. While Lukes, Montefiore, Gutmann, and Shapiro have generally sought to develop this thesis and explore its implications for political discourse, Gray, Barry, Macdonald, Frohock and Clarke have contested it (the latter eccentrically) in one way or another. Shapiro, it should be noted, probes similarities between this thesis and theories of genealogy and deconstruction advanced by French philosophers such as Derrida and Foucault, a topic we turn to in the last section of this chapter.

10. On pp. 30–1 I say that the disputants may share (imperfectly) the point in view from which the concept is formed but contest the central criteria appropriate to it; they may accept many of the same criteria but dispute the point of view from which it is to be formed; they may concur on the criteria and point of view but dispute the extent to which the concept is applicable to the way of life examined. Some analysts would refuse to call this last debate a conceptual dispute, and it is unimportant to the overall thesis if they do so or not, as long as they recognize that disputes of this sort are common and important.

11. Gray, "The Essential Contestability . . ." *op. cit.*, 346–47.

12. One who accepts an intersubjective conception of social life and an expressivist philosophy of language would expect, in fact, that some background dimensions of a way of life potentially contestable will not be available to the self-consciousness of participants. Stuart Hampshire, one of the two originators of the phrase "essentially contested (or disputed) concepts", explores this phenomenon in *Thought and Action* (New York: Viking Press, 1959) and it is a central theme in Charles Taylor's exploration of the history of debates between designative and expressivist philosophies of language, "Language and Human Nature," Alan B. Plaunt Memorial Lecture, Carleton University Publication, 1978.

13. I have considered other dimensions of Foucault's work in "The Dilemma of Legitimacy," in *Political Theory Now*, ed. John Nelson (Albany: State University of New York Press, 1983), pp. 307–42; and "The Politics of Disciplinary Control," paper delivered at the 1982 Convention of the American Political Science Association, Denver, Colorado, September 1–5.

14. Foucault, *Discipline and Punish* (New York: Random House, 1977), p. 193.

15. I have developed a version of this argument in "The Dilemma of Legitimacy," *op. cit.*

16. Hilary Putnam states such an argument against Foucault in *Reason, Truth, and History* (Cambridge: Cambridge University Press, 1982), but I do not think he has considered carefully Foucault's strategy of bracketing the question of truth as a privileged site and probing the mechanisms which give certain rules in a society that privileged status.

17. Adkins, *From the Many to the One* (Ithaca: Cornell University Press, 1970), p. 15.

18. *Ibid*, pp. 20 – 21.
19. I have defended this thesis in *Appearance and Reality in Politics* (Cambridge: Cambridge University Press, 1981), especially chapters 4 and 5.
20. I have explored, though in a highly preliminary way, the question of how to relax the growth imperative and thus to foster more "slack" in the order in "The Dilemma of Legitimacy," *op. cit.*, "The Politics of Reindustrialization," *democracy* (July, 1981): 9 – 20; "Civic Disaffection and the Democratic Party," *democracy* (July, 1982): 18 – 27.

Bibliography

The works listed below will, I think, prove useful to readers who find some plausibility in the themes developed in this study. Each has helped me at least to clarify my thinking on the pertinent issues.

First, to establish philosophical bearings. "If language," Wittgenstein contended, "is to be a means of communication, there must be agreement not only in definitions but also (queer as this may sound) in judgments." Wittgenstein sets the stage thereby for a revised understanding of the concepts that enter into social life. But *Philosophical Investigations* (New York: Macmillan, 1953), is an elusive book; students of politics are well advised to approach its themes initially through the eyes of others who apply them to a more familiar terrain. Peter Winch, *The Idea of a Social Science* (New York: Humanities Press, 1958) and Hanna Pitkin, *Wittgenstein* and *Justice* (Berkeley: University of California Press, 1972) perform that service nicely: Each clarifies Wittgenstein's philosophy of language while developing its implications for social inquiry. Winch's book should be read in conjunction with the work of friendly critics who argue, correctly I think, that his model of understanding unnecessarily limits the ability of the investigator to transcend the perspective of the culture studied or to appraise its life critically. Alasdair MacIntyre places Winch's work in critical perspective in *Against the Self Images of the Age* (New York: Schocken Books, 1971). MacIntyre, Steven

Lukes, Ernest Gellner, and others explore these issues further in Bryan Wilson (ed.), *Rationality* (New York: Harper Torchbooks, 1970).

Charles Taylor brilliantly probes the connection between the concepts and the practices of a society in "Interpretation and the Sciences of Man," *Review of Metaphysics* (Fall 1971): 4 – 51. And Julius Koveski, in a study too little noted by American philosophers and political scientists, argues that the dichotomy between descriptive and normative concepts, which underlies so much work in contemporary social science, has distorted our understanding of these very connections. His short book, *Moral Notions* (London: Routledge and Kegan Paul, 1967), will definitely repay close attention. The argument has affinities to that of another valuable and better known work, John Searle's *Speech Acts* (Cambridge: Cambridge University Press, 1970).

The status of our shared ideas about persons and responsibility and the ways in which they enter into our moral notions are explored insightfully in Richard Bernstein, *Praxis and Action* (Philadelphia: University of Pennsylvania Press, 1971), Stuart Hampshire, *Thought and Action* (New York: The Viking Press, 1959), Herbert Morris, "Persons and Punishment," *The Monist* (Fall 1968): 471 – 501, and P. F. Strawson, "Freedom and Resentment," in *Studies in the Philosophy of Thought and Action,* ed. P. F. Strawson (New York: Oxford University Press, 1968). Hampshire joins W. B. Gallie, "Essentially Contested Concepts," in *The Importance of Language,* ed. Max Black (Englewood Cliffs, N.J.: Prentice-Hall, 1962), in exploring the grammar of contested concepts (he calls them disputed concepts) and in identifying ways to subject the judgments embodied in the shared concepts of a society to critical scrutiny and possible revision. None of these works is specifically about politics, but each helps to deepen our understanding of the connections between conceptual contests and the contours of politics.

A number of political concepts have been subjected to close examination in the recent literature. Perhaps the best place to start is with Brian Barry, *Political Argument* (New

York: Humanities Press, 1965). Barry discusses conceptual analysis in general and also examines the concepts of liberty, interests, the public interest, and justice. Two recent anthologies are also extremely valuable: Anthony de Crespigny and Alan Wertheimer (eds.), *Contemporary Political Theory* (New York: Atherton Press, 1970) and Richard Flathman (ed.), *Concepts in Social and Political Philosophy* (New York: Macmillan, 1973). Each volume includes useful editorial commentary, and together they collect much of the best recent work on the concepts of authority, power, obligation, freedom, equality, justice, and the public interest. Robert Paul Wolff's *The Poverty of Liberalism* (Boston: Beacon Press, 1968) contains a provocative examination of the ideas of liberty, power, loyalty, and community. More specific studies of great value are Steven Lukes, *Power: A Radical View* (London: Macmillan, 1974) and Felix Oppenheim, *Dimensions of Freedom* (New York: St. Martin's Press, 1961). Two books George Kateb, *Political Theory: Its Nature and Uses* (New York: St. Martin's Press, 1968) and Alasdair MacIntyre, *A Short History of Ethics* (New York: Macmillan, 1966), link these recent developments in political philosophy to the classic tradition of political thought. Finally, Glen Gordon and I seek to connect conceptual debates to broader issues in contemporary social theory in our edited volume, *Social Structure and Political Theory* (Lexington: D. C. Heath, 1974).

Excellent introductions to many of the key concepts of political life and to the philosophical dimensions of political inquiry are to be found in the *Encyclopaedia of Philosophy*, 8 vols. (New York: Macmillan, 1967). Its essays on particular concepts such as power (Stanley Benn) and on more general topics such as operationalism (George Schlesinger), behaviorism (Arnold Kaufman), motives and motivation (William Alston), reasons and causes (Keith Donnellan), and ethics (Kai Neilson) provide lucid introductions to pertinent issues and identify a wider literature bearing on them.

Several texts published since the first edition illuminate further the relation between language and politics. Richard

Rorty's *Philosophy and the Mirror of Nature* (Princeton: Princeton University Press, 1979), poses a powerful challenge to epistemic foundationalism, opening the door to an appreciation of the contestable character of the terms of political discourse. Chapter six provides a useful critique of the most recent version of designative philosophies of language. *The Claim of Reason* (Oxford: Clarendon Press, 1979), by Stanley Cavell, delineates Wittgensteinian themes sensitively and links them to the philosophical questioning of Martin Heidegger. Cavell strives to "link the English and Continental traditions, after their long and mutual shunning . . ." A recent essay by Charles Taylor, *Language and Human Nature* (A.P. Plaunt Memorial Lecture, printed by Carleton University, 1978), provides an invaluable overview of the designative and expressive philosophies of language; it clarifies the shifting character of the conflict between these conceptions from early Greek thought to modern philosophical debates. Taylor's luminous defense of expressivism, that is, of language as a medium through which the standards and aspirations of an age or a people are expressed, also provides an excellent introduction to Martin Heidegger's *On the Way to Language* (New York: Harper and Row, 1982). Heidegger's explication of the last stanza of Stefan George's "The Word" ("So I renounce and sadly see: where the word breaks off no thing may be"), allows one to experience the poetic dimension of language more profoundly; it encourages a more intimate appreciation of the relation between using a language and being in a particular world.

An alternative account of the history of conceptions of language, which nonetheless overlaps with those noted above, can be found in Michel Foucault's *The Order of Things* (London: Tavistock Publications, 1970). Chapter three, "The Prose of the World", articulates the conceptions of language, self, knowledge, and nature prevailing in the "episteme" of the late middle ages, and chapter nine, "Man and His Doubles," brilliantly delineates the modern conceptions of language, self, knowledge and nature and the recurrent defeat of attempts to provide them with transcendental backing. This text should be read in conjunction with "The Discourse on Language" in Foucault's *The Archaeology of Knowledge* (New York: Harper and Row, 1972); here Foucault's own Nietzschean conception of discourse as a network of power relations is sketched. Foucault's disruptive deployment of metaphor to unsettle fixed epistemic conventions is best exemplified in *Discipline and Punish* (New York: Pantheon Books, 1977).

Two recent texts help to break down the barriers between Anglo-American reflections on the politics of discourse and those on the Continent. Vincent Descombes, *Modern French Philosophy* (Cambridge: Cambridge University Press, 1979), a text commissioned by Alan Montefiore to clarify the debates in contemporary French philosophy to an Anglo-American audience, succeeds magnificently. Descombes studies theorists such as Deleuze, Derrida and Foucault who "no longer believe that the task of the century (is) to integrate the irrational within an expanded reason," but seek instead to allow "the other" to expose arbitrary elements in the conventions of rationality which now govern us. This text is nicely complemented by one written by an American political theorist, Michael Shapiro, *Language and Political Understanding* (New Haven: Yale University Press, 1981). Shapiro provides a critical review of various philosophies of language informing recent political thought in America and closes with a thoughtful encounter with the conception of "discursive practice" informing the work of Michel Foucault.

Index